This Gospel

A Collection of

MISSIONS SERMONS

DICK BR

D1402317

Published by Abide Publishers LLC
1600 N. Boonville Ave., Suite B&C, Springfield, MO 65803

Cover design, typesetting, and interior design by Lucent Digital
(lucentdigital.co).

ISBN 978-0-9981789-4-3

DEDICATION:

Jennifer,
for patiently listening to and faithfully
praying me through each of these sermons
numerous times.

TABLE OF CONTENTS

INTRODUCTION

The title of this collected book of missions sermons comes from Matthew 24:14: "And this gospel of the kingdom will be preached in all the world as a witness to all the nations, and then the end will come."

Though no man or woman knows exactly when Jesus will come, we have been given some critical indicators.

One is that we must preach the gospel among every people group, such as the gospel according to 1 Corinthians 15:3–8, "that Christ died for our sins according to the Scriptures, that He was buried, and that He rose again the third day," and the gospel according to Hebrews 9:27–28 that "it is appointed for men to die once, but after this the judgment, so Christ was offered once to bear the sins of many. To those who eagerly wait for Him He will appear a second time."

And then there is the sober reality of Revelation 6:9–11, which bluntly offers another critical indicator of when King Jesus comes to rule and reign over all peoples: when more of His faithful followers have been killed for the Word of God and their testimony of Jesus.

Thus, with these indicators in mind, *THIS Gospel* inextricably ties both the preaching of the death, burial, and resurrection of Jesus among every people group and the increased martyrdom of the followers of Jesus to the return of the King.

And so we say, "So be it!" Let's live dead that Jesus comes quickly again in glory.

DICK BROGDEN
Cairo, Egypt
December 2017

the
Promised
Land

EXODUS 17:1-17

NUMBERS 20:1-13

Let's look at two texts from the Old Testament:

> *Then all the congregation of the children of Israel set out on their journey from the Wilderness of Sin, according to the commandment of the Lord, and camped in Rephidim; but there was no water for the people to drink. Therefore the people contended with Moses, and said, "Give us water, that we may drink."*
>
> *So Moses said to them, "Why do you contend with me? Why do you tempt the Lord?"*
>
> *And the people thirsted there for water, and the people complained against Moses, and said, "Why is it you have brought us up out of Egypt, to kill us and our children and our livestock with thirst?"*
>
> *So Moses cried out to the Lord, saying, "What shall I do with this people? They are almost ready to stone me!"*
>
> *And the Lord said to Moses, "Go on before the people, and take with you some of the elders of Israel. Also take in your hand your rod with which you struck the river, and go. Behold, I will stand before you there on the rock in Horeb; and you shall strike the rock, and water will come out of it, that the people may drink."*
>
> *And Moses did so in the sight of the elders of Israel. So he called the name of the place Massah and Meribah, because of the contention of the children of Israel, and because they tempted the Lord, saying, "Is the Lord among us or not?"* (Exo. 17:1–7)
>
> *Then the children of Israel, the whole congregation, came into the Wilderness of Zin in the first month, and the people stayed in Kadesh; and Miriam died there and was buried there.*
>
> *Now there was no water for the congregation; so they gathered together against Moses and Aaron. And the people contended with Moses and spoke, saying: "If only we had died when our brethren died before the Lord! Why have you brought up the assembly of the Lord into this wilderness, that we and our animals should die here? And why have you made us come up out of Egypt, to bring us to this evil place? It is not a place of grain or figs or vines or pomegranates; nor is there any water to*

drink." So Moses and Aaron went from the presence of the assembly to the door of the tabernacle of meeting, and they fell on their faces. And the glory of the Lord appeared to them.

Then the Lord spoke to Moses, saying, "Take the rod; you and your brother Aaron gather the congregation together. Speak to the rock before their eyes, and it will yield its water; thus you shall bring water for them out of the rock, and give drink to the congregation and their animals." So Moses took the rod from before the Lord as He commanded him. And Moses and Aaron gathered the assembly together before the rock; and he said to them, "Hear now, you rebels! Must we bring water for you out of this rock?" Then Moses lifted his hand and struck the rock twice with his rod; and water came out abundantly, and the congregation and their animals drank.

Then the Lord spoke to Moses and Aaron, "Because you did not believe Me, to hallow Me in the eyes of the children of Israel, therefore you shall not bring this assembly into the land which I have given them."

This was the water of Meribah, because the children of Israel contended with the Lord, and He was hallowed among them.
(Num. 20:1–13)

The same people. The same problem. The same place. The same complaint. The same leader. The same God. The same solution.

But due to one small difference, Moses was not allowed to set foot in the Promised Land.

Now, what is your Promised Land? What is your vision, dream, assignment or God-given responsibility? And just as important, what are the factors that could keep you from stepping foot there? From the lessons of these two passages, I want to draw seven points of application.

ERADICATION, NOT SUBJECTION

It seems that Moses always had an anger problem, and in the end, it caught up with him.

You remember young, idealistic Moses. Taking a walk one sandy Sunday he saw one of his own people being beaten. The red mist must have coursed across his eyes and with his bare hands (it seems) he killed the Egyptian offender.

Later, Moses sauntered down Mt. Sinai with two somewhat important tablets in his hands. Imagine what they could have sold for at the auction house Sotheby's if in his anger he hadn't dashed them to bits by smashing them on the rocks below him.

I can relate. Anger is an issue in my life, and the Arab world seems to be especially gifted in exposing it. If you're like me, you have your game face on for the public and then at home you take it off, which sometimes results in your ugliness facing off with the ones you love most.

I remember one day I had a long day at work. I was civil and kind to several people and I helped whomever I could. I finally got home at 5 p.m. after leaving home at 5:30 that morning. I played with my kids for a bit. We had supper, and around 8, my wife and I put the boys to bed. We usually take turns praying and I asked my oldest, Luke, who was 8 at the time, to begin. He was kind of distracted and did not pray. "Luke," I said, "it is your turn to pray." He ignored me. "Luke!" I said a little louder and a little irritated. "Pray!" Again, no response. "Luke, if you do not pray, I'm going to smack you." Nothing. So I lost my temper and slapped him on his back shouting, "PRAY!" He looked startled, and I think God might have been a bit surprised. My buried frustration of the day eventually found its outlet on the shirtless back of poor little Luke.

Your sin issues and my sin issues, though dormant, will rush back and manifest when you are under pressure. Subjection is not enough—our sin must be eradicated. You don't think Moses tried? I'm sure he could have listened to the self-help poets or went for a jog in the desert to let off steam. Moses, like you and me, thought that he could bury his problems. He couldn't and neither can we. These problems have Lazarus-like tendencies; they come back to life—and usually resurrect at the worst time. What have you tried to subdue, hide, or bury in the least seen recesses of your heart? Don't be a fool. They will come back to bite you.

When we lived in Sudan, I received news from a friend there. Buried in the heart were issues of sexual sin—covered, hidden, buried, lurking, living, waiting. And they came roaring back in this person who then committed unthinkable acts.

Oswald Chambers calls this eradication of sins "co-crucifixion": "Have I made this decision about sin—that it must be killed right out of me? … It is the great moment in my life when I do decide that just as Jesus Christ died for the sin of the world, so must sin die out in me, not be curbed or suppressed or counteracted, but crucified."[1]

We cannot cover our sin. We cannot even hold it in subjection while letting it live. It has to be eradicated, removed, yanked from us, and crucified or else it will eventually surface and destroy us.

ABSOLUTE OBEDIENCE

Moses and Aaron did most everything right. When the complaints came, they fell on their face, and the glory of God manifested and the Lord spoke. Moses was even told to take the rod; he took the rod in obedience. But when told to hold the staff and loose his tongue, he loosed both. He spoke and struck the rock.

Jesus asks for our absolute obedience. The problem is we are a people used to democratic decisions so we try to bargain with an absolute Sovereign. While serving a 100-percent God, we are a "majority is enough" constituency. As far as we're concerned, 90 percent is flying colors, 70 percent is a passing mark on an exam, 51 percent wins the election, and 0.08 percent passes the breathalyzer.

Jesus is the "all your heart, all your soul, all your strength, all your mind" potentate, and we are the "I am 80 percent holy, hallelujah and pass the popcorn!" parishioners.

Jesus wants all your money, not just 10 percent. Jesus wants all your time, not just holy days. Jesus wants your entire mind, even your subconscious dreams. Jesus wants all of your heart, even your secret ambitions. Jesus wants all of your words, not just your singing. Jesus wants all of your love; He won't tolerate idols. Jesus wants all of your obedience, not just when it's agreeable.

A 90-percent-plus rate for Moses incurred the wrath of God. What makes you think your 70 percent is acceptable?

Is your all on the altar of sacrifice laid?
Your heart, does the Spirit control?
You can only be blest and have peace and sweet rest
As you yield Him your body and soul[2]

JESUS WANTS ALL THE GLORY

In Exodus 17:5–6, God tells Moses, "Go on before the people, and take with you some of the elders of Israel... I will stand before you there on the rock in Horeb; and you shall strike the rock, and water shall come out of it." The sense here is that God, the elders, and Moses with Aaron are all involved. In Numbers 20:10, Moses rants to the people, "Must we bring water for you out of this rock?" There is a subtle difference between "I did it" (which is easy for us to see as false), "God did it" (which is easy for us to see as true), and "we did it" (which can be true if understood rightly).

I liken this to the story of the Chicago Bulls' Michael Jordan and Stacey King who combined for 72 points in a game. Jordan had 70 of those points, and King a mere two. In an interview after the game King said, "I will always remember the time Michael Jordan and I combined for 72 points." God in His majesty choses to work through the Moseses, Peters, Freds, Ahmads, and Billy Bobs of the world. Yet the proportion of His might and our contribution is surely much more imbalanced than Michael Jordan's 70 to Stacey King's two.

There are three contrary spirits we need to be very careful about in ourselves: I know, I am, and I can. Moses got it confused once and delusion set in, followed by judgment. For Jesus must get all the credit, He must get all the glory, and He must get all the praise. As soon as we wander into the thoughts of "I know, I can, I am," delusion gains a foothold in our thinking. Jesus reminds us that He—and He alone—knows, can, and is. As soon as we think it is by our might or force of personality that water comes from the rock, as soon as we start enjoying the glow or broadcasting to our credit, we are in a world of trouble, hovering on the brink of losing the Promised Land. We must be very careful to give Jesus all the glory.

THE WORD OF GOD IS ENOUGH

Numbers 20:12 is informative. The Lord speaks to Moses and Aaron: "Because you did not believe Me, to hallow Me...." What did Moses and Aaron not believe? What did God say that they did not follow? Well, the only thing they did wrong was to strike the rock. God said speak to it; Moses struck it. The application that must strike us then is that they did not believe the Word of God was enough.

What was Moses' thought? Something like, "Surely, it is not enough to address the rock. I must act. I must add my muscle to God's proclamation. God's Word is not enough. We must wield the heavy lumber."

Do you believe the Word of God is enough? Belief is obedience. Speak, not strike. Proclaim, not act. For Moses, this was the injunction; for us, the question remains relevant. Is the Word of God enough for us? Jesus, the Word of God. God creating with His Word. God sends His Word and heals our disease. Do we, the body of Christ in the twenty-first century, believe that the Word of God is enough?

Pendulums never stop at the center on the first swing. In generations past we were paternalistic. We erred on the side of lacking holism. Today the danger of our humanitarian mission is rooting it in the belief that God's word is not enough. There is a world of difference between feeding the orphan because God's Word tells us to and feeding the orphan because we do not believe the spoken and written Word of God is enough.

What is our motive? We dig the well, feed the hungry, heal the sick because we are ashamed of the Word of God, because we doubt its power to convict sin and point to Christ. If we think that our unexplained actions are somehow more eloquent and inspired than the words "repent for the Kingdom is at hand," then we do not really believe that the Word of God is enough.

When we do not really believe in the life changing power of God's Word, we strike. We strike out the language He chooses.

We strike out in anger at injustice, rather than striking out in love.

To use a baseball analogy, qualified trust in the power of God's Word leads us to strike—but we strike out.

HALLOWED DESPITE US

When Moses struck, when he disbelieved that the Word of God was enough, he did not hallow the Lord before the people. "You did not believe Me, to hallow Me in the eyes of the children of Israel" (Num. 20:12). Now look at verse 13: "The children of Israel contended with the Lord, *and He was hallowed among them*" (emphasis added). Moses did no hallowing of the Lord in the eyes of the children of Israel, yet God was still hallowed among them.

God will be seen as holy, revealed as holy, manifest as holy, with or without my cooperation, with or without my composure, holiness, or character. God will be revealed before the nations as holy.

I would venture to guess that we all have born witness to the phenomena of a minister of the gospel whose life did not match his or her words. People were saved. Many were healed. Scores were blessed and baptized, and over time it was revealed that at the very moment the above ministry genuinely occurred, that vessel was, in fact, marred, and active in habitual sin. We scratch our heads a bit, but two principles emerge.

First, God's Word is true whether or not I am false. To be sure we don't like this and certainly we realize the danger. Yet even if I'm a chronic liar and if I tell you that 2 plus 2 equals 4, whether or not you believe me, it remains true. And for those who hear the message, "repent and be baptized," broadcast from a sinful mouth, it is still true and still powerful. When believed, God honors His Word, even when the medium is sullied.

Second, God is not content to let us remain false. While God honors His Word, He also honors His own nature. Anyone who represents God must ever remember that to speak for God entails living for Him, and if our lives do not match our words, God will remove the microphone. I am acutely aware of this principle in my own life. There may even be someone sitting here, having a very hard time listening tonight because at some point in your memory, my actions toward you did not match these words. If so, I have no excuse, and I ask your mercy and forgiveness.

I was driving with a Muslim background believer (MBB) talking about this very point when a wheel of the taxi next to us gave up its spirit. We heard the loud bang and turned to see the taxi continue to move as it slowly coasted to a stop 100 meters down the road. The tire is the human shell. The air within is the Spirit of holiness. When the Spirit is gone, the car will not—it cannot—continue to move unendingly unless God is hallowed. It was true for Moses. It will be true for me. It will be true for you.

NO ONE IS IRREPLACEABLE

Moses was Mr. Everything to the Israelites. As central as He was, God did not need Him. God did not need Martin Luther. God did not need Mother Theresa. God does not need Billy Graham. And God does not need you!

But oh, the glorious mystery, He wants you! Jesus wants you; He wants to use you. Jesus wants you to work with Him to announce the Kingdom. Jesus wants to love through you, touch through you, speak through you, heal through you, and show mercy through you. Not needed, but wanted. What a freedom this is! God does not need me to help keep this planet in orbit, nor to accomplish His will in the earth. God does not need me to see Muslims saved, discipled, and blessed. There is no pressure, but there is a wonderful invitation.

We are wanted. We are allowed to participate

What a privilege! What a joy!

Oswald Chambers said, "When big men go, we are sad, until we see that they are meant to go. The one thing that remains is looking in the face of God for ourselves."[3]

MOSES NOT ALLOWED IN THE PROMISED LAND

We have gone the long way around in order to set up what I hope you take away as the central point: Moses was not allowed into Canaan.

This seems harsh to us. In my Western, linear, systematic, task-oriented self, I would feel so much better if Moses had simply crossed the Jordan, put one foot in Palestine, and then succumbed to a massive heart attack and died. Somehow my internal feeler would be satisfied. "Aha! He made it. Mission accomplished. He crossed over. Job well done!"

We humans think so tribally, so physically, so geographically when all along for Moses the goal *was not about Canaan. It was about intimacy with God Almighty.*

It is not about Sudan, New York, Juba, or Khartoum. It is not essentially about Bible schools or Muslim evangelism. It is not primarily about street kids or relief and development. It is about walking with Jesus. It is intimacy, union, and saturation with Jesus! Jesus is my destination! Jesus is my Promised Land!

Friends, I do not think Moses failed ultimately. I do not even think that Moses was punished severely. It is my impression that Moses increasingly walked with God. You see, this event happened 20 years before the Jordan crossing.

For 20 more years, Moses led a recalcitrant people.

For 20 more years, Moses served.

For 20 more years, Moses sweated.

For 20 more years, Moses struggled.

For 20 more years, Moses blessed, loved, and provided for Israel.

All the while knowing, he would never step foot into (what we consider) the ultimate destination.

But it was not the final goal for Moses, was it? Yes, he was humble. But more so, deep in his heart, the physical land was not the dream that drove him. Intimacy with Jehovah was.

OUR PROMISED LAND

What is your ultimate goal? We are smart enough, I think, not to say power, fame, or money. But what about missions? Evangelism? Ministry? Can I remind you that those are things of earth? Can I remind you that there will be no evangelism in heaven? Can I remind you that when we turn our eyes on Jesus, the things of earth grow strangely dim?

Intimacy with Jesus—this is our Promised Land. The physical situation has no power or precedence over our journey into Jesus. It is no secret to most of you that I love Muslims. I love to see Muslims saved, free, healed, and forgiven. That is why I am here. That is why my family and I love Sudan. I love Muslims. I want to see them in heaven, and I want them to know that.

But you know what? That is not my Promised Land. Jesus is the sum total of my desire. Walking with Him, loving Him, intimate with Him, known and knowing Jesus, this is our Promised Land.

Let me borrow from two hymns that say it well:

My goal is God himself, not joy, nor peace,
Nor even blessing, but Himself, my God;
'Tis His to lead me there—not mine, but His—
At any cost, dear Lord, by any road.[4]

I'd rather have Jesus than anything
This world affords today.[5]

Reaching Muslims with the Love of Christ

JOSHUA 6

Faouzi Arzouni first presented these thoughts to a meeting of missionaries who work among Muslims. Faouzi was born into a Muslim Shia family from Lebanon and came to Christ in West Africa. He has dedicated his life to loving Muslims. I took his original thoughts and added some of my own.

When we start to think about loving Muslims, we usually think that Islam began in the fifth century with the story of an idolatrous Arabia and the voice that called out for radical monotheism. But I suggest that perhaps we look back a little further.

Galatians 4:4-5 tells us, "But when the fullness of time had come, God sent forth His son, born of a woman under the law, to redeem those who were under the law, that we might receive the adoption as sons."

If you will understand me, God sent Jesus to first century Muslims. The Jews in Jesus' day were legalistic, law-based, community-oriented and hypocritical. If it was possible for a Jew in the first century to embrace Jesus as Lord, it is no harder today for a Muslim. If it was possible then, it is possible now. We face the same objections and the same obstacles. We can take great courage, not only in the testimonies we currently hear from around the world, but at the historical fact that radical first-century monotheists ran, danced, waltzed, leaped and slithered into the Kingdom.

With that understanding, let's look at four snapshots from Scriptures that give us guidance.

REVELATION 12:4

You know the story. A great sign appears in heaven—a woman in labor and great pain giving birth to a son. This son would rule all nations, and then a powerful dragon emerges. "His tail drew a third of the stars of heaven and threw them to the earth. And the dragon stood before the woman who was ready to give birth, to devour her Child as soon as it was born" (Rev. 12:4).

I want to draw your attention to the last phrase "to devour her Child as soon as it was born." When Satan cannot prevent the birth, he tries to kill the child in its infancy. He cannot stop the Israelite women in Egypt from giving birth, so he throws them in the river. He cannot stop Jesus being born, so he kills all the toddlers in Bethlehem.

This is both an encouragement and a warning. The devil is not omniscient. The devil does not know everything. The devil does not have the mind of Christ nor can he discern what God will do. The devil is powerless to stop the work that God will initiate. God will bring life. God will birth what He will. God has brought many Muslims to himself, and He has stirred many hearts to love Muslims. God has done it and it cannot be stopped. But what the devil could not foresee or prevent, he will try and kill in its infancy.

Post World War II, Douglas MacArthur called for missionaries to work among the dispirited Japanese. The country was at an all-time low and MacArthur asked the American church to send 5,000 missionaries. There were no visa problems, only free access. Japan was a country at a crossroads. Their old system shattered; new decisions were possible. MacArthur pled with the American church and total of seven missionaries were sent. Many organizations said "yes" but few followed through. The person in the pew still resented the Japanese. "Those rascals attacked us," they said. "Why should we help them now?"

Today God is giving us incredible opportunities to love the Muslim world. We say "yes" but we do not act on it. "Oh yes, I will love Muslims." Then God opens a door and no one walks through it.

There was a Christian NGO (non-governmental organization) in a Muslim area of Sudan from which the Sudanese staff all resigned due to fear. It was an open door...and we walked away. Through the generosity of Assist International we equipped the Omdurman public hospital with a pediatric ICU unit. Omdurman is a sister city to Khartoum with over 4 million people, and the most Islamic of the Khartoum tri-city area (Khartoum, Omdurman, Khartoum North). The Khartoum Monitor is an English medium paper, and when we visited them concerning the project the editor – a nominal Christian from South Sudan – was furious that we as Christians were helping Muslim Arabs. He was angry that Christian charity was being directed at Muslims.

God is birthing something among Muslims. The devil cannot stop it. The devil cannot deny the birth. But that which he cannot stop being born, he tries to kill while in its infancy. Be glad at what God is doing. Be warned that the devil tries to kill what is birthed in its infancy.

MARK 8:24

This story is also familiar—a blind man at Bethesda. Jesus, contextualizing his healing, puts spit on the eyes of the blind man. This is what the local doctors did in that day. Jesus does this and asked the man if he sees anything. "I see men as trees, walking." What an interesting response. Standing side by side with Christ, side by side with the Creator of both the universe and his very eyes, side by side with the One who raises the dead and sustains the world, the man sees very, very differently.

There was nothing wrong with Jesus. Jesus has and had all power. And yet, even with the presence of the Omnipotent a meter away, this man saw men as trees. Jesus saw men. This man saw trees.

Can I ask this question? How do you see Muslims? As people of God, redeemed and protected by covenant love, you who stand side by side to Jesus, how do you see Muslims?

Many Christians think the best thing for Muslims is that they burn in hell. Faouzi was preaching in the States one year, and as he drove into the parking lot of the church, the car in front of him had a bumper sticker that read "Muslims: Nuke them all." He got out of the car and this man with the "Nuke them all" bumper sticker was an usher in the church—smiling, happy and greeting those arriving.

James and John, walking side by side with Jesus, wanted to call down fire on the Samaritans. Jesus tells them, "You do not even know what manner of spirit you are of" (Luke 9:55).

It happens to people who love Jesus. It happens to us. It happens in this church. Those who love Jesus sing great worship songs, and we walk out of the doors, and in our hearts we call down fire from heaven on those we resent.

How do you see Muslims? As people to be hated? Ignored? Taken revenge on? Or as wonderful chosen humans for whom Jesus died?

MATTHEW 2:1, 9-10

Yet another familiar story, the Wise men bearing a gift. "We have seen his star in the East and we have come to worship Him." Guided by a star. How weird and wonderful is that? Here is the wonderful truth of this method—God in effect says, "I am the God who will do anything and everything to bring those that are far to the truth!" The further some are from the truth; the more dramatic the method may be.

Anna in the temple sees—and she knows—and she rushes to Jesus. Simeon needs a nudge. The shepherds needed an angelic choir. The men from the East needed a star, a dramatic sign in the heavens.

God will move heaven and earth to see Muslims come to Him. What will we do? What price are we willing to pay? What sacrifice will we willingly offer? We rejoice at and anticipate dramatic miracles, but what about the simple things? Are you willing to teach someone to read and write?

Faouzi teaches a young Muslim seeker to read and write. The man becomes interested in the Bible, and they start a Bible study. They go through stories from the Old Testament but they never open the New Testament, and the seeker gets scared and withdraws from the lessons. Then he has dreams, repeated three times, in which there is a light and a voice. Now remember, he never saw the New Testament, nor had they reached the book of Isaiah yet. He tells Faouzi the content of the dream: "Eye has not seen, nor ear heard, nor has entered the heart of man the things which God has prepared for those that love him." The man quotes 1 Corinthians 2:9 perfectly. Faouzi shows him the Scripture, and the man falls on his knees in tears and accepts the Lordship of Jesus in his life.

What are you willing to do to bring the love of Jesus to Muslims? God will move heaven and earth. Will you befriend a Muslim? Teach a Muslim English?

There is a lady in this church. She is from south Sudan. She gives me much joy. She consistently befriends Muslims, loves them, talks to them and laughs with them. I am so proud of her, and Jesus is too.

God moves heaven and earth if He needs to. What will you do?

JOSHUA 5:13

Joshua is thinking like a good military commander. He has crossed the

Jordan and defeated Ai. Now he is ready to attack Jericho. Before that, he goes out for a walk to pray and to clear his head. He sees a warrior with sword in hand. Speaking as one warrior to another warrior, he asks, "are you for us or against us?"

Joshua is a military man. First city to destroy, Ai. Done. Jericho is next. He has forces to muster and plans to make. He meets a big guy with a sword and thinks, "I hope he is on my team." So he asks, "hey, big guy with the sword, whose side are you on?"

What is the response? "Neither."

How would you feel if I reminded you today that God is not on the side of southern Sudan? How would you react if I told you that God is not on the side of political Israel?

The point is that God is not on our side. We must be on His. The point is that we are not in charge of recruiting God to be on our team. He is the Commander of the Army of the Lord and He gives the orders. We get confused, and when given responsibility, we think that means we are in charge. But...

Jesus is in charge, and we better be on His side.

Why was the response "neither"? It was because Joshua was not going to be able to have a logical response to Jericho. It was going to require something non-traditional, something new, something strange. So Joshua asks, "what is the word?" And the answer is something absurd.

Jericho is no problem for God. He will bring the walls down. But that is not the issue at hand. The deal is, Joshua, take off your shoes. You are on holy ground. Joshua, listen. You are in the presence of God. Joshua, listen. You are going to have to do something courageous, something unusual, something non-traditional.

Look around this room. There are hardly any from a Muslim background here. Muslims are not comfortable in our churches. We are going to have to take off our shoes and listen. Are you willing to obey if God tells you to do something foolish?

There was a widow in Brazil with two children and no food. God said go to La Grande, a grocery story with 60 checkout lines. He told her to get enough food for two months and go to checkout counter number 7. She loaded up and queued up in line. She was next in line and the counter closed right in front of her for lunch. They told her to go to another counter and she answered, "My Father told me to come here." So she waited 30 minutes for the line to open again. As they checked out all her groceries, the moment of truth arrived. She had no money. Then over the PA system she heard, "Ladies and gentlemen, to celebrate seven years, check out counter 7 is free."

TWO CLOSING THOUGHTS

I have two closing thoughts from the story of David and Goliath (1 Sam. 17). First, the giant wants to take us out individually, so stay unified. Second, the giant never looked vulnerable until the moment of death. There was no indication he could fall, but then suddenly he did.

So, what is being birthed in you? The devil will try and kill it in its infancy. Do you see as Jesus sees? Are you standing side by side with Jesus and yet see differently? What are you willing to do to see Muslims come to Jesus? Remember God will move heaven and earth. Have you forgotten who is in charge? God is the Commander and He gives the orders. Will you listen, even if it means doing something unusual?

the Inconvenient Lost

1 SAMUEL 14:6-10

As they say in Africa, "My names are Dick Brogden and I am saved." Jesus is my Savior and Lord. I love Him because He first loved me. Jesus is worth it. He is worth everything. And Jesus is not shortsighted.

There are lost in Brazil and Bangladesh. There is despair in Denver as well as Dhaka. The devil and darkness are spread abroad. The universities from which you hail are filled with the perishing. This is true.

It is also true that we have a distribution problem. While the lost are everywhere, the light is not. There are areas of this earth where peoples, tribes and tongues have less access to light than others. This also is true— those without adequate access are the inconvenient lost.

The inconvenient lost are locked behind forbidding borders with hard-to-get and harder-to-keep visas. The inconvenient lost are sequestered in sandy, scorching deserts with inhospitable climates. The inconvenient lost are hidden behind veils, burkas and abayas. They live and die in the shadow of minarets. The inconvenient lost are muzzled by clerics, bound by falsehood and restricted by fatalism. They are not allowed to think, probe or question. The inconvenient lost are best represented by the realm and peoples of Islam.

While I admit there are non-Muslim peoples that are difficult to reach and inconvenient to our grasp, I also propose that Muslim peoples represent the greatest block of the inconvenient lost. There are over 800 distinct Muslim people groups with no witness; 200 of those completely unreached Muslim people groups have populations over 100,000. Eight hundred distinct people groups that are not just unreached—they are unengaged. No missionaries, no believers, no scriptures, no proclamation, no light, no hope. These are the inconvenient lost, for no one works among them.

In March of this year, I was in Bremen, Germany for Christoval, a missions conference with over 20,000 young people who came to celebrate Jesus and to seek His will for their lives. One exhibit was an interactive walk through made up of different tents set up in a cathedral. One tent focused on God's will and why you did not pursue it. As you exited the tent, an oversized blank book was on display and you had the opportunity to write the one reason you were not following God's will.

I flipped through the pages, and in the thousands of entries, one reason was prevalent, written on every page. It was the German word "angst." Over and over and over it was written. It means fear. The greatest hindrance to following God's call is fear. I do not believe that the greatest hindrance to reaching the inconvenient lost is an external foe. Yes, there are demons and devils and powers and principalities that fight against us, but the greatest hindrance to reaching the inconvenient lost lies within us. It is our fear.

Which leads me to ask, "What would you do if you had no fear?" What are the impossible dreams? What are the impassable mountains? If money was not an issue, would you give a year? If personal safety did not matter, would you give your life? What is the challenge God has laid on your heart, so grand that you've told no one? What inconvenience could you rise to conquer? What people would you rush to reach if you had no fear?

Tonight I implore you not to fear. I urge you to look toward the inconvenient lost—not afraid to try, not afraid to cry and not afraid to die.

NOT AFRAID TO TRY

One of my favorite Bible figures is Jonathan, the son of Saul. He was rightful heir to the kingdom, and he delighted in David. But Jonathan was mighty in his own right. In 1 Samuel 14, Jonathan says to his armor bearer, "Nothing hinders God from saving by many or by few. It may be that the Lord will work for us. Let's try. Let's go fight the Philistines. If they say 'come up,' it's a sign; we will go up and fight. If they say, 'We're coming down,' it's a sign; we will stay here and fight."

I hope you see the humor in Jonathan's thinking. He had decided to fight, so whatever the Philistines did, "it's a sign." But here is the main point in verse 6. There was no guarantee of success and Jonathan was not afraid to fail. Jonathan was determined to fight, but he had no assurance of the outcome. "It may be that the Lord helps us," was as cocky as he allowed himself to be. Jonathan was going to try, even though he did not know how it would end.

I'm sure you've heard about the crisis in Darfur, Sudan. Seven years into the conflict, there were 300,000 dead and two million refugees. Arab Muslims slaughtered African Muslims. Khalil Ibrahim is leader of the

Zaghawa rebels and Abdul Wahid is leader of the Fur rebels. These are the two largest African Muslim tribes in Darfur, and they have fought against the government and the Arab Muslim militias.

Brandon Williams was in his mid-20s. He was a missionary in training with us in Sudan. He just finished a year of language school, and we found him an interim job working for a NGO. For various reasons, everyone in the NGO bailed and Brandon found himself country director of this organization. One week into the job, Ibrahim, the leader of the Zaghawa, sent a message to Brandon. "We are tired of fighting," he said. "We are tired of Islam. We want you, the Church, to come help us. We want you to teach our children the Bible. We want you to bring us peace and development."

Wouldn't it be ironic if a clueless 20-year-old missionary in training solved the Darfur crisis? Wouldn't it be delicious if Jesus worked through an unknown to do what the UN, the African Union, Condoleezza Rice, George Clooney and Angelina Jolie all failed to do? Why shouldn't a clueless 20-year-old win the Nobel Peace Prize? Why shouldn't someone in this room one day change the destiny of nations?

Why shouldn't one of you walk out these doors, shake the earth and move its mountains? Why shouldn't someone in this room be the next Samuel Zwemer, apostle to Islam, and lead the King of Saudi Arabia in the sinner's prayer? Why shouldn't someone in this room be the one to pick up the mantle of Billy Graham and in humility evangelize the nations? Why shouldn't we be the generation who takes the gospel to the most inhospitable and inconvenient places on earth?

Is it not fear of the attempt that aborts most victories for the kingdom before they are even born? I urge you. I implore you. I beseech you. Don't be afraid to try—even without a guarantee of success.

"[But] I am not made for perilous quests," said Frodo. "I wish I had never seen the ring! Why did it come to me? Why was I chosen?"

"Such questions cannot be answered," said Gandalf. "You may be sure that it was not for any merit that others do not possess: not for power or wisdom, at any rate. But you have been chosen, and you must therefore use such strength and heart and wits as you have."

"No one answered. The noon-bell rang. Still no one spoke. Frodo glanced at all the faces, but they were not turned to him. All the council sat with downcast eyes, as if in deep thought. A great dread fell on him, as if he was awaiting a pronouncement of some doom that he had long foreseen and vainly hoped might after all never be spoken. An overwhelming longing to rest and remain at peace by Bilbo's side in Rivendell filled all his heart. At last with some effort he spoke, and wondered to hear his own words, as if some other will was using his small voice.

"I will take the Ring," he said, "though I do not know the way."

"I will try. It may be that the Lord helps me," said Jonathan.

"I think that this task is appointed for you Frodo," spoke Elrond, "and that if you do not find a way, no one will. This is the hour of the Shire folk, when they arise from their quiet fields to shake the towers and the councils of the great."

"It is not our part here to take thought only of a season, or for a few lives of men, or for a passing age of this world," said Gandalf. "We should seek a final end of this menace, even if we do not hope to make one."[6]

Let us not be afraid to try. It may be that the Lord helps us—for nothing restricts the Lord from saving the inconvenient lost, whether by many or by few, if we are not afraid to try.

NOT AFRAID TO CRY

In missions, and in the postmodern world today, there is great temptation to dilute our message so that it might be more palatable to the hearer. Transformational development is the buzzword for holism in my circles. Essentially this thinking asks for a balance between word and deed, and most of you would probably agree. I want to ask you to rethink that premise. As pleasant as it sounds, ask yourself if it is biblically supported.

St. Francis of Assisi allegedly said, "Preach the gospel at all times; if necessary use words." I want to remind you that it is always necessary to use words. Humans are receptor-oriented communicators. They assign their own meaning to unexplained deeds.

Not only did St. Francis probably not say that faulty line, he certainly did not live it. Grab a biography of his life. He preached everywhere, even to birds and animals for goodness sake. He also marched right into the camp of the most fearsome Muslim ruler of his day, Saladin, the conqueror of Jerusalem, and preached the gospel to him. How's that for inconvenience?

Here's an illustration. Take the real life case of an SIM missionary to China. He determined to live the gospel, not to preach it. He determined to live such a life of love and service that the Chinese would be drawn to him and ask him about his faith, and then he would explain "the reason for the hope that he has." One year, two years, five years pass. Finally a Chinese man approached. "Can I meet with you in secret?" he asked. "I have been watching your life and have a very important question." The missionary was excited! "Finally!" he thought, "Five years of living the Jesus life, five years of preaching without words, and someone has seen the testimony of my life and wants to know more." They agreed to meet, and the Chinese man earnestly said, "I have been carefully watching your life for five years and I must know, are you a vegetarian?"[7]

If you boiled down the message of the New Testament proclaimers to one word, I submit to you it would be the word "repent." In Matthew 3, John appeared preaching, "Repent." In Mark 1, Jesus began to minister preaching, "Repent." In Mark 6:12, all 12 disciples went out preaching that people should repent. In Peter's Pentecost sermon in Acts 2, he culminated the message with "Repent and let every one of you be baptized." Paul in Athens, the proof text for cultural sensitivity in proclamation, ended his remarks by saying, "These times of ignorance—you blockheads—God overlooked, but now commands men everywhere to repent!"

Jesus in John 6 feeds the 5,000, so they followed Him for more food. "You have to eat me! Does this offend you? What if you see the Son of Man ascend? The flesh profits nothing! The words that I give you, they are spirit and they are life." How radical! How essential. Jesus offended the feeding program beneficiaries. He said that its is His Word that gives life, not food handouts.

And let me highlight John the Baptist, a man not afraid to cry. "Repent! Behold the Lamb of God who takes away the sins of the world!" Jesus said that this John was the greatest of those born of women. Let me ask you then…if Jesus thinks John was the best non-divine we have to offer, who did John feed, clothe or educate? The only water John handed out was in the orifices of the body as he dunked confessors in the Jordan River. John went out in the desert and insulted those who followed. "Snakes, brood of vipers, who warned you to flee from the wrath to come?" And no one born of woman—according to Jesus—had done it better.

Please understand my context. In Sudan, we run schools for the orphaned poor; we drill wells for the parched; we feed the hungry and educate the adult illiterate; and we have volunteers hold convulsing babies so they do not die. We do all these things—and we do them gladly—but this is the reality of fear that I learned along the way. No one likes a proclaimer. No Muslim likes the good news. No Muslim likes to be told that Islam does not cut it and unless he repents, he is headed towards hell.

No missionary likes constant rejection. No missionary likes to be always thought a fool. No missionary revels in being the village idiot with the heretical message. We get tired of the scorn. We get tired of the rolled eyes and not-so-subtle mocking. And as the years go by, we want to be liked, thanked and respected. We tire of the inconvenience of an unpopular message, so we offer something that is wanted. We build a school; we dig a well; and we pass out medicine. And guess what? We're the good guys again. We are praised and blessed. They interview us on TV and put our picture in the newspaper. This is a temptation I fight. It is a battle not yet finally won. Yet in essence we are proclaimers and we cannot be afraid to cry.

Nik Ripken is a missionary who works among Somalis. There were 100 Muslim background believers when the persecution began. Ninety-six of those 100 were killed. Ripken says, "The goal of the devil in persecution is not to chase us away. It is to silence us. When we shut up in the face of fear, we side with the persecutors. When we stand and continue to proclaim, we stand with the persecuted."

Recently a girl from Saudi Arabia came to faith. Her father was a member of the religious police. He found out about her conversion. He killed his own daughter—but not before he cut out her tongue. It's graphic, but demonically symbolic. The devil wants to shut down our crying. He does not necessarily want to remove us. If he silences us, he has rendered us ineffective. And he uses fear to do it—fear of man, fear of trouble, fear of rejection, fear of scorn.

After 96 of his 100 friends were martyred, Nik began an in-depth study around the world on this topic. At the end of it, one staggering point emerged: "The main thing we learned from the missionaries," the Muslim background believers said, "was how to fear."

One missionary gets kicked out for witness, and all the other missionaries decide to lay low for a while and not proclaim so that they not get in trouble. At the first sign of civil unrest or insecurity the missionaries leave. The first bombs have hardly fallen and the missionaries are largely gone.

We cannot be afraid to cry. Yet our crying does not have to be shrill. Our crying does not have to be annoying nor flamboyant.

Let me tell you a true story from Darfur. We have an English center in Darfur. The director's wife is a young mother with three children under three. One day she was sweeping the compound when an illiterate woman came by asking for help. Our missionary invited her in and offered her work instead. Daily they would sweep the compound together and our missionary would share stories of Jesus. She also showed her short portions of the Jesus film and the God story video. After a short time, this illiterate refugee came to Jesus.

Our missionary began to draw simple stick figures to illustrate Bible truths. A process of discipleship began through stick figure drawings. The illiterate woman would use the stick figure drawings to help her remember the lesson and she would return home to share the lessons with her husband and brother. She also took her husband and brother a Bible. Through stick figures and Bible reading, her husband and brother came to Christ.

One day her brother who worked as a driver for a NGO was attacked by jinjaweed (Arab bandits in the Darfur conflict). They were looking for a compressor. Furious because they didn't find one, they beat him within an inch of his life. Bloody, battered, and broken, he was sent to the government hospital in Omdurman (part of the capital 1,000 kilometers from home) for treatment. Waiting outside the hospital for his doctor's appointment, he sat down in a little shop that belonged to an Arab merchant. The Arab merchant began talking to him and then invited him to his nearby house. Upon entering the house, the Arab merchant revealed he was a secret follower of Jesus, a MBB, and prayed for the wounded man in the name of Jesus. They stayed together, and for three months, the healed Darfur man received discipleship.

After returning to Darfur this man lived and shared his faith everywhere and many came to the Lord. One day he was driving to another village in Darfur and an old blind man was in the car. He prayed for this old blind man and the old man was instantly healed. The healed man invited the man to his house to teach more about the gospel, but the neighbors found out and kicked them out. So the old former blind man sent 11 young men back to the refugee camp for teaching. These 11 men came to the Lord and started a house church. There are now several house churches in the village of the old blind man. They have even on their own initiative conducted a water baptism service using old barrels!

Here is the point: The inconvenient lost of Darfur are being reached. Why? Because a mother of three children under three was not afraid to cry, because she was not embarrassed to witness nor disciple through stick figures.

I beg of you. Don't be afraid to try. Don't be afraid to cry. And lastly, don't be afraid to die.

NOT AFRAID TO DIE

It was the spring of 1940. Germany had overrun the defenses of France and Belgium. England had sent its army, the British Expeditionary Force, to help. The cowardly Belgian king surrendered with hardly a fight; the French pulled back in fear; and the British Army ran for their lives, huddled together at Dunkirk. There 350,000 men were about to be wiped out by superior German forces. It was a desperate day.

King George IV sent this message by radio to the shaken troops: "The decisive struggle is now upon us. Let no one be mistaken. It is no mere territorial conquest that our enemies are seeking. It is the overthrow, complete and final, of this Empire and of everything for which it stands: and after that, the conquest of the World. It is a life and death struggle for us all. And if their will prevails, they will bring to its accomplishment all the hatred and cruelty which they have already displayed. But confidence alone is not enough. It must be armed with courage and resolution, with endurance and self-sacrifice. Keep your hearts proud and your resolve unshaken. Let us go forward to that task as one man, a smile on our lips, and our heads held high."

King George received a reply from his Army commanders trapped at Dunkirk. It was only three words: "But if not...." I do not know if you recognize those words. Biblically illiterate America today might miss it, but 1940 Britain knew their Bibles.

Three Hebrew youth refuse to bow to Nebuchadnezzar's image of gold. He built a murderous fire and gave them one more chance to bow. "We have no need to answer you, O King. Our God is able to deliver us and He will deliver us. But if not, let it be known to you that we do not serve false gods. We will not bow." Our God is able to deliver us, but if He does not, I am not afraid to die. I am not afraid of the inconvenience of death.

You have heard this famous quote from the church fathers: "The blood of the martyrs is the seed of the church." If this is true—and it is—then is it also true that we have not yet seen great breakthroughs in the Muslim world, we have not yet seen an indigenous church widely spread simply because we have not planted enough seed—enough bloody seed? If it is true—and it is— that the death of martyrs leads to the life of the Church, then why are we so afraid to die? And why will we not send missionaries to the Somalias of the world? And why do we shy away from the very thing that will lead to life?

I was talking with someone about sending personnel to Somalia. "Not now," you may say, "It is too dangerous." Yes, it is dangerous; faith does not deny facts. But perhaps Somalia is unreached because it has not yet been watered with enough martyrs' blood. We have been stingy with our seed. We have scattered seed largely where it is safe and convenient. We have forgotten that seeds must die in order to bear fruit.

In the movie *The Lord of the Rings*, Galadriel says,

> The power of the enemy is growing. Sauron will use his puppet Saruman to destroy the people of Rohan. Isengard has been unleashed. The Eye of Sauron now turns to Gondor, the last free kingdom of men. His war on this country will come swiftly. He senses the Ring is close. The strength of the Ringbearer is failing. **In his heart, Frodo begins to understand. The quest will claim his life.** You know this. You have foreseen it. It is the risk we all took"[11] (emphasis mine).

I do not talk about death cavalierly. We are not twisted jihadists who madly destroy ourselves. In Christianity, if you try to be a martyr, it does not count! I am talking about fear and not being afraid to die, not being inconvenienced by death, not making life choices based on fear. Dying biblically is not reserved for one heroic moment. We die daily.

In 1988, I was a young college freshman. Two prominent professors at North Central University fell into moral sin. Our academic dean Dr. Meyer addressed us in chapel that week. "You do not wake up one morning and decide to commit adultery," he said. "All large choices are merely the culmination of a series of daily decisions." The decision to die for Jesus in the heroic sense is not ours to make. The decision to die daily is. When we choose to die to our own desires, our own wills, our own flesh, our own convenience; when we submit to our authority, our roommate, our peers; when we yield our rights, our opinions, our preferences; when we say "yes" to the Holy Spirit; when we say, "I will give my life for the inconvenient lost"; and when we lay down our dreams to take up His, we hack away at the fear of dying. We prepare ourselves for the inconvenient lost.

I love the dwarf Gimli, just before attacking Mordor: "Certainty of death, small chance of success, what are we waiting for?" I am not a prophet.

I do not know the dreams God has laid on your heart. I do know that God has expectations and plans for you far beyond what you know. I do know that God wants us to shake this earth. I do know that left to this generation are the inconvenient places and peoples of earth. I do believe that the most inconvenient for us to reach are Muslim peoples. I do know that Jesus is asking us to do something about it. It IS up to us.

I also know that the primary hindrance to reaching the inconvenient lost is fear. It is not convenient to give your life for Muslims. It is not convenient to walk away from a relationship. It is not convenient to defer graduate school. It is not convenient to forgo job opportunities. It is even not so convenient to die.

Yet in the name and Spirit of Jesus, overcoming through His aid all inconvenience, we will not be afraid to try, not be afraid to cry, and not be afraid to die. We will reach the inconvenient lost. It is up to me. It is up to you.

A Day of
Good News

2 KINGS 7

It is an honor to celebrate 110 years of the Assemblies of God in Egypt. Today certainly is a day of good news.

We are all following the news in Syria. Yesterday, I read an amazing story about Syrians. Part of the Syrian army surrounded a city, and no one was allowed to go in or out. All food and supplies, cut off. Famine in the city became terrible. People ate the heads of donkeys and the droppings of pigeons to survive. As terrible as it was, some, in their desperation, even ate their own children.

Four men from that city became desperate, and they said to themselves: "If we stay here, we die. If we go to the Syrian army and beg for bread, maybe they will kill us or maybe they will give us food. But if we stay here, we die for sure. Let us at least go and beg bread at the Syrian camp. If they kill us, we shall only die."

At sunset, the four men snuck away from the city to beg at the Syrian army camp, but when they got to the camp—it was now dark—they were amazed. A rumor had spread through the camp that the Turks and Egyptians were attacking, and the whole Syrian army had fled, leaving all their supplies behind. The army camp was deserted. These four men found food supplies and ate immediately. They found money, clothes, and even gold and silver. The Syrians were so afraid, they left their tents and valuables lying there. There was so much money and clothes that these four men collected it and left the camp to hide what they found. They worked through the night collecting and hiding. They came back and got a second load of treasure and hid that as well. After the second load, they thought about their friends back in the city and they said to one another: "We are not doing right. This day is a day of good news, and we remain silent. If we wait until morning light, some punishment will come upon us."

This is a true story, but it did not happen this week. It happened 2,500 years ago, and it's recorded in the Bible. You can read the story in 2 Kings 7.

WE MUST NOT KEEP SILENT

Friends, this is a day of good news, but we remain silent, and if we wait until morning light, some punishment, some disaster will come upon us.

What would you think of a person if he invented the cure for AIDS but did not tell anyone? Would you consider him a loving person?

What would you think of a person if she invented the cure for cancer but did not tell anyone? Would you consider her a good person?

What would you think of a person who found a crying baby in the street but walked by and did not help that baby? Would that be an honorable person?

What would you think of a person who saw a woman being abused in the market but did not intervene to rescue her? Would that be a respectable person?

What would you think of a family member who received billions and billions of dollars, more money than he could ever spend in 100 lifetimes, but did not help his children, parents, uncles, nephews, or his village in their need and hunger? What type of person keeps good, help, and *life* from those he loves?

Now let me ask you this: What type of church keeps ETERNAL life away from those they love?

We, indeed, celebrate 110 years of the Egyptian Assemblies of God. We are not celebrating buildings. We are not celebrating a license or a permit. We are not celebrating schools or orphanages or institutions. We are not celebrating programs.

Let us not forget what we are celebrating. We are celebrating the fact that we were beggars, we were starving, we were dying, the devil had us surrounded, we were killing each other, we were destroying our own children, we were blind and deaf and lost, we were on our way to eternal death in hell, and Jesus saved us. Jesus delivered us. He rescued us, and He saved us from our sin. Jesus satisfied our hunger with spiritual food. Jesus covered our nakedness with righteousness and reconciled us to God. Jesus gave us peace from war, protection from the devil, and hope of eternal life! This is a day of good news, and we must not keep silent, or some disaster will come up on us.

LEARN FROM THE OLD MAN IN MAURITANIA

In 1992, I was working in Mauritania. There was a famine on the border of Mali, and I went with some friends to help. We delivered meat to the people so they could eat. One of those friends was an old man. This man was very sincere about his faith, and his faith was different than mine. One day, he sat with us and shared about his faith and with tears in his eyes, he begged us to embrace his faith. He was so worried about our eternal life. He was so sincere about his faith that he wept as he invited us to join him. He wept because he loved me. He did not want me to die and go to hell. He believed that only his religion could save me.

Friends, if we really love someone, we will tell them how they can live forever. I did not and do not agree with that old man in Mauritania. His religion is different than mine, but I love him for loving me. And I learned from him, that if I am to love others, I must tell them how to have eternal life, even if they disagree with me.

We are not doing right. This day is a day of good news, and we remain silent. If we wait until morning light, some punishment will come upon us.

Here in Egypt, there are millions who do not know Jesus is the only Savior. If we do not tell them this good news, we are not doing right—and if we wait, some punishment will come upon us. In the Arab World, there are millions who do not know Jesus alone can save them from hell. If we do not tell them this good news, we are not loving them—and some punishment will come upon us. In Afghanistan, Turkey, India, Bangladesh, the Maldives, in Somalia, Zanzibar, Indonesia, and Pakistan, in Iran, Russia, Palestine, Greece, and Germany, there are billions who have never heard that there is deliverance from the devil's armies, that there is food and clothes and supply for spiritual needs—*and if we remain silent, punishment will come upon us.*

Friends, let me be clear. We are celebrating 110 years of the Assemblies of God in Egypt. We are not strong. We are not large. We are but beggars, trying to survive. And in our weakness Almighty God allows us to live. He has provided and will provide; He has protected us from enemies; and He has given us hope and life—for one reason: The Assemblies of God exists to proclaim to the world that there is salvation, hope, life, and deliverance, and that deliverance can only be found in Jesus Christ!

The Assemblies of God exists to share the hope of eternal life with the world. We must overcome our fear and selfishness. We must open our mouths in love. We must lift up Jesus—the only Savior. We must invite all men and all women of every race and religion to find *life* in Jesus! We must share with neighbors, friends, visitors, and even strangers that Jesus has made a way for all *nations* to have eternal life.

This is a day of good news, and we *will not* remain silent, *for if* we wait until morning light, some punishment will come upon us. But if in love, we open our mouths and proclaim to all the world that Jesus can save them from their sins, then truly, there will be something to celebrate about the Assemblies of God.

My Father, My King

The title of my message today is "My Father, My King." The big idea is that our Father and King is looking for fearless messengers who will represent him faithfully among the nations. Our text from Scripture is Psalm 2. Let me initially reflect on this text by means of a fable.

I grew up in a palatial castle. I was a prince, a child of the king. My first memories were the twinkling blue eyes of my father as he played with me in my nursery. I didn't know he was king. I didn't know what a king was. All I knew was the strong arms of my papa as he carried me around. I can close my eyes and remember his comforting embrace, his soothing voice, his silly jokes, and his infectious laughter.

My papa was strong and kind, loving and gentle. All was right in my little world. We wrestled together, played together, giggled together. He loved me, and I was safe. He was so tender. He was so approachable. He was my friend, my father, my comfort, and my peace.

I grew up with this loving man who cared for me and showered mercy, joy, love, and grace upon me.

As I grew, I noticed that not all treated my dad as I did. We had servants who stood straighter and talked less when he came into the room. I could tell they adored my dad as I did, but they were very respectful of him. They used this "king" word—always with anticipation and delight. Like when papa would travel and be expected back, they would say: "THE KING IS COMING!" Then there would be a surge of activity to make sure the castle looked perfect.

I thought it funny and somewhat unnecessary. It's just my dad, and if they could only see him roll around the floor with me, they wouldn't be so guarded or circumspect around him.

It all changed for me one day when I happened by the throne room (changed in the good way, I mean, change that gained something, not a change by loss). I walked past the throne room, and the curtains were agape. I could see in, without being seen, and I could see my dad, and he didn't look pleased.

As I watched some rebels were brought in. I don't think I've ever seen my father so furious, nor the faces of his generals so solemn. I was a little bit surprised.

The rebels did not repent. They cursed my father—even I felt the insult. They threatened, mocked, and insulted the king! That made me tremble. I could only stare at my papa, for I saw things on his face I had never seen before. I didn't really understand what I was seeing—the wrath and the narrowing of his eyes, I had not seen that look before.

My father the king stood up and with a quiet voice, but with fire in His eyes, said, "You have plundered my kingdom, cut down my forests, and polluted my rivers. You have mistreated my animals. You have lived by greed and cruel self-interest. Worse than that, you have ravaged the crown jewel of my creation. You have aborted and abused my children. You have dishonored and enslaved my women. You have disrespected and perverted my men. You have misled the young and abandoned the grey haired. Worst of all, you have not represented my interests or character. You have defamed and slandered my good name. You have rejected my rule. You have twisted my truth. You have insulted and offended me, and you have done so repeatedly with deliberate and evil intent"

The hall fell silent at the angry passion of the king, and then the judgment fell. "Take these rebels and hang them in the public square, and then send some of my best and bravest officers to their stronghold. Send an offer of peace on these inviolate terms: If they will lay down their arms, if they will repent of their wrongs, I will have mercy on them and bring them under the protection of my kingdom. They can eat from my table, and I will shower them with love and affection. But if they will not turn from their rebellion, they will face the full force of my wrath. This is not a discussion, a dialogue, or a negotiation. They must either repent or perish.

I slipped away from the throne room and went to my chamber. My heart hammering. My head exploding. I couldn't quite understand what I was feeling, but when I thought about my father, the king, something expanded within me. I wanted to cry and fight all at the same time.

I heard footsteps and turned. My dad walked in. He suddenly looked bigger and stronger. I ran to him. He embraced me, and I him, and in that intimacy, I was both son and subject. The one holding me was both my father and my king.

Most of us, and fittingly so, first came to know God as Father. This is beautifully fitting. In our brokenness, He loved us, saved us, cared for us, and nurtured us. This love of the Heavenly Father has been our milk, and long will Love's nutrients strengthen our spiritual bones. But now it is time to add the meat.

A maturing child does not treat his father in private as He does in public.

The intimacy of the home and the honor of the office are not in tension. The Father who nurtures and loves us sits on a throne. Yes, a throne we can boldly approach, but still a throne. The children who run to sit on the King's knee must grow into men who prostrate with all of His other warriors.

Is it not awe-inspiring that this most famous of Old Testament verses on missions— "Ask of me, and I will give You the nations for Your inheritance" (Psalm 2:8)—is set in a Psalm about the Messiah and His regal triumph?

We are so used to preaching missions from a John 3:16 perspective, "God so loved," that we have neglected the "God is so angered." In truth, preaching God's love without preaching God's wrath is akin to running an Olympic 100-meter race by hopping on one foot. That one leg may indeed be robust, but without the synergy that comes from a second healthy leg, no prize will be won. One robust leg paired to a shriveled one makes it impossible to run straight, much less to run in such a way as wins the crown. A boat rowed with one arm vastly stronger than the other will reach no harbor but will aimlessly spin in circles. An airplane with one wing curved for lift and the other flat will not safely land, but will swiftly crash.

The nations rage. The people plot vain things. Rulers take counsel against the Lord. The King's authority is questioned. The great throne of heaven is disrespected. The eternal court is despised. Our sovereign God is insulted and demeaned. And now our King raises Himself up from His throne in righteous anger. Now the gavel of judgment descends and falls. Now He who sits in the heavens stirs. He has a message for us to transmit to the nations: "Kiss Him. Placate Him. Bow before Him. Humble yourself. Confess Him as Lord. Make peace with Him 'while it is day, for the [angry] night [of judgment] is coming when no one can work' (John 9:4)."

And oh, by the way, ask of Me and I will give you the nations. The very nations are in rebellion, a rebellion that will be crushed. The great high King is looking for war time ambassadors, representatives to Libya, Somalia, Iran, Afghanistan, and Kashmir. God is searching for fearless proclaimers who will go to the Muslims of China, the Buddhists of Thailand, and the Hindus of India.

He is seeking ambassadors to join their voices to John the Baptist and cry, "Repent! Flee the wrath the come" (Matt. 3:2, 7); to join Jesus in crying,

"Repent, the kingdom of heaven is at hand" (Matt. 4:17); to join Peter in crying, "Repent, and let every one of you be baptized" (Acts 2:38); to join Stephen who cried, "You stiff-necked...you always resist the Holy Spirit" (Acts 7:51); and to join Paul who cried, "These times of ignorance God overlooked, but now commands all men everywhere to repent" (Acts 17:30). The urgent cry goes out from all the King's ambassadors, "Repent! Flee the wrath to come! Kiss the Son. Make peace with Him before He makes an end of you!"

For the fable I told is, indeed, based on fact. Our loving Father is also the insulted, offended, and angry King. In this biblical reality, this is a world where the nations are in rebellion against the King, a world rushing toward the poured-out wrath of God.

Here are the facts:

- There are 7.5 billion people in the world today.

- These 7.5 billion are collected in over 200 nations and 16,000 people groups.

- One nation (political entity) can have multiple ethnicities. Pakistan, for example, is one nation with 400 people groups.

- These people groups align in major affinity blocks, affinities that reach across borders.

- Globally, 32 percent of the world is Christian; 22 percent, Muslim; 16 percent, secular; 14 percent, Hindu; five percent, Buddhist; and 10 percent is a collection of other religious affiliations (Jewish, Sikh, Mormon, Baha'i, etc.).

- For the specific focus of the Antioch Initiative, the Muslim, Hindu, and Buddhist affinities make 41 percent of the world's 7.5 billion peoples, or 3.15 billion people.

- These 3.15 billion people are found in approximately 7,000 unreached people groups.

- An unreached people is understood to be less than two percent evangelical and without the power to reach themselves. They are still in need of missionary presence.

- Of these 7,000 unreached, almost half (3,500) are unengaged peoples: no resident missionaries, no local churches, no access to the gospel, no news of either the King's wrath or of His love. They don't even know what trouble they are in, let alone that there is a loving means of deliverance.

- To add insult to injury, even though the Muslim, Buddhist, and Hindu consortium is 42 percent of the world and about half of the global population, it only receives three percent of the personnel and finances. The King is sorely under-represented to our grief and shame. There are 3.15 billion people who don't even know how badly they have insulted King Jesus. They have no idea that judgment looms. They have no idea that eternal disaster is about to strike.

We are here today, along with friends and leaders, to make an appeal for ambassadors. Fresh from the lands that tremble, fresh from the fields who reject and resist the divine authority of our Father the King, we wonder: *Is there anyone here who will fearlessly and faithfully represent the King among the nations?*

Before you respond, let me expound on the job description with the help of prophets, parables, and apostles, for I don't want to mislead you. The assignment is not for the faint of heart and ambassadors of the King do not achieve prophetic results without prophetic pain.

ISAIAH

Psalm 2 is not the only misrepresented missions text in the Old Testament. Another is found in Isaiah 6. Most missions messages end with the "Here am I! Send me" (Isa. 6:8). I propose we start there and consider carefully what follows.

Let's pick up the familiar story in verse 5: "Woe is me, for I am undone... For my eyes have seen the King, the Lord of hosts." Isaiah sees the King, is undone, is cleansed and forgiven, volunteers, and is then given his assignment in verses 9 to 11: Go, speak to a people who will hear but not understand, will see but not perceive, will have dull hearts, heavy ears, and shut eyes, and go in this futile proclamation until cities are laid waste, houses are without a man, the population is decimated, and the land is filled with forsaken places.

Essentially, the "here I am, send me" of Isaiah 6:8 leads to what feels like a fool's errand in which no one listens. In fact, "here I am" leads to failing 90 percent of the time. I say a 90 percent failure rate because verse 13 offers the hope of a tithe (10 percent) as a remnant, as a stump that remains when the oak is cut down, with holy seed in that stump.

"We are men of action," Wesley said to Prince Humperdink in "The Princess Bride." "Lies do not become us."[13] So here is the unvarnished truth of our call. We see the King. We are commissioned to those who will not listen. We are called to fail 90 percent of the time. "Broad is the way that leads to destruction... Narrow is the gate...which leads to life, and there are few who find it" (Matt. 7:13–14). The missions road is one of heartache. The prophetic call is one of rejection. The rank of ambassador is for those who can handle insult and hold their head high. You will be refused more than you will be accepted. You will appear to fail 90 percent of the time. But the seed is in the stump, and 10 percent of 3.15 billion means 300 million Muslims, Buddhists, Hindus and others will be around the throne, worshiping the King.

Is the King not worth the pain that praise demands?

JEREMIAH

Jeremiah, too, was ordained a prophet to the nations (1:5). "Whatever I command you, you shall speak. Do not be dismayed before their faces. I will make My words in your mouth fire" (1:7, 17; 5:14). His message, so counter to popular opinion, was a burden he could hardly bear: "O Lord, You induced me... You are stronger than I... I am in derision daily... I shouted, 'Violence and plunder!' Because the word of the Lord was made to me a reproach and a derision daily. Then I said, 'I will not make mention of Him, no speak anymore in His name.' But His word was in my heart like a burning fire shut up in my bones; I was weary of holding it back, and I could not" (20:7–9).

What was this message of fire? It was not love, grace, mercy, favor, and blessing. How Jeremiah longed to give those sermons! How he longed to be the good parson for once! No, the message of the prophet was judgment, violence, wrath, punishment, and disaster. The message caused Jeremiah to be hated, and who likes to be hated, either by kin or kingdoms?

We have been told that we must serve in such a way as to be liked, but Jesus says: "Woe to you when all men speak well of you" (Luke 6:26). We have been told that we must unite with those that oppose the gospel. Jesus says: "I did not come to bring peace but a sword" (Matt. 10:34). We have been told to make our voice winsome. Jesus says, Lift up your voice and wail, sons and daughters of Jerusalem, "because you did not know the time of your visitation" (Luke 19:44).

Jeremiah 23:16–20 and 28–29 says,

> *Do not listen to the word of the prophets who prophesy to you... "You shall have peace." For who has stood in the counsel of the Lord, and has perceived and heard His word? Who has marked His word and heard it? Behold, a whirlwind of the Lord has gone forth in fury... It will fall violently on the head of the wicked. The anger of the Lord will not turn back... In the latter days, you will understand perfectly. And he who has My word, let him speak My word faithfully. "Is not My word like a fire?" says the Lord, 'And like a hammer that breaks the rock in pieces?"*

EZEKIEL

Ezekiel understood what it meant to break rocks. In Ezekiel 3, God tells him:

> *Son of man... go, speak to the house of Israel. But the house of Israel will not listen to you. Behold, I have made your face strong against their faces, and your forehead strong against their foreheads. Like adamant stone, harder than flint, I have made your forehead; do not be afraid of them, nor be dismayed by their looks. Son of man, receive into your heart all My words. Tell them, "Thus says the Lord God," whether they hear, or whether they refuse.* (Ezekiel 3:1, 7–11)

Ezekiel says in verse 12, "Then the Spirit lifted me up, and I heard behind me a great thunderous voice: 'Blessed is the glory of the Lord from His place!'" And the hand of the Lord was strong upon him. (v. 14).

It is this encounter with the King, similar to Isaiah's encounter, that leads to the prophetic assignment: "Son of man, I have made you a watchman… When I say to the wicked, 'You shall surely die,' and you give him no warning…that same wicked man shall die…but his blood I will require at your hand" (vv. 17–18). Ezekiel is then told to be mute at times, but when God speaks to him, "Open your mouth, and you shall say to them, 'Thus says the Lord God.' He who hears, let him hear; and he who refuses, let him refuse; for they are a rebellious house" (vv. 26–27).

If you do not open your mouth and tell the Somalis right outside your door that they are in rebellion, that they insult the King, and that wrath descends upon them, then their inevitable blood will be upon your head. Are Somalis hard-headed, bound by Satan, and deceived in Islam? Yes, but God has made the foreheads of His prophetic people like adamant stone, harder than flint. If we do not yell warnings from the ramparts, if we do not shout disturbing news from the walls, if we do not point out the descending wrath, then we have not loved. We have only subtly hated. In wanting to be liked, we have loved ourselves more than we have loved the lost. We have been more concerned with being appreciated than being ambassadors that save lives. If we do not move among Buddhists, Muslims, and Hindus with hard foreheads and soft hearts, we have not represented the King and the blood of three billion people is upon us.

NEW TESTAMENT

And lest you think that this radical messaging is only for Old Testament prophets, consider these New Testament examples.

Luke 12 tells the story of servants waiting for the master's return. "Be ready, for the Son of Man is coming at an hour you do not expect" (v. 40). And what will the Son of Man—gentle Jesus—do to the unfaithful and unready servant? What is the fate of the servant who does not do what he is told to do or does not say what he is told to say? He will be "cut in two" and appointed "his portion with the unbelievers" (v. 46) and "be beaten with many stripes" (v. 47).

Luke 19 is just as graphic. Jesus is asked about the appearing of the

Kingdom of God, and he responds with the parable of the talents. The culmination? What will the Master do when He comes? "Bring here those enemies of mine, who did not want me to reign over them, and slay them before me" (v. 27). These are the words of an angry and insulted ruler.

In Mark 13:3, Peter, James, John, and Andrew ask Jesus about the signs of the end. Jesus details all the terrible things that will happen and says that we must be His ambassadors before rulers and kings. Verse 10 (like Psalm 2) is context for the wonderful missions promise, "And the gospel must first be preached to all the nations," where we must speak whatever is given to us in that hour (v. 11) and where we will be hated by all for His name sake (v. 13).

Is it not remarkable that the gospel going forward to all the nations comes at the cost of being hated and not being loved? Do you doubt this? Does this surprise you? What then of Matthew 24 and 25? These two chapters are all about apocalyptic eschatology. That's the fancy way of saying the end of human-centered history when Jesus comes in power and glory to judge the wicked, vindicate the righteous, and set up His eternal reign.

Matthew 25 ends with: "When the Son of Man comes in His glory… He will sit on the throne of His glory. All the nations will be gathered before Him" and He will judge the sheep and goats (vv. 31–33). In Matthew 24:3, Jesus is asked, "What will be the sign of your coming, and of the end of the age?" Jesus responds, "They will deliver you up to tribulation and kill you, and you will be hated by all nations for My name's sake. And then many will be offended… Many false prophets will rise up…" (vv. 9–11). This is the striking context—being hated and refused.

In the spirit of Psalm 2, Isaiah 6, Jeremiah, Ezekiel, and Mark 13, we have the famous missions declaration of Matthew 24:14: "And this gospel of the kingdom will be preached in all the world as a witness to all the nations, and then the end will come."

In Acts 4:17, post-Pentecost outpouring, the apostles are commanded "to speak to no man [in the name of Jesus]." Peter and John respond in verses 19–20: "Whether it is right in the sight of God to listen to you more than to God, you judge. For we cannot but speak the things which we have seen and heard." Peter and John give a report to the other apostles in Acts 4:24, whereupon they all raise their voices to God with one accord and say:

"Lord, You are God, who made heaven and earth…" Then they quote Psalm 2: "Why did the nations rage, and the peoples plot vain things? The kings of the earth took their stand, and the rulers were gathered together against the Lord and against His Christ (vv. 25–26)." They continued, "Now, Lord, look on their threats, and grant to Your servants that with all boldness they may speak Your word (v. 29)." The passage goes on to say, "And when they had prayed, the place where they assembled together was shaken; and they were all filled with the Holy Spirit, and they spoke the word of God with boldness" (v. 31).

Psalm 2, Isaiah, Jeremiah, Ezekiel, Luke 12, Luke 19, Mark 13, Matthew 24–25, Acts 4, a vision of the King and a burning compulsion to defend His honor and to speak for His fame. Is it strange to hear a missions call linked to the anger and honor of the King? Is it strange to be told that what's needed today—as has always been true—are prophetic ambassadors, apostles who in fidelity to the insulted King proclaim fearlessly that rebellious nations are under wrath and they must run to the King and His cross to escape the judgment to come? Is this discomfort with the reality of our Scriptures and our Sovereign not an indictment on all of us? Has our awe of the King fallen so low that now what motivates us is opinions and causes of men, and not the King Himself? Are we inspired more by the beauty of the earth or the beauty of the King? Are we offended more at man's hatred of man or man's hatred of the King? Are we sickened more when men violate women or when men violate the King? Are we energized more by temporal justice or by the King's eternal laws? Is our goal to be amicable or ambassadorial? Are we driven more by being popular or by being prophetic? And in mission itself, have we taken up the causes of the King as our fuel, or is it the King Himself, His honor, His Name, His glory that gives us life, purpose, and calling?

DARE TO BE

Our loving Father, the King, yet rules. He casts a searching eye over His subjects and commands: Dare to be a Daniel; dare to stand alone. Dare to say "Here am I" with Isaiah for a 90 percent failure rate. Dare to stand on the wall, yelling warning with Jeremiah, tears streaming down your face.

Dare to bang your head with Ezekiel against the stone walls of hell-bound hearts. Dare to join the hated voice of apostles and martyrs of the last two millennium in a gospel proclamation that is faithful to the honor of the King.

We convene to align our attention on the world of unreached peoples. It is right and fitting that we do so. We are accustomed to how our Heavenly Father interacts with the lost in kind, merciful, gracious love. This is most precious to us and ever shall be. But what the rebellious nations need now is not weak and fearful theologians. What is not needed are ambassadors who hop on one leg, flail with one arm, or flap with one wing. The Muslim, Hindu, and Buddhist worlds, 7,000 people groups with 3.15 billion people, need a new Isaiah. They need another Jeremiah. They need a fresh Ezekiel. They need not Joan of Arc, but a new Joan the Baptist. What is needed among the unreached today are fearless and faithful ambassadors, plenipotentiary of the King of Kings, men and women who will proclaim God's wrath and love with equal passion.

Confessions of a God Hater

of a

God Hater

PROVERBS 6:16-19

In the worldwide depression of the early 1930s, a desperate young Greek man named Vasilly Koulamantas found himself destitute. He boarded a ship for New York City. There he found menial work and met a beautiful German girl. They fell in love and became engaged to be married when she became deathly ill and died. Brokenhearted, my grandfather shipped the body of his fiancée back to Germany and returned to Greece.

Mourning his loss, he agreed to an arranged marriage. My mother was the twelfth born of thirteen children in the middle of World War II. And my family was rough. They were known as the crazy Koulamentases. One relative got so ticked at God that he took a shotgun outside and fired at the heavens. My grandmother lost several boys at birth, and the local medium told her that my aunts (her daughters) were the cause. To break the curse my grandmother put one of her own daughters in the walk-in oven to roast to death. My aunt was only saved by the timely intervention of her siblings. Food was so scarce that the family ate weeds and thistles to survive, and when my mother was born, she suckled right from a donkey!

After the Nazis invaded, the war made life more difficult. Soldiers surrounded my grandfather's farm, and on his naming day (like a birthday), the Nazi Commandant paid a visit. Sitting in my grandfather's farmhouse, the Nazi officer looked over at the fireplace. Suddenly, he jerked his chair back and jumped to his feet. Every Nazi officer in the room leapt to their feet as well. His face red, he pointed to a picture on the fireplace mantle and demanded: "Where did you get that picture?"

Stunned, my grandfather replied that it was his deceased fiancée. The German officer began to cry and embraced my grandfather. Between sobs he explained that she was his one niece, his favorite niece. He then turned and barked an order to his junior officers that not one person or possession on that little Greek farm was to be touched. If anyone disobeyed his order, he would shoot him himself.

After the war, my grandfather once again sailed to New York. By washing dishes, he brought over my aunts and uncles one by one. Last to come were my mother, her youngest brother, and my *yai yai* (grandmother).

My grandfather was a stern, hardworking man. He started a little restaurant off Wall Street serving rice pudding and other things. When ladies came in showing too much cleavage, he stormed up to them, pinched their bosoms, and growled: "If you don't want them pinched, don't expose them!" When he saw women in trousers, he marched up to them and shouted, "What are you trying to do? Become a man?" He then threw them out of his restaurant. If men complained about his cooking, he threatened them with a butcher knife. He was verbally abusive to his wife and family. He was so angry and mean that my mother hated him. She and her brother planned how they could kill him in order to protect their mother.

One day my grandfather got saved in a little Greek Pentecostal church, and he became a work in progress. He witnessed to others, and if they would not get saved, he started swearing at them: "What is the matter with you, you stupid, blank-ety blank? Why won't you get saved?" His Greek Orthodox family rejected and ostracized him. He took my mom to that little church in Manhattan on 34th Street where she was one of about two young people. The other was a young expressive Greek who was not too shabby on the piano. His name was Kartsonakis, Dino Kartsonakis.

In that church, my mom gave her heart to the Lord, and God gave her a different spirit. Instead of hating her father, a wondrous love for him grew inside her. She felt pity for him, that his family rejected him. She waited for him at the door and when he came home from work, weary and spent, she got him into a chair, took off his dusty shoes, and lovingly washed his feet.

My mom worked with David Wilkerson in those early years. She walked among the gangs of New York with Nicky Cruz and others, evangelizing and demonstrating the power of God. She then went to Bible college and received further training in Zion, Illinois. She met my father. They married and in 1967 headed to Africa. She was pregnant with my older sister, and they had $50 in monthly pledged support.

In spring 1970, I was born. My father was away on ministry, and I came into the world in a tiny bush clinic by a Quaker doctor. My mom screamed in tongues at the top of her voice for the whole delivery (you theologians make what you will of that; the Quaker doctor is still a little confused). A week later, I was circumcised in that little shack and during the circumcision a storm rushed in and blew the tin roof off (you psychologists make what you will make of that).

I grew up in paradise. My father was a genuine man of God. Like most men of God, he mixed fun, adventure, music, and joy with prayer, sacrifice, and sweat. He was passionate about the unreached and took me up among the nomadic, rugged Turkana people of northeast Kenya.

I remember my mom gave out used T-shirts to the topless women. They were so delighted that the next week they all came to church proudly wearing their used shirts with two big holes cut in the front, so they could nurse their kids. And everybody nursed everybody. Old grandmas, saggy and baggy, plopped their rock-in-a-sock appendage into any crying infant's mouth. I'll never forget watching an old granny shuffling down the desert path. A young baby was strapped by goatskin to her back and when the baby started crying, grandma didn't miss a beat or a step. She just shuffled along, put her hand under her saggy breast, and flipped it over her shoulder to the baby on her back who dry suckled away contentedly.

Yes, wrinkled nudity was normal. I had church outside under thorn trees, killed snakes, jumped off cliffs into volcano lakes, chased lions on my motor bike, explored caves and jungles, all under the protection of a mother and father marvelously in love with Jesus.

I went to North Central Bible College where godly men and women influenced me. I headed off to Mauritania for an internship, married a stunning wife, and learned about ministry in Kenya for two years. We learned mostly what not to do. Then in 1996, Jennifer and I entered the Sudan. We both had Christian heritage. We both had encouraging friends. We both had excellent training. We both had wise mentors and counselors. We were in the service of the King. We lived amongst unreached people. We were giving our lives so that those who never heard might hear.

After several years in Sudan, we got a phone call in the middle of the night. No one calls with good news at 3 a.m. We took the call and heard one of our closest Sudanese friends, Sarah, crying. Her 20-year-old daughter who had a 3-month-old infant just died. Sarah was at the hospital and didn't know what to do. I rushed downtown and found Sarah wailing and walking barefoot in the street. We collected the body from the morgue with other relatives and put it in the back seat of my car. The body laid across the laps of three relatives with dead bare feet pressed up against the window glass.

We drove in silence through the dark night. An Arabic worship tape played softly and Sarah sang along with tears. The moon was full when we arrived at Sarah's slum house. The body was laid on a sisal rope bed in the middle of the mud walled courtyard. Friends and family emerged from the darkness and began to mourn.

I sat watching for a while. Then I distinctly heard the Lord tell me to go and pray for that dead body. I felt the Lord tell me to pray that she would rise from the dead. I argued with Him for a while but eventually walked over to the bed. Several relatives sat on the bed around the body, so I reached past them and put my hands on her head and said, "Get up!" And her head began to lift.

I AM A GOD HATER

I have not yet gotten to the title of this message: "Confessions of a God Hater."

There are two simple, related truths: (1) God is great, awesome, and perfect in all His ways, slow to anger, abounding in love, compassionate, merciful, pure, holy, true, great in counsel, and fearful in wonders, with none like Him; and (2) I am vile, wicked, rebellious, and no good thing dwells in my flesh—and you're the same.

From your youth, most of you have been fed the message that God loves you. Someone sold you a simplified Jesus who begs you to accept Him. Your culture has cheapened the gospel and thereby insulted it. In it, Jesus comes begging, hat in hand, hoping meekly that you will deign to accept Him. As if the God of glory needs your patronage!

"We have taken the infinitely glorious Son of God," writes David Platt in Radical, "who endured the infinitely terrible wrath of God and who now reigns as the infinitely worthy Lord of all, and we have reduced him to a poor, puny Savior just begging for us to accept him."

We somehow think God needed us, that He was lonely as He sat enthroned in eternity. We think that His earth is the center of reality and we are the center of that world. Life revolves around us—our needs, our wants, our pains, our grief, and our glory! We live unto ourselves and Jesus is merely fire insurance. We have no sense of His majesty, and we treat Him so cavalierly. We are not undone in His presence. We do not walk softly in His house. We lost the fear of God and are corrupted by love without truth. We mitigated our rebellion, excused our sin, and rationalized away holiness, and we have no idea of the concept of wrath. And we certainly don't think we deserve it!

I don't know who you see standing before you. But not knowing the evil depth of my own heart, I know enough to confess. I confess that in my flesh, in my unredeemed state, in my natural inclinations, in the testimonies of my actions, I confess that I am a God hater. A Puritan prayer puts it well:

> *Save me from myself*
> *From the artifices and deceits of sin*
> *From the treachery of my perverse nature*
> *From denying the charge against my offences*
> *From a life of continual rebellion against thee*
> *From wrong principles, views, and ends;*
> *For I know that all my thoughts, affections, desires*
> *And pursuits are alienated from thee*
> *I have acted as if I hated thee, although thou art love itself.*

GOD LOVES AND HATES SINNERS

I have two simple points for you to wrestle with here: (1) God loves and hates sinners, and sinners hate Him back; and (2) God has a wonderful plan for sinners like you and me. I know these are shocking to hear, but stay with me and allow the Spirit to confirm what He will.

First, God loves and hates sinners. It's a shock for us to think of God in terms of hate, isn't it? But the Bible is very clear that God hates. We are conditioned to think that hate is wrong. Logic tells us that to love evil is wrong and to hate evil is just, right, and fitting. It is the object of the verb and motive of the heart that justifies hate for humans. God, by nature, is just in all He does, even when He hates. Let me pause here to unpack this, because if you don't understand what I mean here, you won't be able to digest the rest of this.

Our emotional response to hate is that hate is wrong. This is because hate has fueled humans to do horrible things. But hate is in fact neutral, and when you think about it, it's good to hate some things. Elie Wiesel says that the opposite of love is not hate, but indifference. When a loving God hates, it means He is against, so passionately against, that He will destroy. The Bible defines hate as being so against something that one will destroy it. Some things should be destroyed; some things should be under wrath. To hate child abuse, rape, pornography, all of these are appropriate emotions, are they not? We should want to destroy these things. And when I say hate, I mean to be so passionately against something that is wrong that you take active steps to destroy it.

The Bible is full of references to God hating, to God being so against something that He commits it to destruction and places it under His wrath. And yet we know that God is good and we know that God is love, yet clearly a good God hates. Just look at these references:

You shall not set up a sacred pillar, which the Lord your God hates. (Deut. 16:22)

For I, the Lord, love justice; I hate robbery for burnt offering. (Isa. 61:8)

However I have sent to you all My servants the prophets, rising early and sending them, saying, "Oh, do not do this abominable thing that I hate!" (Jer. 44:4)

I hate, I despise your feast days, and I do not savor your sacred assemblies. (Amos 5:21)

The Lord God has sworn by Himself, the Lord God of hosts says: 'I abhor the pride of Jacob, and hate his palaces. (Amos 6:8)

"Let none of you think evil in your heart against your neighbor; and do not love a false oath. For all these are things that I hate," says the Lord. (Zech. 8:17)

For the Lord God of Israel says that He hates divorce. (Mal. 2:16)

Thus you also have those who hold the doctrine of the Nicolaitans, which thing I hate. (Rev. 2:15)

It is clear that God hates. "Yes," you say, "God hates the sin but loves the sinner." That is nice modern nonsense, a faulty philosophy traced back to Ghandi. It's partly true—God does love sinners. But it's partly false—God also hates sinners. God will destroy sinners. He did at the flood, and He will do it again.

God is against the wicked, animate and otherwise. God is angry at the wicked every day, the Scripture says. God will destroy wickedness and the wicked both—His righteousness demands it. God is against—God hates the wickedness and the unrighteousness in me! My sin is not removed from my person. My sin is not a disembodied appendage of who I am. I am tainted, soiled, evil in every cell.

It is not abstract sin alone consigned to hell. Hell is filled with people who are eternally under the destructive wrath of God, the hate of God. Do you doubt me? Look at these stark Scriptures:

> *The boastful shall not stand in Your sight. You hate all workers of iniquity.*
> (Psalm 5:5)

Note: God hates the worker of iniquity, not just the abstract iniquity itself.

> *The Lord tests the righteous, but the wicked and the one who loves violence His soul hates.* (Psalm 11:5)

Again, the text says God hates the wicked person.

> *These six things the Lord hates; yes, seven are an abomination to Him: A proud look; a lying tongue; hands that shed innocent blood; a heart that devises wicked plans; feet that are swift in running to evil; a false witness who speaks lies; and one who sows discord among brethren.* (Prov. 6:16–19)

People are under the wrath of God. People are under His destructive commitment. God hates the false witness—the person. God hates the one who sows discord.

All their wickedness is in Gilgal, for there I hated them. Because of the evil of their deeds I will drive them from my house; I will love them no more. (Hosea 9:15)

This reference is the most alarming. It states that not only does God hate wicked people, but it also declares that He will love them no more. God hates! God is against sin and sinner!

G. K Chesterton puts it this way in his book Manalive: "The goodness of good things, like the badness of bad things, is a prodigy past speech; it is to be pictured rather than spoken. We shall have gone deeper than the deeps of heaven and grown older than the oldest angels before we feel, even in its first faint vibrations, the everlasting of the double passion with which God loves and hates the world."[15]

We do ourselves a disservice, and we are not faithful to God's nature because we are embarrassed about the wrath of God against sin and sinner.

God is good.

God is love.

God is pure.

God is holy.

God is supreme.

God is great.

In God's greatness, He has no tolerance for my rebellion or for yours. There is no one innocent—not the addict, the sex slave, the abused, or the white missionary kid from Kenya.

Don't you see that before we were victims, we were all rebels? Don't you see that God is so *God* that all of us are in our selves repugnant? Don't you see that day-old babies and 89-year-old saints are horrible creatures, disgusting in the extreme, when contrasted to God? But I also believe the Psalmist: "Behold, I was brought forth in iniquity and in sin my mother conceived me" (51:5). I agree with the hymn writer, "Foul, I to the fountain fly."

Our righteousness is like soiled menstrual cloths, says the Scripture. Who wants to touch that? Don't you see that God hates sin and sinner? God is against sin and sinner. God will destroy sin and sinner. Don't you see that the greatness of God demands He be intolerant of sin and sinner alike?

And don't you see we have hated Him back?

We are by nature sons of wrath.

We are natural enemies of God.

We are selfish.

We are prone to wander.

We are rebellious.

We are conniving, hypocritical, foolish, lying idiots.

We love ourselves and excuse our weaknesses.

We are the masters of partial surrender and manufactured reputations.

We live to exalt self and seek our own glory, and all this must be called what it is—it's hating God.

We don't really want Him to rule and reign. We want His subsidy for our ambitions. We can't even claim the satisfaction of hating God first. Due to indwelling sin, we were rebellious at birth, born with a bent heart (Gen. 8:21). The wave of God's wrath towered over us before our first breath. Before we knew that we hated Him, we were under His condemnation.

None are innocent.

None are good.

None love God.

This is the unyielding testimony of both Scripture and history. All have hated God. God hates, and God is against sin and sinner. He must be by nature. We have hated Him back for our nature is rebellious in the extreme. These horrific truths make my next point all the more staggering.

BUT GOD HAS A WONDERFUL PLAN

Some of you were raised in a Christian home as I was. I am so thankful. But one danger of being raised in Christendom is an ironic inoculation from God's wrath. If you have never come to terms with how sinful you are, how disgusting you are in your flesh before God, how the holiness of God demands that He hate sinners, how the goodness of God requires He destroy sinners, if you have not understood the wrath of God, not really understood God's hatred of sin and sinner, God's opposition of you in your uncovered self, then you cannot really understand His great love.

Picture yourself with me standing behind the cross. As we lean out past the bleeding feet, we see a huge wave coming towards us. This wave is the wrath of God. It towers over us. It is 1,000 miles high and stretches beyond east and west. It is unstoppable. It is a tsunami of holy anger against rebellious sin. It rushes down upon us, and we are doomed. This wave of the wrath of God, inescapable, descends on us. It is what we deserve.

And Jesus opens His mouth and drinks it.

Drinks it all.

When Jesus drank the full cup of the wrath of God because He loved us, when Jesus drained the cup of my sin and your rebellion, it killed Him. It was not the nails and flogging that killed Jesus. It was love, the love that drank the full cup of the wrath of God on our behalf. The Scriptures establish that God hates sin and sinner. Think. Stretch us further with this scandal: "He made Him who knew no sin to be sin for us" (2 Cor. 5:21). Think on that. Recoil on that. A God who hates sin—and will destroy it—made His Son to be sin for us! The wrath of God poured out on Jesus, the hate, the opposition, the destructive passion of God, poured out by the Father and swallowed by the Son.

How can this be?

What kind of love is this?

What kind of God is this?

I, so twisted within, so self-righteous, so riddled with false motives, lust, anger, flesh, pride. I, a God hater under His wrath. I, so loved by God that Jesus swallowed the wrath of God for me. "Be of wrath the double cure, save from sin and make me pure."

God sends the destroying angel, sees the blood, and passes over me. In Jesus, wrath and mercy meet! Jesus frees us from our bent toward sinning. Romans tells us that God is both just and justifier.

Before the throne of God above
I have a strong and perfect plea
A great High Priest whose name is Love
Who ever lives and pleads for me.

When Satan tempts me to despair

And tells me of the guilt within
Upward I look and see Him there
Who made an end to all my sin.

Because the sinless Savior died
My sinful soul is counted free
For God the Just is satisfied
To look on Him and pardon me
To look on Him and pardon me.

And:

Yes, Jesus loves me.
Yes, Jesus loves me,
Yes, Jesus loves me
The Bible tells me so.

Because this is true, because Jesus loves me, there really is only one response I can give. I must live a life to make much of God. I must live a life to make much of God. I have heard it said, "We have many conversions through life, not just one," and I have found that to be true. I hope that today is a conversion day for you. I hope that today the shock of God's hate, God's passionate necessity to destroy sin and sinner heightens your worship of Him as you realize afresh His great love, protected by Jesus from the wrath of God. Perhaps like me, you have lived long under Christ's protection, but lived largely for yourself.

WHAT HAPPENED WITH THAT DEAD BODY?

When I laid my hands on that woman's head and prayed, her head lifted up. My heart leapt. Then the head fell back down. A hefty relative chose that moment to get off the sisal bed, and the shifting ropes caused the corpse to move.

As I drove home, the sun began to rise and I entered a conversation with God. "Why?" I asked. "I trusted you and looked foolish. You left me hanging." As I drove, the gentle Holy Spirit prompted me to ask myself: "What would I have done if she had been resurrected?" I thought about it and realized that I probably would have headed straight home to write an email. I would have been very careful to make God the center of the story but just as careful to indirectly let readers know I was involved. The Spirit said to me, "I cannot trust you with My power, for you still want to share in the glory." My disappointment turned to dismay. God is not willing to share His glory with another. Others were left un-helped because I could not be trusted. Over and over, other events have supplemented that incident to continue to show me that I don't live to make much of God. But oh, I want to! I want to live a life that makes much of God. I want to live consumed for His glory!

Here I am, Lord, with Isaiah, undone, glimpsing again Your greatness, ashamed at my smallness. Here I am, Lord, with all that I am not. Here I am, wicked but loved and forgiven. Is it possible, Lord, that You can use my small life to make much of You?

WHAT IS GOD'S PLAN FOR ME, FOR YOU?

This is the plan of the God who loves you: Make much of Him! Make much of Jesus! Live to make Him famous! Live to proclaim the unsearchable riches of Christ!

You may have been sexually abused. You may be Miss Goody-Two-Shoes. It doesn't matter. In our flesh, you and I are disgusting before God. We all sullied ourselves before others soiled us. But Jesus swallowed God's wrath. We now are accepted, covered, and cared for in the beloved, loved eternally. Therefore, let's live to make much of God!

This is in the end why mission is so vital for us all! A world under the wrath of God, men and women in rebellion from every tribe and tongue, all hate Almighty God. To see their poverty, pain, needs, and longings is important, but it's senseless if you don't see their rebellion and their God-hating hearts! They stand under the wrath of God about to perish!

Who will warn them? Who will value them enough? Who will shout out the good news of the wrath swallower? Who will plead, "Turn from your wicked ways. Escape the wrath to come. Receive the love of Christ, that times of refreshing may come"? Who will live to make much of God? Who will come to terms with the horror of who we were that we might live in the wonder of who Christ has made us?

That I a child of hell,
Should in His image shine—the comforter has come!

Who will live dead? Who will live to make much of God?

Oswald Smith tells the story of Alexander Duff. Duff was a veteran missionary to India who returned to Scotland to die. As he stood before the General Assembly of the Presbyterian Church, he made his final appeal, but there was no response. In the midst of his appeal, he fainted and was carried off the platform. The doctor bent over him and examined his heart. Presently Duff opened his eyes. "Where am I?" he cried. "Where am I?"

"Lie still," said the doctor. "You have had a heart attack. Lie still."

"But," exclaimed Dr. Duff, "I haven't finished my appeal. Take me back! Take me back! I must finish my appeal!"

"Lie still," said the doctor again. "You will go back at the peril of your life."

In spite of the protests of the physician, the old warrior struggled to his feet, and with the doctor on one side and the Moderator of the Assembly on the other side, he again mounted the steps of the pulpit platform and as he did so, the entire Assembly rose to do him honor. Then, when they were seated, he continued his appeal.

"When Queen Victoria calls for volunteers for India, hundreds of young men respond, but when King Jesus calls, no one goes." He paused. There was silence.

Again, he spoke. "Is it true," he asked, "that the fathers and mothers of Scotland have no more sons to give for India?" He paused again. Still there was silence.

"Very well," he concluded. "Then aged though I am, I'll go back to India. I can lie down by the banks of the Ganges and I can die, and thereby I can let the people of India know that there was one man in Scotland who loved them enough to give his life for them."

In a moment, young men all over the Assembly sprang to their feet, crying, "I'll go! I'll go!"

When the leaders and causes of this world call for volunteers, thousands of young men respond, but when King Jesus calls, when God calls, it's a few brave women alone who tend to respond. Is it true that the churches and families of America have no more sons to give for the nations? Is it true there is no person hearing this who will live a life that makes much of God? Will no one give his or her life to make much of God among the nations?

For the Mouth of the Lord has Spoken

ISAIAH 40

> *The voice of one crying in the wilderness: "Prepare the way of the Lord; make straight in the desert, a highway for our God. Every valley shall be exalted and every mountain and hill brought low; the crooked places shall be made straight and the rough places made smooth..."*
> (Isa. 40:3–4)

In 1900, the Arab world, ranging from Mauritania to Iraq, stretching from Lebanon to Yemen, reaching across North Africa, the Middle East and the Arabian Peninsula, was 13 percent Christian.

In 2012, Iraq had 2.3 million Christians. Today it has about 230,000. That is a 90 percent loss due to immigration and persecution.

In 2014, Syria was 19 percent Christian. Now nine of its 17 million people are displaced—internally or externally unable to live in their own homes. The percent of Christians is unknown, possibly as low as five percent.

About five years ago a revolution began in Tunisia. It spread to Egypt, and since around 2013, 250,000 Christian families, over one million people, have left Egypt for friendlier climes. Add to that, the reality that nearly one million Muslim Egyptians are born each year. You can quickly deduce that in the last three years Egypt has lost a million Christians and gained three million Muslims—a net plus/minus of around four million Muslims. In order to gain ground in Egypt, we would have to lead over a million Muslims to Jesus every single year.

In 2016, the Arab world is now four percent Christian, down from 13 percent in 1900, and it will continue to decline to three percent over the next few years.

Faith does not deny facts, and the facts are these: While it is true that never in history have we seen so many Muslims coming to Jesus, it is also true that never in history have the valleys been so dark; the highways crooked; the mountains of wrath, violence, and defiance so towering; and the powers of darkness so enthused. The facts are these: Simply due to persecution, immigration, and high Muslim birthrates, we are losing ground and we are losing the battle. Never in the history of the world, never in God's redemption timeline has the Arab world been less Christian than it is now.

And it is to this hour and these realities that the prophetic word of God insists: "The glory of the Lord shall be revealed, and all flesh shall see it together; for the mouth of the Lord has spoken" (Isa. 40:5).

Isaiah prophesied during the reign of four kings of Judah — Uzziah, Jotham, Ahaz, and Hezekiah. He witnessed the advance of antagonistic powers. He rode the waves of revival and rebellion in Judah. He witnessed the menace of invaders and the gathering clouds of war. His day was not significantly less fearsome than ours, thus we take up his prophetic declaration for our times and we make verse five our outline for today.

THE GLORY OF THE LORD SHALL BE REVEALED

What a comfort that God has allowed us to peek at the end of the book! Surrounded by darkness, faced with unsavory choices in local politics and global economics, losing freedoms and common decency in the public sphere, we have not lost the hope of the promises of God. We have the prophetic word.

Standing on the promises that cannot fail
By that living word of God we shall prevail.[16]

We know that Jesus is coming in glory. We know Revelation 5:9 guarantees around the throne we will assemble with every tribe, tongue, people, and nation. We know that every knee will bow and tongue confess that Jesus is Lord, to the glory of God the Father. We know that Somalis, Arabs, Moors, Turks, Malay, and Uighurs — every nation, every tribe on this terrestrial ball — will Him "all majesty ascribe and crown Him Lord of all."[17]

We have read the back of the book and we know the last headline of human history is that Jesus wins and the Glory of the Lord shall be revealed.

Lift up your heads, O you gates!
And be lifted up, you everlasting doors!
And the King of glory shall come in. (Psalm 24:7)

I heard a beautiful story this week from North Africa. A Muslim woman fell in love with Jesus. She was isolated and had no Christian friends, but she knew she wanted Jesus to be her King of glory. With no church background, never hearing about the sinner's prayer or catechism or membership classes, she did not know what to do, she just wanted to invite the King of Glory in. So, she made a huge, lavish feast. She prepared numerous dishes in the Arab style—multiple meats and grains and fruits and vegetables. She set the table with her finest. She laid out the food in appealing style. And she prepared two places at the table. Then she went to the door of her house, opened it and welcomed in the King of glory. "Come in Jesus, dine with me," she said. This was the only way she knew to welcome Him in. This was her turning point, her entry into faith. She made a banquet for Jesus, and He set His banner of love over her.

This is a beautiful revelation of glory. The Old Testament word for glory is usually *khavod*, and it most literally means weight. When Jesus comes, you can feel His presence. When Jesus comes, there is a tangible wonder to both body and spirit. When Jesus comes, all else is unimportant.

Oh yes, Jesus is coming again. Jesus is coming in power and great glory. The glory— the tangible, weighty, presence of the Lord — will be revealed. In that great and glorious day, all who have glorified him will be vindicated and all who have rebelled will be eternally and painfully punished. "The kingdoms of this world have become the kingdoms of our Lord and of His Christ, and He shall reign forever and ever" (Rev.11:15). It is our blessed hope in a world gone mad.

But it is just as true that Jesus is going to come to His people before He comes for His people. Have you prepared a lavish feast for Jesus? Have you gone to the door and welcomed Him in? Has the glory — the tangible, weighty, soul-satisfying presence of Jesus — filled your heart? If the glory of Jesus is not real to us, if caffeine does more for us in the morning than the presence of Jehovah, if we are not awed and enriched by the dynamic, current, consuming, intimate glory of Jesus, how can we claim that wonder for others? If we are not desperate for Jesus, how can we expect a revelation of His glory? If His glory is not revealed to us, how will reach the world?

Beloved, have you opened the door for Jesus? When was the last time you invited Him in for a lavish feast? When was the last time, the presence of the Lord was so strong upon you, so strong in this room, that all else stopped, all else paled. The glory of the Lord *will* be revealed to God's people *and* to the world. Or as in the second phrase of Isaiah 40:5...

ALL FLESH SHALL SEE IT TOGETHER

The Live Dead movement is dedicated to the glory of Jesus among all peoples. We affirm that God is the center of mission; that all peoples and all things are only fully satisfied when they are satisfied in Jesus; and that God is most glorified when He is all we want, and all we need.

In Live Dead we have three non-negotiables: Church planting, unreached people groups, and teams. We are committed to planting churches where churches do not exist — that is among unreached peoples — and we are committed to doing that in teams. For not only will all flesh see the glory of God together, all flesh must proclaim the glories of God together.

When we talk of mission, it is foolish to think we can do it alone. It is foolish to think the Assemblies of God in America can reach the world. It is foolish to think all flesh will see the glory of God if we only work with those we like. If all flesh shall see the glory of God together, then all the church must spread the glory of God together. *We are going to have to be just as desperate to work together as we are to see the glory of God.* It is, after all, the "together" in glory that makes it ever sweet.

Let us not forget the privilege we have to assemble together. In the Arab world, recently there has been revolution and bloodshed. You probably remember the 21 men, mostly Egyptians, who had their heads cut off in Libya in 2014. In 2015, a Libyan Muslim from a wealthy clan witnessed the violent slaughter of several Sub-Saharan Africans in his village—simply because they were nominal Christians, not Muslims. The barbaric act in the name of Islam disgusted him and disillusioned, he fled.

He knew no one, and alone and afraid in a North African country he began to search. Finding a website that glorified Jesus, he read about the love of God and within one week decided to follow this Lord of love. Scripture alone led him to desire baptism, so by himself he went into his bathroom and splashed some water on himself. "I knew I could not use water from the toilet tank" he said, "but I didn't think sprinkling was enough. So, I found a bucket and doused myself again." Now, that's the real Ice Bucket Challenge.[18] (By the way, as difficult as it is to stomach all these atrocities by radical Muslims today, there has seldom been a better time to witness, for the gospel has never looked so good!)

Islam as it is broadcast is disenfranchising Muslims by the scores. In fact, in Egypt the largest growing demographic is atheists. The Muslim Brotherhood surged to power in 2012 by claiming, "Islam is the answer." But the masses are finding that Islam is the problem. And who would have thought, with our Cold War past, that we would rejoice when someone became an atheist! For we know that atheism cannot satisfy the glory void and that it is but a step in the flesh towards our glorious Savior.

An isolated Muslim woman in an Arab nation wracked by war came to Jesus. She had no Christian friend and was aware of no other Christian in her nation. She longed for a Bible, just to hold the Word of God. This brave new believer could not rest without getting a Bible, and at great peril to her life, she traveled across her war-torn nation to a neighboring country, to meet a missionary just to get her hands on a Bible. They arranged the meeting by phone in clandestine fashion. Upon meeting, the missionary tried to engage in conversation but the new believer wanted none of it, brusquely demanding to see the Bible. The Bible was produced and presented, and this brave woman with eager, anxious hands reached out soberly for it. For the first time in her life she had the trusted Word of God in her hands. She had never even seen one before this moment. Reverently and with emotion, she brought the Bible to her lips and kissed it. Then without opening it, she slowly extended her hands out. She gave it back to the missionary saying, "If I take this back to my home, they will kill me. I just wanted to see and hold it once." And we who have multiple bibles in our homes or on our devices, when was the last time with shaking hands we kissed the precious revelation of God's glory?

Another disenfranchised family in North Africa rejected Islam and decided as a group to seek what is eternally glorious together. The family of six divided up the major religions of the world for study, and each member of the family began to research a religion. One daughter had a dream and in her dream, she saw a Bible floating in the air — nothing above it, as if to say there was no higher authority, and nothing below it, as if to say it need not rest on any other truth. She shared her dream with her family, and they concluded the Bible alone must be true, and they must find one together. Searching online they found an advertisement for a free Bible, so they asked for one to be sent to them. After several weeks, a follow-up inquiry was sent to see if the Bible arrived. It had not; it had been captured in route. So, the missionaries said, "We will bring you one!" and a meeting was arranged.

After the meeting was arranged, the family began to wonder, "Is this a trap? The sent Bible had our address on it. Could this be security trying to arrest us? If one of us goes to meet the ones bringing a Bible and it is a trap, will we disappear?" The family wrestled with their fear, but their longing for the trusted Word of God overcame their fear. One daughter said, "I will go meet these people. We need a Bible. And if I perish in a trap, then I perish." Her sister could not bear the thought of her going alone, so she pledged to go with her. With tears and shaking, these daughters hugged their family goodbye, not knowing if they were walking into danger or delight and nervously headed to the rendezvous point. What glad delight they had when they saw those appointed to meet them were foreigners so they knew they were not security police. The Bible was received, and all flesh saw it together. The whole family of six has come to Jesus and have all been baptized! The glory of the Lord shall be revealed and all flesh shall see it together.

There is but one chronological indicator of Jesus coming in glory: Matthew 24:14. "The gospel of the kingdom will be preached in all the world as a witness to *all the nations* and then the end shall come" (italics added). The Spirit will be poured out on *all* flesh. The gospel preached to *all* people. *All* shall see it together. Which in mission is why we must ask the critical question of "where" — where is there flesh, where are there peoples that have never heard about Jesus and who have never known or seen the glory — the tangible presence of a loving God. It is there that we must send. It is there that we must spend. It is there that we must go, live, and die that *all* may see Him together. Is there someone here today God is calling to the Arab world?

Yes, the glory of the Lord will be revealed. Yes, all flesh must see it together, for thirdly...

THE MOUTH OF THE LORD HAS SPOKEN IT

My family and I live in Cairo, surrounded by lostness. The Arab world has between 300 and 400 million inhabitants. Egypt has almost 100 million citizens. This means that more than one quarter of the Arab world lives in one country. Cairo has 25 million people. Greater Cairo, a one-hour radius or so, has about 40 million people. Within one hour of my house lives about a tenth of the Arab world.

Islam is the premier issue of our day. War, terrorism, Islam, the politics of oil, Israel in an Arab sea, all demand the attention of the globe for good, for bad, for the gospel and for otherwise. The center and origin of Islam is the Arab world. If all flesh is going to see the glory of God together, then something dramatic is going to have to go down in the Arab world.

Lostness can overwhelm you. How can a city of 25 million be reached when we struggle to reach our neighbor? As I noted earlier, if almost a million Muslims are born into Egypt annually, we would need to reach a million each year just to gain one inch of ground. And in the last year our team has led two Muslims to Jesus.

Yes, there are other teams. Yes, there are national brothers seeing more fruit than us, but even when we put together all the new believers of all God's people, we don't even reach 1,000, with a million new souls added to the crippling numbers of the lost. How on earth are we going to reach Cairo, Egypt, the Arab world, and the Muslim world?

There is a hill called Mt. Moqqatam on the east bank of the Nile in Cairo. You can drive to the top of this hill for a panoramic view of the giant city. I was there last week, and the week before, praying with a team over the city. I looked down the hill and saw a military base. It had a dusty soccer field, and some children of officers were playing soccer. One of those teenage boys was wearing a bright green shirt. It was vibrant and stood out on a dry, sandy background. I thought of him walled in that military compound, walled in a coercive ideology, insulated by a mass of humanity 25 million strong. How on earth do we reach Him, Lord? Does he even have a chance?

I got in our Speed the Light[19] car and began to fight the Cairo traffic heading home. Honestly, I was depressed as I poked along in traffic.

Absentmindedly, I turned on the radio and my iPhone randomly selected the remix version of Handel's Messiah. Sandi Patti with her incomparable soprano voice begins to belt out Isaiah 40:5: "For the glory, the glory of the Lord shall be revealed, and all flesh shall see it together, and all flesh shall see it together." And the music begins to swell, and faith begins to rise in my heart (as tears likewise in my eyes) and I began to pound the steering wheel and crank the volume up as high as my 45-year-old ears can take. "For the glory, the glory of the Lord shall be revealed for the mouth of the Lord has spoken it!"

This priceless vision is not guaranteed to us by some charlatan! This promise of the knowledge of the glory of the Lord covering the earth as the waters cover the sea (Hab. 2:14) is not the word of some street magician. This oath that *all flesh* shall see it together is not guaranteed by a salesman or a politician. This declaration that the hardest sinner can repent; the vilest nation can be changed; the highest mountain humbled; and the most crooked highway straightened — this affirmation that He will be the praise of every tongue eternally — these promises are not given by mortal men, nor even angel tongue, but the mouth of the Lord has spoken it! Spoken it!

APPLYING ISAIAH 40:5

First, if you really want the glory — the weight of the presence of Jesus to be made known globally — you must intimately experience it personally. When was the last time you prepared a banquet for Jesus? When was the last time you personally, privately lavished your attention on Him? Do you want to change the world? Your heart must once again be madly, exclusively in love with Jesus. One application is to say, "Jesus, I've been distracted, neglected you, my pearl of great price, but I want to adore you. I want to banquet with you alone, just the two of us, under the banner of your love."

Second, if you really want all flesh to see it together, you must ask the where question and be willing to be part of the answer. Where is Jesus not glorified? Those places and peoples will be our priority. One application is to join the Live Dead family in our Wednesday fast. Wherever you are, fast Wednesday lunch and pray with us for unreached places and people.

Another application is to say yes to Jesus to join one of our church planting teams in the Arab world. No matter your age, gender, or education, to say, "Yes, Lord, I'll be part of the all flesh that sees these last days' miracles together."

Finally, if you really believe that the mouth of the Lord has spoken it, then your mouth will also speak. God has brought Muslims to our schools and offices and neighborhoods. If you really believe that the glory of the Lord will be revealed, that all flesh will see it together because the mouth of Jehovah has spoken it, then one application is to befriend a Muslim right here in your world and speak, love, and pray them to Jesus. Another application is to give sacrificially of your finances so this same proclamation can happen in the hardest places of earth.

Abide, Apostle, Abandon

JONAH 3

This chapter includes my sermon from the Centennial Celebration of the Assemblies of God in August 2014, an event that marked the 100 years of the church fellowship in America. Thus, the references to the Assemblies of God in the text.

We've probably all heard about what has happened in Iraq: Children butchered, women raped, men forced to convert to false religion, villages attached, fear spread throughout the region, heads cut off and displayed to intimidate any who dare resist. You know what I'm talking about, don't you? I'm of course talking about the Assyrians in the time of Jonah, 2,500 years ago.

Nineveh, Assyria's capital, was in present day Iraq—the same land where Islamic fanatics now rage. The Assyrians were a violent, bloodthirsty, intimidating aggressor bent on world domination, just like the Islamic caliphate in Iraq and Syria today.

To me the great miracle of Jonah is not that the sea calmed when Jonah was thrown in or that the fish swallowed Jonah in order to save him. To me the great miracle is that the intimidating, bloodthirsty, disobedient, false-religion-spouting city of Nineveh repented! And if God did a miracle like that once, can He not do it again? Is He not the same God with the same glory? If God can change the hearts of the Assyrians, He can certainly change the heart of radical Muslims. All He needs are a few Jonahs.

At the end of this chapter, I will ask if there are any modern-day Jonahs: Jonahs who will stop running to comfort and away from danger, Jonahs who will walk fearlessly to the most dangerous places and peoples of this world and boldly preach Jesus, Jonahs who will give generously of their resources for the glory of God among all peoples.

Perhaps you're wondering how this can possibly happen? How can God take the magnified folly and weakness of our flesh and current church culture, and turn it into the wisdom, power, and authority of God among all nations? It is my conviction and it is the belief of Live Dead that the impossible can once again occur in the Ninevehs of our day.

If we will abide.

If we will apostle.

If we will abandon.

IF WE WILL ABIDE

First, we must abide. We must return to and maintain the simplicity of just having Jesus.

In John's missionary gospel, John simply states the heart of mission: "If you abide in me and I in you, you will bear fruit, and your fruit will remain" (John 15). In other words, Jesus is saying, "The only way to make disciples and plant the church among unreached peoples is if you spend extravagant time with me!"

Paul puts his mission perspective in this light: "I determined not to know anything among you except Jesus Christ, and Him crucified" (1 Cor. 2:2). Paul worried that his disciples would drift away from "the simplicity that is in Christ" (2 Cor. 11:3).

In 1992, I was 22-years-old. I graduated from North Central University and left the U.S. for the Islamic Republic of Mauritania in West Africa. Mauritania is 99.9 percent Muslim. A civil war, in which Arab Moors killed African Pulars, had just ended, and the team I went to join was not happy to have me. It was a multi-national team, and in a tense, war-torn nation, they thought a young American would jeopardize them and the work.

I walked out of the modest airport where the acting team leader, a big, strong, rugby-playing Brit, met me. He wore the Mauritanian robe and a frown. His arms folded across his chest. He greeted me with these words: "We don't want you. You are not welcome. Get back on that plane and leave."

We argued for some moments in the hot summer evening in the parking lot and I refused to get back on the plane. Reaching an impasse, my leader told me: "If you will not leave, this is what I will do. I have arranged a one-room rental for you in the middle of the slum. The room shares a courtyard with a widow and her grandchild. There is no water, no electricity, no furniture, and no kitchen or supplies. There is only a one-inch foam mat on the floor and there is a pit toilet in the courtyard. I will drop you off with this woman in the slum and leave you for two weeks. If you survive those two weeks, I will consider allowing you to join our team."

And that is what he did. I spoke no Arabic. I knew no one. It was just Jesus and me all day long. I woke up at 5 a.m. and prayed until the sun came up. I read my Bible. I walked the streets and watched where local people bought bread. I pointed to the bread and opened my wallet and let the baker pick out what he wanted. I spent my days praying, crying out to Jesus for help, alone and afraid. At sunset, I walked outside the slum to the large fields of garbage that stretched from the city to the Atlantic. I walked among the garbage and sang to Jesus. There was no else I could talk to. I had no one. I had nothing. All I had was Jesus.

In those African sunsets, Jesus came and walked with me. Oh, how sweet His presence was. Oh, how close He felt. I sang and cried and poured my heart out to Him—and Jesus came near. He was very near. The nearer Jesus came the worse I felt about myself. I prayed to Jesus at least four hours every day. I read massive amounts of Scripture. Yet, the closer I came to Jesus, and the nearer He came to me, the more ashamed I was of my sin, the more astounded I was by His grace, the more shattered I was with His love for the lost. I sang songs like,

I was sinking deep in sin—very deeply stained within and

I stand amazed in the presence—and wonder how He could love me, a sinner condemned, unclean and

I need Thee, oh, I need Thee.

I cried and rejoiced that Jesus saved me and I felt as if I would burst in His presence. I cried and mourned that everyone around me was going to hell. I felt like I would explode with His passion.

Jesus was all I had—and all I wanted and all I needed. It was incomparably sweet—to have nothing but simply Jesus. From that simplicity, the fullness of having nothing but Jesus, from the sweetness of abiding with Him, from the nothingness of being unable to help anyone, came incredible power and favor.

Friends, we won't change the world because we are young. We won't reach the nations because we are many. We won't evangelize the lost because we have energy and enthusiasm. Our power is not in our ideas. Our power is not in ourselves. Our power is in the precious presence of Jesus, in abiding in Him.

When Jesus thrills our souls, He cannot be contained in our hearts. He swells in our spirits and He is a fire in our bones. He bursts forth from our tongues. When Jesus is all that we want, we find that He is all that we need. Being full of Him, we stand before men and women with faces shining and eyes piercing and tongues praising. It is the ongoing experience and reality of Jesus that empowers witness.

Do you want to change the world? Do you want to shake the nations? Do you want to see Jesus glorified in the darkest, vilest, most demonized places of earth? It can only be done if you learn to abide in Jesus. The only ones who will change the world for eternal good and the glory of God are those who give Jesus extravagant daily time in the word and prayer. The real world-changer is the one who has learned to abide in Jesus. "Turn your eyes upon Jesus," said Lillias Trotter. "This, this is my secret!" said George Mueller. "The word of a gentleman," wrote David Livingstone. "The exchanged life," Hudson Taylor called it.

Do you want to change the world? You must abide. You must learn to spend extravagant time every day in the presence of Jesus, in the Bible and in prayer. If you do not learn to abide in Jesus, you will merely travel the world and add your vile sinful self to its corruption. All those that walk into darkness must first learn to abide in the light. It is Jesus, and Jesus alone, who will change this world, and you and I better be full to the bursting with Him.

IF WE WILL APOSTLE

Next, we believe we can complete the Great Commission if we will apostle, if we will advance together in planting the church where it does not exist.

In Romans 15, the Apostle Paul talks about what God has accomplished. "[Through me God has made] the Gentiles obedient…in mighty signs and wonders, by the power of the Spirit of God, so that from Jerusalem and round about to Illycrium I have fully preached the gospel of Christ" (v. 18–19).

Oh, praise and glory to Jesus! For the honor of His name, the Assemblies of God has preached the gospel fully from Los Angeles to Boston, from

Boston to Nigeria, from Nigeria to Mauritius, from Mauritius to southern India, from southern India to the Philippines, from the Philippines up to China, from China over to Fiji, from Fiji to Argentina, from Argentina to Mexico, and from Mexico back to the Bible Belt of America. Praise and glory and honor to Jesus that the full gospel has been fully preached. Praise Jesus that over the years, the frontiers have been penetrated, and indigenous churches have been established. This is marvelous in our eyes and our hearts rejoice at what God has done.

In the light that the gospel has been fully preached in some places, Paul continues in Romans 15:20: "I have made it my aim to preach the gospel not where Christ was named, lest I build on another man's foundation."

"I have made it my aim," Paul tells the Corinthian church that he pioneered, "to preach the gospel in the regions beyond you" (2 Cor. 10:16).

Let me be very clear, even if I offend you. Some of you have been told that everyone is a missionary. This is sheer nonsense. For as British historian Stephen Neill said, "If everything is missions, nothing is missions." Biblically and logically, missions is critically distinct from other important ministries. If you take Paul as your model missionary, missions must mean the regions beyond. If you take Jesus as your model missionary, take note—missions is not toward Christians, not to the saved, not to the found, not to the household of faith. Otherwise, Jesus could have stayed in heaven ministering to the angels, filling celestial pulpits and singing in multiple languages in sanctuaries of heavenly comfort.

Missions is not even strictly an issue of lostness, for there are lost people everywhere in the world. Missions is an issue of access. Missions means that we take the gospel where it has not gone. Missions means we pray with an open Bible and an open map. Where does the church not exist? Where has the gospel not gone? Where are there unreached peoples? God does not love the Muslim more than He loves the homeless pagan outside your door—but He certainly expects that we give our lives so that all might hear!

In these last days before Jesus comes, can we not commit ourselves to live and die for Him far from our homes? Cannot someone live and die for Jesus in Mogadishu? Cannot one young man and woman say, "Yes, Lord, I will go to Afghanistan? Cannot one young lady say, "Yes, Lord, I will preach Christ in Libya or Mali?" Cannot one leader say, "Yes, Lord, Yemen for the cross of Christ!" Cannot someone echo John Knox of Scotland and say, "Give me Somalia or I die? Give me the Rashaida or I die? Give me the Bedouin or I die?" Is there no one who will risk life and limb that some Syrian turns to Jesus? Is there anyone willing to go to jail in Saudi Arabia that the Saudis might be free?

We must apostle, and our apostleship is not to be rendered in the shadow of a thousand steeples. Our apostleship must drive us into the shadowlands— to Libya, Iraq, Syria, Kashmir, Iran, Uzbekistan, and Somalia. Our apostleship must cause us to bear God's glory into darkness, and we must witness and suffer and live and die in the most unstable locations that Christ might eternally win the hearts of unreached peoples.

The end of our missionary task, therefore, cannot be holding starving babies or drilling wells or building schools or coaching soccer. These are temporal kindnesses; they are not eternal annunciations. These are means, but not ends.

Missions takes the gospel where the gospel has not gone. Missions plants the church where the church has not been planted. Missions finds the people who have no believers and makes disciples. Missions makes disciples and plants the church in the valley of the shadow of death.

How can it be that tens of thousands of American youth have signed up to serve and die for our country in Iraq and Afghanistan, but none sign up to live and die for Jesus in those same places? Why do our parents allow us to die for our country but not for our King? Why is it that the American church is enamored with ending the sex trade, promoting free trade, saving the environment, without the greater passion of crying over lost souls and agonizing over the billions marching straight to hell?

You want to be a missionary? "Die to your small ambitions," said Francis Xavier. Launch out into the most dangerous places of the world. Resign yourself to going and staying where it is dangerous, dark, lonely, unstable, resistant, and difficult, and where it might very well cost you your life. You want to be a missionary? Apostle! Commit yourself to taking the gospel where it has not gone, to planting the church among unreached peoples.

In the mid-1800s, Bishop French of India made a call for five of God's brightest young missionary men to penetrate the Arabian Peninsula. No one went. So, Bishop French in his 60s decided to go. He sailed for Muscat, Oman, whereupon he promptly succumbed to sunstroke and died. A. E. Moule wrote this epitaph for him:

> *Where Muscat fronts the Orient sun*
> *'Twixt crashing sea and heaving steep,*
> *His work of mercy scarce begun,*
> *A saintly soul has fallen asleep:*
> *Who comes to lift the cross instead?*
> *Who takes the standard from the dead?*

We can only be obedient to the Great Commission if we apostle.

IF WE WILL ABANDON

When we abide and when we apostle, we must be clear that it will cost us. We must also abandon. We must embrace suffering for Jesus' sake as our normal reality.

Because this point is so critical, and for so many in the West obtuse, let me first build a biblical case.

Ananias was told to rise and go to a street called Straight to tell Paul, God's chosen vessel, God's apostle, how many things he (and those who followed him as he followed Christ) must suffer for Jesus' sake (Acts 9:11–16):

- Labors, stripes, prison, deaths, lashes, rods, stoning, shipwrecks in the deep, perils of waters, perils of robbers, perils in the city, perils in the wilderness, perils in the sea, perils among false brethren, weariness and toil, sleeplessness, cold, and nakedness. (2 Cor. 11:23–27)

- Tribulations, needs, distresses, stripes, imprisonments, tumults, labors, sleeplessness, fasting, dishonor, unknown, dying, chastened, sorrowful, poor, and having nothing. (2 Cor. 6:4–10)

- Hard pressed on every side, perplexed, persecuted, struck down, carrying about in the body the dying of the Lord Jesus, and delivered to death for Jesus' sake. (2 Cor. 4:8–12)

- Trials of mockings and scourgings, chains, imprisonment, stoning, being sawed in two, tempted, slain with the sword, wandering destitute, afflicted, and tormented. (Heb. 11:36–40)

- "Crucified with Christ" (Gal. 2:20)

- "Crucified the flesh" (Gal. 5:24)

- "The world has been crucified to me, and I to the world." (Gal. 6:14)

- Strengthened for all suffering with joy (Col. 1:11)

- "Bound in the Spirit, not knowing...that chains and tribulations await" (Acts 20:22–24)

- "Chains are in Christ...to die is gain...granted on behalf of Christ, not only to believe in Him, but also to suffer for His sake." (Phil. 1:13, 21, 29)

These, too, are promises of Jesus. It's likely you have been fed the pleasant promises of God since you can remember. May we cry, "Yes, Lord, we embrace them! But these verses are Your promises, too. You promised us suffering and we commit to submitting to the whole of Your will for our lives."

A young Sudanese man I discipled in Khartoum ended up discipling me. Full of vision, he stood before our team and exhorted them with fire: "We must charge the mountains and stand in the rivers with scorpions in our pockets!" My team echoed back an "amen," not entirely sure what he meant but somehow understanding that challenge and scorpions were in our mutual future.

Bashir now recovers from the trauma of torture and prison, from watching men slaughtered right before his eyes. Bashir knows that it is by many tribulations we advance the kingdom of God.

The biblical and Christological precedent is not unmitigated growth and progress from victory to victory to victory. Thanks be to God who always leads us in His triumph—from victory to cross to victory to cross to victory to cross to victory to cross.

Jesus was favored, anointed, protected, and blessed that He might march with flinted face to Golgotha. Servants are not greater than our Master. Why should our trajectory be any different? Where do we get the audacity to think that any Christian will experience unbroken success or peace until the return of our Lord? The Christian of your generation will be a suffering, abandoned one.

Something about suffering for Jesus' sake defeats demonic powers! When Jesus is so precious that we willingly embrace trial and loss for Him, some force is unleashed in the spirit realm, something divine is hurled against and splinters the gates of hell. When our missionaries suffer and die, we are not unmoved—it wounds and crushes us all—but we rejoice because their sacrifices are not in vai, to abandon all for Jesus. We long to decrease that Jesus might increase, for God chooses the weak and foolish things of the world to shame the wise and mighty, that no Christian should glory in His presence. We hunger for our cross, not because we want to die, but because we long for Christ to live in us, because our hope is in resurrection, because death has no terror to a Christian that believes in resurrection. "I have been crucified with Christ," says Galatians 2:20. "It is no longer I who live, but Christ lives in me; and the life I now live in the flesh, I live by faith in the Son of God who loved me and gave Himself for me." And if Jesus did this for me, shall I not be willing to do the same for others?

Many of you reading this have a destiny, a destiny that lies on the other side of Calvary. Your immediate future is one of suffering. Jesus bore His cross, not ours. We yet have a cross to bear. We must take up our cross, He says, and follow. We yet must follow Jesus in abandon.

Have you experienced suffering? Have you already been abused and rejected? This is no disqualification. Jesus is adept at turning your pain towards His purposes. You who have suffered unwillingly because humanity is evil, will you now willingly suffer because God is good?

We will only reach our world if we abandon ourselves to this costly call. Perhaps you have been brought to this place at this time to understand that you have been favored and allowed to grow or afflicted and allowed to suffer for one purpose: That you go with flinted face to your cross. That you suffer for Jesus' sake and that you suffer well. That you lose your sense of privilege. That you no longer care about prestige. That you are forever immune to a desire for wealth. That popularity makes you vomit. That you are willing to lose your life, to joyfully abandon the deceiving comforts of an American life, that you become less that Jesus rises, that Jesus shines, that Jesus is glorified. We who believe in Spirit-led births, let us not tremble at Spirit-empowered deaths.

Christ loved us enough to die for us. Do we love Christ enough to die for Him? If the price of world evangelization is our own discomfort and demise, will we not willingly and joyfully pay it? If the price of the glory for Jesus among all peoples is that we go, outside the camp, to suffer for His sake, to be crushed and killed by ignorant people hostile to the cross, shall we not willingly and joyfully pay it? If the price for lifting the cross over every ideology and falsehood is that we are crushed, derided, marginalized, abused, scorned, and vilified, shall we not willingly and joyfully pay it? You who have danced at the altar, will you not place yourselves on it now, weeping for the sake of the world?

IF WE WILL CHANGE THE WORLD

We will only change the world as we learn to abide—if we return to the simplicity of just having Jesus. We will only be missionaries if we apostle—if we plant the church where the church does not exist. We will only glorify Jesus among all peoples if we abandon—if we embrace suffering and persecution for Jesus' sake.

Will you commit yourself today to abide, apostle and abandon, to walk fearlessly into the Ninevehs of our day? Will you say yes to Jesus and to His mission, to a passion for all peoples of this earth? Yes, Lord, we will abide, we will apostle, and we will abandon.

One Short Life

MATTHEW 1:1

Let's start at the very big ending. Picture the scene in heaven with every tribe, tongue, people, and nation in worship. These nations biblically are not geo-political entities. They are ethnic communities or distinct people groups. They have their own language and culture. They are communities such as my friend Mohammed's who is from the Rashaida nation. There are 150,000 Rashaida in the Sudan. Not one Christian. Not one church. Not one of Mohammed's family is in heaven. Not yet anyway. But at the big ending, the ending of this broken world, at the beginning of our heavenly forever, God has guaranteed that Rashaida will be there.

Now it is somewhat ludicrous to talk of beginning and ending when talking about God. God has no beginning and He has no end. God is eternally glorious. God was before man existed; He will be forever exalted. The span of man on earth is brief indeed, and if the span of human history is short, then your appearance on the scene is shorter still. A breath, and then you're gone.

One short life, you might as well make it count. When your life is done, when your heaven begins, will anyone be there because of you? Specifically, will anyone from an unreached nation enjoy heaven forever because of how you live? Will your life count?

Fatima's life counts. Born in Saudi Arabia, the veil on her heart was lifted and her tongue confessed Jesus as Lord. So, they cut it out and killed her. They snatched away her one breath, and by killing her, sped her on to joy. Her new tongue now sings His sweetest praise.

"Missions is about the worship of Jesus," says author David Mathis. "The goal of missions is the global worship of Jesus by His redeemed people from every tribe, tongue, and nation. The outcome of missions is all peoples delighting to praise Jesus. And the motivation for missions is the enjoyment that His people have in Him. Missions aims at, brings about, and is fueled by the worship of Jesus."[20]

Missions is about the worship of Jesus. This is the record of Scripture. The Bible across time reveals God's passion for all nations. "Jesus Christ, the son of Abraham, the son of David," says Matthew 1:1. Abraham was blessed to be a blessing to all nations. Bedouin Abraham — a friend of God — interceded for homosexual Sodom. Joseph marries an Egyptian. Moses receives the law in Saudi Arabic (how ironic). Naaman comes from Syria. Jonah proclaims in Iraq. A Sudanese pulls Jeremiah from a well. David sings the nations into gladness and starts a dynasty that Jesus will crown a kingdom that will include every ethnic group. Luke the Greek gives us a Gospel and Acts, Jesus finds the greatest faith in Italians and Phoenicians. Half-breed Samaritans declare, "You are the Christ, the Savior of the World." A Libyan carries the cross. Arabs, Iranians, and Kurds get saved at Pentecost. The first churches are planted in Turkey. Galatians, Ephesians, Philippians, Colossians, Thessalonians are all missionary letters to church plants. Philip meets a Sudanese in Gaza. Timothy and Titus are non-Jew missionaries.

The Bible record is the account of the gospel unleashed. Mobile temples thrust out to every people. People like the Uyghur of Western China, Kazakhstan, and Kyrgyzstan, about nine million total. The Uyghur became Muslims a millennium ago; thus, Xu is a 25th generation Muslim. His father is in hell, and his father is in hell, and his father is in hell, and his father is in hell, and his father is in hell, and his father is in hell…. You get the sobering picture. Twenty-five generations of Xu's family rot in hell because a Muslim missionary was sent.

Missionary biblically means "sent one" — sent where there is no church, no Christian, no congregation, where the ethnic people have never heard of Jesus. Missionaries are those sent to plant the church in virgin soil. Missionaries are like firemen. They rush in where all others run out.

Missionaries rush to places of oppression and death, to places where they are not welcomed or wanted, to unreached peoples like the Shagiya. Ahmad is from the Shagiya nation. His nation has no church. The Shagiya are tough, materialistic, and enterprising, and they exert their will on others. Other Sudanese tribes resent the Shagiya. There is a proverb in Arabic about the Shagiyya: *Lau talga shagi wa dabi fi tariq, uktul ash-shagi wa khali ad-dabi.* It means, "If you find a Shagiya person and a snake in the road, kill the Shagiya and let the snake go free." Jesus didn't come to kill the Shagiya; Jesus was sent to crush the serpent's head. Who will be sent to let them know? Who will be a missionary to the Shagiya? Who will help plant the first Shagiya church?

When God poured out His spirit anew 100 years ago, He did so through multiple fountainheads: Scandanavia, India, South Africa, and Canada. All experienced revival and renewal in the Holy Spirit. One such fountain was a mixed-race chapel on the poor side of Los Angeles, on a little street called Azusa. Men and women, hungry for more of Jesus, came together. They began to pray and praise, and God filled them with a power to witness, full of love for Jesus. Those filled by the Spirit marveled at the unity of worship — black, white, brown, men and women, young and old. The Holy Spirit rushed upon them all and gave them purpose — their purpose was to live for the glory of Jesus among all peoples.

Fueled by a passion to see all nations know this wonderful, uniting Jesus, this little group of fellowship grew and cooperated to send missionaries to places that had no churches. Some were sent to Buddhist Tibet; some to Muslim Indonesia; some to Hindu India; some to animist Africa; and some to their deaths in the Amazon jungles. Others lived and died on remote islands of the sea. They and others like them went to breathe their short breaths, to light their one light where there was only death and darkness. In 1914, this group of missionary senders organized. "We can send missionaries better together," they realized, and the Assemblies of God (AG) was born.

In 1921, they resolved again that mission work must focus on where there was no church, no Christian, no light — and a wonderful thing happened. Take, for example, Carlos. Carlos is from Brazil. For years his nation was pagan. In centuries past they sacrificed babies to idols and worshiped demons. The conquistadors came and baptized Carlos' ancestors in blood and converted them to Catholicism. For centuries Carlos' family was bound by religion, lost in legalism. Carlos was freed because of missionary endeavors, and his people, too, have seen the light. Carlos is one of 22 million AG believers in Brazil. Yes! Twenty-two million in Brazil! Of the 60 million AG believers around the world, more than a third reside in the great country of Brazil. Glory, praise, and honor to God!

That is just counting one denomination, but the body of Christ is bigger than just one. There are now 2.2 billion Christians in the world! Missionaries were sent to Korea, and today there are 15 million Christians in Korea. Missionaries were sent to Argentina, and now there are 36 million

Christians in Argentina. Missionaries were sent to Nigeria; today there are 81 million Christians in Nigeria. Missionaries were sent to China, and Chinese Christians number 100 million.

To the glory and praise of Jesus, who loves all nations, the church has been planted among many of the world's unreached peoples. National churches thrive; buildings are built; ministers graduate from schools, orphans are fed; and wells are dug. In many lands, national believers do all of these things. The gospel works; the gospel is alive and well! For this we truly rejoice. Praise to a glorious God who builds His church. Honor to the men and women who were sent! Respect for those who sacrificed, labored, and died to see the Church worldwide blossom to where it is today.

We stand on their shoulders, and because we do, we see things they longed to look into. We see that believers in Qatar grew by 100 percent last year from one to two! We see 6,500 unreached people groups untouched by the gospel. We see 40 percent of our world has no access to Christ. Every day 150,000 people on this planet die, and 45,000 of them die without having heard of Jesus. Because two billion people around the world don't have a Christian friend. Because no one was willing to pay the price necessary that all might hear. This is the greatest injustice in history. Who will be sent to those who have never heard?

The personal income of Christians in 2011 (according to the International Bulletin of Missionary Research) totaled 31 trillion U.S. dollars. Of that 31 trillion, 1.8 percent went to Christian causes and 0.1 percent of total went to foreign missions, and one-tenth of that went to reach the unreached.

These numbers are staggering so let me simplify it. Find a penny and hold it in your hand. For every $100 earned by Christians in 2011, about two dollars went to help the poor, about one penny went to sending missionaries, and about one-tenth of a penny went to reach unreached peoples, those who have never heard about Jesus. Do you know how much Christians value the unreached? About a tenth of a penny on every $100.

Emir has never heard. Emir lives in the "Zero Zone." The Zero Zone is in the northeast corner of Turkey. Zero churches, zero Christians, zero missionaries. Zero breath wasted on telling Emir of the love of God; zero risk taken; and zero lives laid down that Emir and his people might live.

Surely the Lord of the nations intends all His children to have access to His grace!

It is not an issue of lostness; it is an issue of access. The sinner in Mogadishu is just as lost as the sinner in Dallas or Minneapolis, but Minneapolis and Dallas have the fastest growing churches in America — and Mogadishu has none! No churches, no witness, no light!

Hassan is a Somali from Mogadishu. He spends most of the day chewing kat. Kat is a drug that makes Hassan forget. Kat helps Hassan forget that his Somali nation has gone to hell and no one really cares. Surely Hassan, hungry for just one crumb, he has a right to some Living Bread.

I am not saying that everyone should go to Somalia, the Zero Zone, Western China, or the Shagiya nation. I am saying we share a common responsibility: Someone must go! Every Christian is responsible for the unreached, whoever you are, whatever you do, however young or old, rich or poor, no matter where you live, no matter your gifts, talents, callings, or limitations. God's missionary heart insists that your will be bent towards His, that your passion reflects His, that you will use your life, your one breath for those who have never heard about Jesus.

We are all called to populate heaven with unreached people. We will pray for the unreached. We will give to the unreached. We will advocate and influence our children, our peers, our students, and our world to live and die for those who have never heard about Jesus. We may not all be called to pioneer among unreached peoples, but we are all called to see that someone does, to use our hands and hearts and minds, to give our talents and treasure and time toward the glorious end goal of God that every tribe, tongue, people, and nation in worship.

There is an African proverb that says, "To kill an elephant, you cannot stab its shadow." The elephant of our age is Islam. The heart of Islam is the Arab world. Cairo sits in the center of the Arab world as its biggest city. Twenty-five million people live in Cairo. Muslim missionaries are trained from Al Azhar University. The Qur'an is sent globally from Egypt's printing presses. Islam is preached everywhere from Egypt's media outlets. The Islamic party gains ascendancy there, as it does across the Muslim world.

What better place to be?

What better time to go?
Let courage rise with danger and strength to strength oppose.

the
Kingdom
Available

MATTHEW 4-5

Count Zinzendorf was the founder of the Moravian Missionary Movement. The Moravians were dedicated Europeans who sold themselves as indentured servants in order to cross the seas and preach the gospel. A crystallizing moment for Count Zinzendorf took place in an art museum where he stumbled across a picture of a bloody and crucified Jesus. Underneath the caption were the words: "I have done all this for you. What will you do for me?"

Any missions endeavor begins and ends with Jesus.

He is our King. He is our General.

It is His passion that fuels us. It is His resource that sustains us. It is His wounded arms that heal us.

William Carey and the great coastal missions' movements followed the Moravians. Sailing along behind the galleys, missionaries infiltrated the port cities of the world.

Then the inland regions lifted their lost voice and Hudson Taylor went to interior China. The African Inland Mission chopped into the darkness of Africa's heartland.

Then C. T. Studd and the student volunteers joined the fray. Cameron Townsend, Jim Elliot, and friends adjusted the radar to people groups and the unreached, and in the last few decades the guns of the Lord of Hosts have swung around to take on what George Otis calls "The Last of the Giants"—Islam.

In this our greatest challenge, the church must rise to its finest hour. Islam stands as the last great un-penetrated bulwark. It is time for Islam's gates to "not prevail." It is my honor and mandate to proclaim to you that in greater numbers than ever before Muslims are fleeing the ranks of their doomed castles and running into the arms of the King of glory.

This is our hour of opportunity. This is the hour to strike. This is the hour to risk our all and to sacrifice our best. This is the hour for which so many have bled and died. As Brutus on the eve of attacking Philippi said so well:

> *Our legions are brim-full, our cause is ripe.*
> *The enemy increaseth every day.*
> *We, at the height, are ready to decline.*
> *There is a tide in the affairs of men,*

Which, taken at the flood, leads on to fortune;
Omitted, all the voyage of their life
Is bound in shallows and in miseries.
On such a full sea are we now afloat,
And we must take the current when it serves
Or lose our ventures.[21]

Now is the time for taking the tide in missions to Muslims. We must seize the opportunity or lose our ventures.

To focus our attention on God's plan for the Muslim world, I want to look at Matthew 4 and 5. Though the text might be familiar, please tune in for I am going to read from an uncommon translation.

> *And Jesus went about all Galilee, teaching in their synagogues and preaching the gospel of the kingdom, and healing all kinds of sickness and all kinds of disease among the people. And His fame went throughout all Syria; and they brought to Him all sick people who were afflicted with various diseases and torments, and those who were demon-possessed, epileptics, and paralytics; and He healed them. Great multitudes followed Him—from Galilee, and from Decapolis, Jerusalem, Judea, and beyond the Jordan* (Matthew 4:23–25).
>
> *And seeing the multitudes, He went up into a mountain. And when He had sat down, His disciples came to Him. And He opened His mouth and taught them, saying:*
>
>> *"Blessed are the Bedouin Beja,*
>>   *For theirs is the kingdom of heaven.*
>> *"Blessed are the murdering Mujahideen,*
>>   *For they shall be comforted.*
>> *"Blessed are the victims of war,*
>>   *For they shall inherit the earth.*
>> *"Blessed are the Muslim fundamentalists,*
>>   *For they shall be filled.*

> *"Blessed are the pagans,*
>> *For they shall obtain mercy.*
> *"Blessed are the mentally handicapped,*
>> *For they shall see God.*
> *"Blessed are the Arab politicians,*
>> *For they shall be called the sons of God.*
> *"Blessed are the Southern Sudanese slave children,*
>> *For theirs is the kingdom of heaven.*
> *Blessed are you when men call you "Abd" and "Kafir" and give you the old bread in the dukan [market], and call you a dog and stupid, for My sake. Rejoice and be exceedingly glad, for your reward in heaven is great, for so they persecuted the prophets who were before you.*
> (Matthew 5:1–12, my paraphrase)

A little Muslim shepherd boy was given a special lamb for a present. This lamb grew into his favorite sheep and he loved it dearly. One year during the Eid, the sheep disappeared, and the boy looked for it frantically. He was afraid someone had stolen it to be used as a sacrifice. The young shepherd came across other shepherds who had mingled their herds. He asked them if he could search for his sheep among the throng. He was told that he would never be able to identify his sheep among so many. He replied: "Of course, I will. My sheep knows my voice." The young shepherd called out and his sheep came running out of the masses.

About ten years later, a missionary gave this Muslim man a New Testament. He began to read the Gospels and came across the words of Jesus: "My sheep hear my voice, and I know them, and they follow Me" (John 10:27). At that moment, the Holy Spirit reminded him of his childhood friend and he surrendered his life to Jesus.

THE KINGDOM IS OPEN

In the time of Jesus (and even today) there was a wrong misunderstanding of the kingdom. It was thought that the Kingdom of God was for the special and privileged—you have to be good, you have to be special, you have to earn or deserve the Kingdom. In the time of Jesus, people thought it was the scribes and Pharisees who were in. In our day, we have our own perceptions about who is good, who is safe, who is reachable, who can come in and who cannot. In the text, we read that Jesus had gone all around the countryside with a simple message: "The Kingdom is available. My Kingdom is open. Everyone is invited; come on in." The Beatitudes are not a miserable "be like this" list. Jesus is not saying that you have to be poor and miserable to enter the Kingdom. His whole message is actually the opposite—rich and poor, well and sick, strong and weak, master and slave.

You do not have to be disadvantaged to enter the Kingdom; rather, no disadvantage can keep you out. The Kingdom of God is open to you, no matter how fortunate or unfortunate you are. Rich? Come on down! Poor? Come right with him! "My Kingdom is open," Jesus informs us, "and I want you in it!"

Let us look at his invitation in the context of Sudan.

BLESSED ARE THE BEDOUIN BEJA, FOR THEIRS IS THE KINGDOM OF HEAVEN

You have probably heard the children's rhyme "Fuzzy Wuzzy":

Fuzzy Wuzzy was a bear,
Fuzzy Wuzzy had no hair,
Fuzzy Wuzzy wasn't very fuzzy,
Was he?

Writer and explorer Rudyard Kipling, while traveling through Sudan, encountered a Hamitic people, dark-skinned, wearing white *jellabiyas* (robes) and blue vests with long broad swords on their side and on their heads, large afros. British soldiers had given them the nickname "fuzzy wuzzy." Kipling wrote a poem using the term "fuzzy wuzzy" that praised the people for their fighting skills:

So 'ere 's to you, Fuzzy-Wuzzy, at your 'ome in the Soudan;

You're a pore benighted 'eathen but a first-class fightin' man;
An' 'ere 's to you, Fuzzy-Wuzzy, with your 'ayrick 'ead of 'air—
You big black boundin' beggar—for you broke a British square![22]

The Beja are a resistant Muslim tribe—fierce warriors, proud, heavily into the occult, illiterate and nomadic. Of the three million Beja, we know of about three believers. Let me tell you the story of one of them.

Hassan was an adamant, hardheaded Muslim. He consistently and passionately rejected the witness of a friend until one night when he had a dream. In his dream, someone Hassan recognized as Jesus approached him carrying a cross. He walked up to Hassan and smacked him over the head with the cross. Hassan woke up disturbed, walked around and eventually went back to sleep. The same dream repeated—Jesus returned and clobbered him again. When Hassan woke up, he decided he had better investigate this Jesus a little more sincerely. When Hassan was later asked how he knew it was Jesus, he said, "Easy! Jesus was dark-skinned and wore a white jellabiya, blue vest, and big Beja hair."

Blessed are the Bedouin Beja, for theirs is the kingdom of heaven.

Those whom Jesus called blessed are the spiritual zeros. Blessed are those who do not have a clue. Blessed are those who to this point have never heard of me, never seen a Bible, never watched one frame of the Jesus Film, never darkened the door of a church, and never ever even met a Christian. Blessed are those who spiritually know nothing, for the Kingdom of heaven is now available to them.

There is nothing good about spiritual poverty. Let us not twist it into a positive; yet let us rejoice with Jesus, that His Kingdom is not just for those who have memorized the whole Bible in seven different languages. It is also for the "know nothings," wherever they may wander on this, His blessed earth.

BLESSED ARE THE MURDERING MUJAHIDEEN, FOR THEY SHALL BE COMFORTED

You might be familiar with the Arabic word "mujahid." It comes from "jihad," and means 'the one who struggles for the faith." Saadiq was one such person. It was his mandate to travel through southern Sudan to convert Christians to Islam. He told me the most effective method was to hold a gun to a Christian's head and tell him he had a choice—either accept Islam or be shot. "In one day alone," he told me, "I blew the brains out of 60 people."

One day Saadiq entered the mosque to pray. He performed the ablutions. He knelt down in an ordered row, and as he prostrated, he saw a bright light and heard a voice: "Saadiq, you cannot kill my people anymore!" He jumped up and ran outside. He washed again, fearfully tried to pray, and again heard the voice and saw the light: "You cannot kill my people anymore."

Saadiq approached his leaders for counsel. They suggested he take some time off and get some counseling. The counsel he received from man did not help—but the Counselor was working overtime.

Saadiq was overwhelmed with grief and guilt. He began to mourn. He found a group of Christian pastors and related the vision and the voice to them. The pastors took out their Bibles and read from Acts 9, the Damascus road conversion of Paul. When Saadiq heard the Scripture, he broke. He fell on his face and wept uncontrollably. He cried out: "That is me! That is what I have done. Is there any hope?"

And of course, there was—and is! And a mujahid mourner found the Prince of Peace. This world is full of pain and sorrow. You may be the victim. You may be the culprit. Your pain and loss is not a disqualification. Come to Jesus and be comforted. His Kingdom is open to you.

BLESSED ARE THE VICTIMS OF WAR, FOR THEY SHALL INHERIT THE EARTH

Over the years, we have heard many horror stories coming from southern Sudan—soldiers using the skulls of their victims as cups, pregnant women tied to a tree and bayoneted through the stomach, schools and hospitals bombed, Christians locked in churches and the churches burned to the ground, civilians thrown from airplanes at 20,000 feet, pastors crucified, children raped.

Somewhere in the plains of southern Sudan, a Dinka shepherd boy steps on a hidden landmine. He has no interest in the war. He is too young, too meek, to even yet understand the issues. The landmine explodes and blows both of his legs off. Jesus smiles down at him from the Sermon on the Mount and says, "Blessed are you, Deng, for legs or no legs, fear not! The Father's desire is to give you the Kingdom. You shall inherit the earth."

And all those like Deng who have no one to advocate for their rights are invited to the Kingdom of Jesus. He will be their eternal Champion.

BLESSED ARE THE MUSLIM FUNDAMENTALISTS, FOR THEY SHALL BE FILLED

A few years ago, in Omdurman, Sudan, the Lord led a pastor to go to the market and publicly proclaim Jesus. Though restrictions have eased recently, at that time, especially in Omdurman, the heart of conservative Islam in Sudan, this was a dangerous proposition.

Since 1989, Sudan has been ruled by Sharia law, a law that is rigid and stern, a law that demands any Muslim who turns to Christ be punished by death. Into the teeth of this fundamentalism, the pastor felt Jesus was calling him to go. The pastor asked his church to pray and fast for three days, and then he bravely headed for the open market. Setting up a table in a crowded area, he filled the table with Bibles. Then he began to preach.

Immediately a fundamentalist was incensed and tried to shout him down. But as soon as that angry man tried to shout, he was convulsed by a coughing fit. He tried several times, but all he could produce was a fit of coughing. So in embarrassment, he shuffled away. The crowd was intrigued. The pastor finished his message and gave an invitation. Not a soul moved, not a mustache twitched. The pastor decided to close in prayer.

There is something in Sudan called a *haboob*, a dust storm. Desert winds sweep over the city throwing dust in the air and darkening the sun. Severe haboobs can be extremely sandy and visibility is lost. As the pastor prayed, a severe haboob swept through the market and in the cover of the sandy darkness, the listening crowd rushed the table. Upon the closing "amen," the pastor opened his eyes to find all of the Bibles and crowd…gone.

The systems of this world cannot satisfy whether they are Islamic fundamentalism, materialism, atheism, or any hybrid thereof. Anything and anyone other than the Bread of Life leaves you hungry. And Jesus wants fundamentalist Muslims to know the Kingdom of the heaven is also available to them. Come, all who hunger and thirst, and you shall be filled.

BLESSED ARE THE PAGANS, FOR THEY SHALL OBTAIN MERCY

In an air conditioned office of an oil company in Khartoum North, with a brand new Toyota Land Cruiser sitting outside, a Khawaja muses over his cigarette and the cold beer in his hand (which he smuggled out of the Pickwick Club). He burps to himself as he types at his Pentium 5 computer and makes a donation to the street boys program in Haj Yusif.

Jesus looks down from the heavens and says, "Blessed are you, merciful pagan, for you shall receive mercy. I have come that you might have life and have it abundantly. My heavenly kingdom is available to you."

BLESSED ARE THE MENTALLY HANDICAPPED, FOR THEY SHALL SEE GOD

In typical Arab fashion, Sudanese like to marry within the family. Originally this helped to keep the money in the family, but a difficult byproduct is a higher than normal rate of Downs Syndrome children. Many of these children become an embarrassment and are locked away in private inner rooms.

My maternal cousin, Alex, is mentally disabled. He used to have a vile mouth and when he would walk his dogs in the early mornings, through the streets of New York City, he would curse so loudly that the neighbors could hear him. One day my father sat down with Alex and in a very simple way explained the Scriptures and prayed with him. From that moment, Alex was reborn.

Whenever he drank a glass of water, he sat down and folded his hands: "Thank you, Jesus, for this glass of water. Amen." He began to praise the Lord on his early morning walks, and through the dangerous New York City streets, he walked, proclaiming with all his energy: "Thank you, Jesus.

I love you, Jesus. Praise you, Jesus!" And all the neighbors who used to listen to him curse, now heard him praising the Lord. A few years ago, my father took Alex to a church for a prayer meeting. As they left, Alex turned to my father and said: "Uncle Dick, I sense the presence of God in this place."

And Jesus turns to Alex and says, "Blessed are you, O pure heart, for you shall see God. Blessed are all the simpletons and naïve of this world. Blessed are the handicapped and the mentally unstable of Sudan and the world. For My Kingdom, for I myself am available to them."

BLESSED ARE THE ARAB POLITICIANS, FOR THEY SHALL BE CALLED THE SONS OF GOD

Last year Jimmy Carter won the Nobel Peace Prize in part for his efforts to bring peace to Sudan. This year, for the first time, the Nobel Peace Prize went to an Iranian Muslim lady.

Sudan has been at war for the last 20 years and fighting for 40 of the 50 years of its independence. We are now on the verge of a breakthrough. Politicians are bargaining, making deals, sacrificing friends, compromising here and refusing to talk there. There are many Arab politicians who do not know the Lord Jesus. They have not fallen on their knees in repentance and confession. Most probably have flawed motives and a selfish agenda, that for whatever reason, fair or foul, Ali Osman Mohammed Taha and John Garang are working for peace.

And Jesus tells both us and them, "Blessed are you, Taha and Garang, for I want you in My Kingdom. Blessed is every Arab and southern Sudan politician. Blessed are the crooks and the honest. Blessed are the strong and the bribed. Blessed are the fair and the foul, for to them also My Kingdom is made available.

Whether you like it or not, the Kingdom is available to Abel Alier and Hassan Al Turabi, to John Garang and Omar Al-Bashiir, to Mohammar Qadaffi, Mubarak, Museveni, Moi, and every other politician involved in the peace process.[23] The Kingdom is available to them.

BLESSED ARE THE SOUTHERN SUDANESE SLAVE CHILDREN, FOR THEIRS IS THE KINGDOM OF HEAVEN.

Blessed are you when men call you "slave" and "infidel" and give you the old bread in the store, and call you a dog and stupid, for My sake, for to you also is the Kingdom of heaven.

In Sudan, there are some who have suffered terribly in the last few years. Children have watched their parents tortured and killed, and then walked hundreds of miles through the bush looking for safety. Children have been abducted, misused, and abused by both sides.

The Christian Sudanese people are treated like second-class citizens. The rules of law and society favor Muslims. Christians are cheated, abused, neglected and despised. The General Overseer of the Sudan Pentecostal Church, Fermo Ogilla told me, "My first memory in life is of my mother screaming as she ran with me to hide in the forest as the Arabs ran into our village killing, raping, and looting."

A friend accepted the Lord two years ago, and from the mother who loved him dearly, from the mother who had never spoken to him in anger, he received a beating. As a grown adult he stood there and took it—the emotional pain far outweighing her feeble slaps.

Whether the ill treatment is torture—with converts' fingernails pulled out. Whether it is prejudice—with unfair treatment in the courts, buses, stores. Whether it is neglect—with lack of electricity, water, and schools to Christian areas.

We understand that Christians are mistreated in the Sudan. To all those who are tired of being second class citizens in their own country, to all those who are weary of discrimination and scorn, to all those who are fed up, angry, and even bitter, Jesus says: "Blessed are you, for the Kingdom of God is absolutely available to you."

If you are a little uncomfortable with my translation of the Beatitudes, then I have done my work well because this was the very point of Jesus. He came to establish His Kingdom, His rule amongst men, but "men" had predetermined who was worthy of God's Kingdom, "men" had decided that the Kingdom was only for those "who had it all right." The Kingdom was only for those who were clean, organized, and religious. The Kingdom was only for special people. The Kingdom was an elite grouping that few could merit.

And Jesus thunders against that. "My Kingdom is available to everyone," He says. There is nothing that can preclude you from the Kingdom. I want everyone to be a part, and in this hour of history specifically, I am longing for Muslims to come in, in their millions.

WHAT GOD WANTS EACH OF US TO PROCLAIM

The same kingdom that is available to you is available to others—no matter their condition, their wealth or poverty, their humility or pride, their background, or their history. Man, including you and me, does not set the parameters on who is invited. God has declared His Kingdom open. It is available to you and it is available to every Muslim in this land—in Sudan and beyond- that will come to Jesus on His terms.

There was a couple on our team with a little daughter named Adeline. Adeline loved people and she loved to talk. On their second day in the country, Adeline walked out of their apartment into the street and waved at the Muslim family that was smiling at her across the street. Then with lifted voice she began to shout and point, "They are the Muslims. We are the missionaries." Her parents rushed out to stop her. It took Adeline all of one day to blow her family's cover, but you know what? Little Adeline had it right. We were not commissioned to "Go ye into all the world to conceal the gospel, hiding from security, inquirers, and neighbors, being as irrelevant and ineffective as possible." Neither were we instructed to work hard in Sudan so that our children could have a better life, so that their children could work hard, so that their children could have a better life. What kind of empty and imprisoning cycle is that?

We have been commissioned to get the gospel out. We have been commanded to proclaim. We have been ordered to live our lives moment by moment so that the nations of the world may rush into the Kingdom of the King of Ages!

The African tale is told of a lion instructed by God not to eat any of

God's people. One day the lion entered a village and ate the whole populace. God rebuked the lion and reminded him he was not supposed to eat God's people. The lion apologized and explained, "Sorry God, I started to eat them at their feet and I found no trace of you until I reached their lips." May you not respond to this message with lip service and empty words, but would you, too, make your will and life available to however the Spirit leads you to respond? I do not know what kind of response the Lord is asking from you, but it usually falls within one of three areas. What are these three areas? The hymn "O Christians, Haste" gives us the simple options:

Give of your sons to bear the message glorious
Give of your wealth to speed them on their way
Pour out your soul for them in prayer victorious
And all your spending Jesus will repay.[24]

In Sudan, we are in desperate need of message bearers, those of you who will say, "Yes, I will give my life to tell Muslim people about Jesus. Yes, I want training on how to reach Muslims with the gospel."

In Sudan, we desperately need your wealth. We want to send missionaries all over Sudan and even to other nations. We cannot do that unless you give to missions.

In Sudan, we desperately need your victorious prayers. Islam is demonic and binding. We will only be effective as a mission church in Sudan and we will only see millions of Muslims saved if we have faithful warriors lifting up the church, our missionaries and the nation in prayer.

Following Jesus

Jesus came to seek and save the lost. At the end of this message, I will ask you to follow Jesus in the giving of your life for the unreached. I will ask you to lay down your plan for your life to do as Jesus did. I will ask you to consider that when Jesus commanded us to go into all the earth to preach among all the *ethne* (nations) to make disciples of every people, He actually meant you. Here I want to suggest that He who searches all hearts, that He who is sovereign over your life and mine, is present today, looking for missionaries who will go.

E. M. bounds said,

> Men are God's method. The Church is looking for better methods. God is looking for better men... [What is needed in missions now] is not more machinery, or better new organizations, or more and novel methods, but men whom the Holy Ghost can use. The Holy Ghost does not come on machinery, but on men. He does not anoint plans, but men... It is not great talents or great learning or great preachers that God needs, but men great in holiness, great in faith, great in love, great in fidelity, great for God—men always preaching by holy sermons in the pulpit, by holy lives out of it. These men [and women] can mold a generation for God.[25]

As we consider following Jesus, let us be clear that Jesus is not impressed with silly promises: "I will follow you wherever you go" (Matt. 8:19) or "Even if all betray you, I never will" (Matt. 26:33). Even knowing what is in us, Jesus does not commit himself to any man (John 2:24–25). Jesus knows that the cross is His destination. So, to all who profess to Him, to all who say to Him, "I will follow you *wherever* you go," Jesus asks these simple questions.

ARE YOU WILLING TO FOLLOW ME TO NOWHERE?

> *Jesus said to him, "Foxes have holes and birds of the air have nests, but the Son of Man has nowhere to lay His head."* (Matt. 8:20)

Jesus doesn't belong to this world. He is not at home here, and neither should you be at home.

There will·always be a father to bury. There will always be another responsibility, for to be present is to be responsible. Love finds a need and meets it wherever you are. If you stay here in your homeland, there will always be valuable and valued work to do. There will be noble and needed duties that must be done. The call to follow Jesus is stunning, for it is a call away from legitimate and important responsibility, definite and certain activities, towards unfriendly and uncertain places and circumstances.

At the end of the day, we are only truly free when we follow Him, not knowing where we will lay our head.

Gladys Aylward was a poor Irish cleaning lady who felt called to China. But she was such a dim student that she flunked out of missionary training. She decided to go anyway and determined to raise the money for one-way passage to China. She became a maid in the household of Sir Francis Younghusband, but the travel to and from her job at his estate wiped out nearly all her savings. In fact, she had only two and a half pennies left. She laid them in a row on top of her Bible. A sense of hopelessness came over her.

Authors Janet and Geoff Benge pick up the story:

Gladys was certain [China] was where God wanted her to live and work, and if that was where God wanted her, surely He would help her get the money she needed to get there. She placed her hands over the money and in a loud voice prayed, "Here is my Bible. Here is all the money I have. Here is me. Find some way to use me, God." Gladys worked hard for many weeks and then went down to a shipping agency with three pounds.

"How much is a one-way ticket to China?"

"And to what part of China?"

"Any part will do."

"The cheapest ticket is 90 pounds... That's 30 times more than you have!"

"Is there a cheaper way?"

"There is—by train through Russia, but Russia is at war with China. It's unlikely you would arrive at your destination, wherever that might be…"

"It's my life that would be at risk, so it's my choice. I would like to open an account to pay for a train ticket to China. [Remember, this is 1930.] Take the three pounds, I'll be back every Friday until I have paid off the ticket."[26]

It took months to save the money, but she raised it and left England. She was kicked off the train at the end of the line in Russia, near the Chinese border. Bombing and fighting made crossing the border impossible, and Russian soldiers order Gladys to walk back the way she came. She walked all night back up the tracks, nearly freezing to death walking through the Siberian winter, braving wolves and inclement weather. She eventually made her way to the city of Vladivostok, only to be captured by a pimp. A dangerous escape led her to Japan, from whence she found her way to China. She travelled for weeks by train or foot, arrived at a village where the road ended, and was carried up into the mountains in a basket on the back of a mule.

In her first days, she had mud thrown on her as a "foreign devil." She witnessed the decapitation of a thief by the Mandarin's order, and the head rolled right to her feet. She ran home crying, overwhelmed at the nowhere to which following Jesus had brought her. Her elderly co-worker died, so in order not to starve, she opened an inn for mule caravans called the "Inn of Eight Happinesses." Gladys and her trusted Chinese helper shared Bible stories with all the mule caravan guides, who then spread the gospel wherever they traveled.

The Mandarin then asked Gladys to be his "Honorable Foot Inspector" and to tour the district to ensure that the binding of young girls' feet ceased.[27] Gladys agreed on one condition, saying: "Wherever I go on behalf of your excellency, I will speak of my God and my faith, and I will try and make others believe as I do."[28] Shocked, because no one spoke to the Mandarin that way, much less a woman, he agreed, and Gladys proceeded to share the gospel in every village of the district as she helped wipe out the practice of foot binding. Believers came to Jesus, and churches formed.

A prison revolt occurred as poorly treated prisoners went wild, took over the prison and slaughtered one another in chaotic violence. The Mandarin sent Gladys to the prison. The soldiers with her were too afraid to go in themselves, but said to Gladys: "You must go in and stop the fighting! You are always telling everyone you have the living God in you, so how could they kill you? You and the living God can go in there and get the men to stop fighting. Otherwise none of them will be left alive."[29] Gladys fearfully entered the prison. She found blood splattered everywhere. Men were dead or dying all around her.

A prisoner rushed at another one next to her with machete raised above his head to strike. Gladys yelled, "Stop at once, and give me that machete!"[30] With evil eyes, he turned on her, arm frozen in the air. He dropped the machete, and it clattered to the ground. The noise startled the other fighting prisoners. Gladys shouted, "All of you! Drop your weapons and come over here. Get into a line in front of me here. I have been sent here to find out the problem and solve it, but I can't talk to the governor on your behalf until you clean up some of this mess. Clean up this mess and then we will talk about how I can help you."[31] Spoken like a true maid, who knows the power of clean! The prisoners cleaned up the mess. Order was restored. Only then did the governor and all his male soldiers re-enter the prison. Gladys confronted the governor on the animal-like treatment of the prisoners and instituted a program for prison reform, jobs, money-making initiatives, farming for nutritious food, study, and gospel lessons.

World War II began, and the Japanese bombed the inn. Gladys was buried alive in the rubble. After being dug out, she walked her orphan children (more than 100) over the mountains. It took weeks, but they all survived. Starvation, fatigue, and a blow to the head from the butt of a rifle when she stopped Japanese soldiers from raping Chinese women sent her into a coma at the end of the forced march. In recovery, she traveled to Tibet and shared the gospel with 500 Buddhists monks. She worked in a leper colony and shared the gospel there. She got the lepers to serve and preach the gospel in the prison.

Gladys started a university ministry and led many university students to faith, just before the Communists took over the university. The communists made the 500 university students take a test and asked them to indicate if they stood for or against the communist party. Two hundred students said they were against the Communists. When questioned by the Communist authorities, those 200 said they converted to Christ through Gladys' preaching and now supported Jesus Christ and no one else. The furious Communists called the 300 Communist student sympathizers to a secret meeting and told them to harass the 200 Christians for a month. They handed out another questionnaire, and this time those not supporting the Communists was more than 200! Again, the Communist students were called upon. Harassment led to beatings of the Christians and breaking up of prayer meetings, but a third examination of loyalty showed that not one of the Christians wavered. Infuriated, the Communists assigned 10 Communists to each individual Christian with orders to break them down. Christians were not allowed to talk to one another. They were mocked and every word recorded.

After three months, a public meeting was called in the town square for all students. Communist troops marched over 200 Christian students into the town square. Each Christian had a report. The Communist leader picked up the first report, a new convert, a 17-year-old young girl from Peking. He looked at that young girl who had been pressured for three months. Gladys stood in the square watching. "Who do you support now?"[32] The girl spoke loudly and clearly, "Sir, three months ago, I thought Jesus Christ was real, and I thought the Bible was true. Now after three months of your hatred, I know Jesus Christ is real, and I know the Bible is true."[33] The official, his face white with rage, yelled to one of the soldiers on the left. The girl was pulled to the center of the square and shoved to her knees. A sword was drawn and her head was lopped off. Seventeen years old. Gladys stayed while each of the more than 200 Christians were similarly questioned. Not one of them betrayed Jesus. Every one of them beheaded. Two hundred Christians followed Jesus to nowhere.

As she slowly walked home, Gladys thought, "If they must die, let them not be afraid of death, but let there be a meaning, O God, in their dying."[34] Those 200 young students followed Jesus to nowhere, and their heads had nowhere to rest but in the bloody town square.

Are you *sure* you are willing to follow Jesus? It might lead you with

Gladys to the back side of nowhere—to war zones, to long walks through frozen forests, to abuse by pimps, to poverty, sickness, prison, bombings, refugee status, pain, or trial—for following Jesus to nowhere, certainly means trouble.

Which leads us to our second question.

ARE YOU WILLING TO FOLLOW JESUS TO TROUBLE?

> *Now when He got into a boat, His disciples followed Him. And suddenly a great tempest arose… Then His disciples come to Him…saying, "Lord, save us! We are perishing!"*
> (Matt. 8:23–25)

Paul Bettex's linguistic training served him well on the mission field. He was proficient in 13 languages. He put his scholarly and theological abilities into practice by living among the people to whom he ministered. Stories of the hardships he faced in South America circulated among American Christians, and he returned in 1903 as a missionary hero. Upon his return to America, Bettex taught at Central Holiness University in Oskaloosa, Iowa. He attended meetings at the Azusa Street Revival in Los Angeles, joined the ranks of the Pentecostals, and in 1910 headed for China as a missionary.

Bettex published a periodical, *Canton Pentecost*, of which there are no known surviving copies. His wife, Nellie, died in China in 1912. In 1916, Bettex disappeared and was never again seen alive. Chinese Christians expended great energies in searching for Bettex and finally found his body, buried six feet in the ground with three bullet holes in his chest.

During his missionary work in South America, Bettex wrote:

And the more truly a Christian is a Christian, the hotter rages the battle about him. All heaven and hell take part in his fate. Here there is no place for amateur Christians. It is a fight for life and death… Few are the martyrs on whose heads crowns have been lighted while they were asleep. Their preparatory school has ever been sorrow, suffering, poverty, year-long fulfillment of duty.[35]

Paul Bettex and those early Pentecostal missionaries all knew that following Jesus meant heading into storms. Following Jesus meant trouble.

Fast forward 50 years or so to Ecuador. Elizabeth Elliot wrote in *These Strange Ashes* of her first years as a Bible-translating missionary in South America. She tells the story of a man named Macario who was "God's answer to prayer...the key to the whole of the language work; he was (God knew) the only man on earth who spoke both Spanish and Colorado with equal ease."[36] But he was senselessly murdered, shot to death. Their translation work "now came to a sudden full stop."[37] Later a flood and then a theft robbed the translators of their card files, in which they had invested years of work. They had to start all over again.

And after all this, Elisabeth married Jim Elliot, one of five young missionaries who were trying to reach out to the then-isolated and hostile Waorani people of the Amazon rain forest. One evening they sang a hymn, "*We Rest on Thee, Our Shield and Our Defender.*" The next day they traveled into the forest, met a party of Waoranis, and were all speared to death, leaving behind many widows and orphans.

In her 1996 epilogue to *Through Gates of Splendor*, the account of these missionaries' deaths, Elliot wrote:

> We know that time and again in the history of the Christian church, the blood of martyrs has been its seed. We are tempted to assume a simple equation here. Five men died. This will mean x-number of Waorani Christians... Perhaps so. Perhaps not... God is God... I dethrone Him in my heart if I demand that He act in ways that satisfy my idea of justice. It is the same spirit that taunted, "If Thou be the Son of God, come down from the Cross..." There is unbelief, there is even rebellion, in the attitude that says, "God has no right to do this to five men unless..."[38]

Jesus says that the hour at which God's glory was most brilliantly revealed was on the cross (John 12:23, 32). Do we realize that when we sing worship songs that say "Show us your glory" in these air conditioned and comfortable chapels and churches that we ask to be shown the glories and agonies of the cross?

Elisabeth Elliot argues in one of her fictional works *No Graven Image* that if God always acted the way we thought He should, if God only supports *our* plans, if God only does what we want, then He is a God of our own creation, a counterfeit God? Such a god is really just a projection of our own wisdom, of our own self. If He does something we don't like, we want to "fire" Him or "unfriend" Him as we would a personal assistant or acquaintance who was insubordinate or incompetent.

Are you willing to follow Jesus to trouble? Are you willing to follow Jesus if that means your husband dies? Are you willing to follow Jesus on His cruciform terms? Are you willing to follow Jesus if you disappear with Paul Bettex, buried in a grave with three bullets in your chest? Are you willing to follow Jesus if you end up like Jim Elliot and four of his buddies with spears in their side, floating down an Amazon river? Are you willing to follow Jesus with no guarantee that you personally will see the harvest, with no guarantee that your sacrifice will directly lead to fruit? Are you willing to follow Jesus to trouble, tempest, and storm? Everyone here enjoys a romp through the green pastures past still waters, but is anyone here game for the valley of the shadow of death?

Guess what? The missions pleasure cruises are all booked up with a waiting list. But the boat for Afghanistan still has plenty of seats.

Next question…

ARE YOU WILLING TO FOLLOW JESUS TO FEARLESSNESS?

> But [Jesus] said to them, "Why are you fearful, O you of little faith?"…
> So the men marveled, saying, "Who can this be…?"
> (Matt. 8:26–27)

In summer 2017, a bold young believer in North Africa, only 19-years-old, began to share his faith publicly on social media to friends and his family. In a country with less than 50 known believers, he stood up fearlessly for his faith.

So public was his witness that the militia followed and threatened him. Sensing the net closing around him, this young man made a video for broadcast. This what he said:

> Hello, I'm a citizen of [a North African country]. I'm a Christian. If you are [hearing these words], it means either, I have been persecuted and disappeared…or that I am dead somewhere.
>
> This is a message to my brothers and sisters, to the Christian nation, and to the secret believers everywhere in the Islamic world.
>
> I died for Jesus. I died for saying the words of the gospel. I couldn't stop talking about Jesus because of what I felt and what I believe in.
>
> I'm probably with God now. It sounds weird to say [it] but: Don't let my blood go to waste. You…my brothers and sisters, you secret believers in the Islamic world, go out there, stop fearing!
>
> We never lose. When you are with God, you never lose. If you die, you win. If they persecute you, you win. If you fly to another country, you win. You are winning anyway…why are you afraid?
>
> Have some passion. Even Jesus said, "The one who denies me…I will deny before My Father." So, you have to accept Jesus.
>
> I have been reduced in my movements in the country here. I am being followed everywhere. Stop fearing. He is here… He is everywhere.

Days after this video was taken, this teenager was abducted by Islamic militia. He was beaten for 20 days. They broke his ribs, sternum, and clavicle; a rib punctured his lung. When they released him to emergency care in the local hospital, it was with the warning that if he every opened his mouth again about Jesus, they would kill him.

In Isaiah 57:11, the Lord asks us, "And of whom have you been afraid, or feared, that you have lied and not remembered Me?… Is it not because I have held My peace from of old that you do not fear Me?" There is only one way to be truly fearless—and that is to fear the Lord. We fear the Lord, so we don't have to fear anything or anyone else.

Do you want to follow Jesus? One of the preconditions is that you respect Him so highly that you don't fear anyone or anything else. When we fear man, we are afraid to open our mouth. When we fear God, we are afraid of the damage done to the lost if we do not open our mouth. When we fear man, we are afraid to go to dangerous places. When we fear God, we are afraid of the eternal pain the unreached will suffer if we do not go. When we fear man, we are afraid to send our children to the unreached. When we fear God, we are afraid of the consequences to their own soul if we do not bless and send them. When we fear man, a multitude of terrors can incapacitate and limit us. When we fear God, nothing else on earth can intimidate or shake us. Following Jesus means that there is room in our heart for only one fear.

Let me ask one more question about following Jesus…

ARE YOU WILLING TO FOLLOW JESUS TO JUDGMENT?

> *And suddenly they cried out…*
> *"Have You [Jesus] come here to torment us before the time?"*
> (Matt. 8:29)

Fierce evil knows who is King. In Matthew 8:29, the demons in the two demon-possessed men recognized that judgment was coming, and in verse 31, the demons beg. Even the demons know there is an appointed time for the King to come and judge. Have you forgotten that Jesus is coming to judge?

Do not forget that the New Testament is an interpretation of the Old Testament message. Adam fell and sin entered the world. God made covenant promises with Abraham, but Abraham's children were a mess. God brought His people from Egypt in the Exodus, but Moses' flock quickly worshiped idols. God delivered through judges and kings, but the kings broke the covenant and became wise in doing evil. The prophets lamented the complete failure of man. They looked to the promised Messiah and proclaimed a second Exodus to come.

Messiah will come as King. He will not only deliver us from sin. He will eradicate sin, death, despair, and evil. Messiah will come to judge, destroy, rule, and reign forever. Messiah will exodus us from this broken world and enter us into the new creation, new heavens, and new earth. That is our blessed hope.

When the New Testament references the day of the Lord, it is *that* day, that *glorious* day. And when the New Testament references kingdom, it looks forward to that time when Messiah comes to judge.

John Harrigan points out that

> the first coming and the second coming of the Messiah are the two primary elements of the apostolic witness. God has appointed Jesus as Judge in the eschatological lawsuit against humanity, and Jesus has called His disciples to testify as true witnesses in anticipation of that day (Acts 10:42). So as Allison A. Trites incisively summarizes, "Jesus has a lawsuit with world. His witnesses include John the Baptist, the Scriptures, the words and works of Christ, and later the witness of the apostles and the Holy Spirit." Mark 13 and Matthew 24 tell of the persecution to come. The ultimate reason for this persecution will be to bear witness before them (Mark 13:9) so that "this gospel of the kingdom will be preached in all the world as a witness to all nations, and then the end will come" (Matt. 24:14). Though commonly interpreted as a positive testimony, context suggests that this gospel is an indictment upon all the nations who are hating and persecuting the saints.[39]

Brothers and sisters, do you want to follow Jesus? You must follow Him—as did all the prophets—by becoming incredibly unpopular. The missionary message is a prophetic message—it's not going to win you friends. The missionary has the difficult assignment of going into all the world to tell religions and cultures, tribes and tongues that they are wrong, to announce pending wrath, for the gospel only makes sense if we start with the bad news.

There is an eternal King. This King, despite His tender mercies, has been offended. This King, despite His generosity, has been insulted. This King of all nations is coming in wrath to judge. Flee, oh peoples of the earth, flee the wrath to come! Repent, turn, beg for mercy! Run to this King and throw yourself at His feet and beg for mercy. It is your only hope.

You want to follow Jesus? It is an ongoing descent into unpopularity, for you must announce the judgment to come. You must plead with arrogant and rebellious peoples to repent—and they are going to hate you for it. For the disciple, indeed, is not greater than the master. They hated Jesus. They are going to hate you. Are you willing to follow Jesus to judgment? Most modern Christians are not. We no longer have the fortitude to judge or be judged. We have lost the courage to stand up and say, "This is right, and that is wrong." Yet, if we want to follow Jesus, we must do so before both kings and in the public commons. We must do so before the nations.

IS THERE ANYONE HERE

"And behold, the whole city came out to meet Jesus. And when they saw Him, they begged Him to depart from their region." (Matt. 8:34)

In one of the most stunning stories of Scripture, two demon-possessed men are healed. And once the people of the city saw the right-minded men, they begged Jesus to leave because they preferred their pigs. Some things have to go if you want Jesus to stay.

Do you prefer your pigs?

You can't follow Jesus and keep your current status. You have to follow Him to nowhere. You can't follow Jesus and live a protected life. You have to follow Him to trouble. You can't follow Jesus and live in a sanitized castle. You have to follow Him to places of terror, unmoved by demons and dragons. Because you fear God more than you fear fear, you can't follow Jesus and be popular. You have to follow Him to judgment.

It's no surprise that so few truly follow Jesus. Narrow indeed is the way that leads to life. Narrower by far is the path that leads to the nations. But there are men and women here today that God is calling to that path.

God is calling you to represent him among unreached peoples. God is calling you to glorify Him in Saudi Arabia, Libya, Syria, Yemen, Malaysia, Indonesia, Pakistan, Turkmenistan, India, Russia, Iran, China, Somalia, Mauritania, and Chad.

And Jesus doesn't trick you. He lays out the realities: Follow Me to nowhere. Follow Me to trouble. Follow Me to fearlessness. Follow Me to judgment. It is both the hardest and the best job in all the world.

Is there anyone having heard the difficult disclaimers just described who would say, "Yes, Lord, with fear and trembling, sobriety and hope, knowing it will cost me all, I will follow You wherever You go"?

Worthy of Jesus

of

Jesus

MATTHEW 10

There are three critical things to talk about today:

- It's critical that we confess Jesus as God.
- It's critical that we die to self.
- It's critical that we live dead.

IT'S CRITICAL THAT WE CONFESS JESUS AS GOD

In every age, Jesus has called men and women to Himself. In every age, Jesus has given them power. In every age, Jesus has asked them to bear their cross and lose their life.

I just talked to Ella, a team member in Cairo. She is Romanian and grew up in Italy, and she was saved two years ago. When she shared with her mother that God had called her to missions, her mother said, "You are dead to me." They have had no contact since. Brave little Ella confessed Jesus before her mother, and has paid a price for it.

I begin today with the clear reminder that the supreme issue historically and globally is what we do with Jesus. The intentional drugging of the devil has made reality unclear—the reality that nothing is as important as the supremacy, the deity of Jesus. Every "ism" at its core is rebellion against King Jesus. The enemy wants to soften our stance and our allegiance; he starts by trying to mute our proclamation. A weakened, silenced voice leads inexorably to weakened heart loyalty.

We cannot yield to the siren song of respectability. We must embrace being hated, resented, scorned, and despised. We have to speak out for and stand up for King Jesus—like the Arabic congregation in Damascus, Syria. A visitor relayed how he crossed bombed-out streets and wire barriers to get to this vibrant congregation. The building packed full. The congregants standing in the face of violence and terror, singing at the top of their voices:

Stand up, stand up for Jesus, the trumpet call obey
Forth to the mighty conflict in this His glorious day
Ye that are men now serve Him against unnumbered foes
Let courage rise with danger and strength to strength oppose.[40]

These Syrian Christians know what the mighty conflict is—and it's not physical war or human justice. It's not essentially anything else than this: Jesus is fully man and fully God. He is the King of Kings and the Lord of Lords. He is worthy and desirous of the praise of every tongue, the worship of every nation. Every demon in hell and ideology of man agitates against the deity of Jesus! *This is the mother of all battles!* All else are skirmishes. Don't lose sight of the fight for the confession of the deity of Jesus! Don't listen to the diabolical call of materialism. It's not about your job. It's not about your house. It's not about the education of your kids. It's not about family holidays at the cabin on the lake. No! The stakes are so much higher than these temporal and important realities—for there is a higher issue, a greater good, a mighty conflict.

A truth that must be publicly confessed, believed, and trusted is Jesus is the God of glory! Jesus must be the center of our affections. Jesus must be the center of our approach. Jesus must be our focus. Jesus must be on the throne of our conversation, activity, and mission. It's not about Mary as Theotokos, God Bearer—it about Jesus, God among men! It's not about Mohamed as prophet—it's about Jesus, the God who saves! It's not about democracy and unrestrained indulgence—it's about Jesus, the God who sets free! It's not about secularism, pluralism, universalism, or idiot-ism—it's about Jesus, God, the I AM, Jehovah, Lord of angel armies, the only Way, the only Truth, the only Life, Lord of glory, coming in power, the Ancient of Days.

Every "ism" of history and current thought, every demon of hell, and every effort of the devil in some way assault the majestic authority and supremacy of Jesus, who is very God of very God. Any voice, being, or ideology that denies the deity of Jesus is an insult to the very nature of God—God in three persons, Father, Son, and Holy Spirit. The Son, fully man and fully God—fully man, a perfect sacrifice, and fully God, a perfect High Priest. Jesus is worthy of all honor and praise, this is the issue! And upon the public confession of our allegiance to Jesus, the battle will be won or lost. As Matthew 10:32-33 reminds us, confess Jesus as God and be confessed before the Father, but deny Jesus as God before men and be denied before the Father in heaven.

Raymond Nonnatus was a thirteenth century Spanish missionary to Muslims. He went to Valencia where he ransomed 140 Christians from slavery. He then traveled to North Africa where he ransomed another 250 captives in Algiers. Then he went to Tunis where it is said he surrendered himself as a hostage for 28 captive Christians when his money ran out in keeping with a special fourth vow taken by members of his order. He suffered in captivity; a legend states that the Muslims bored a hole through his lips with a hot iron and padlocked his mouth to prevent him from preaching.

Matthew 10:34–35 is disturbingly clear. It reminds us that Jesus did not come to bring peace on earth. Jesus is the great divider, even among families, and the division is determined based on two decisions:

- What we will do with Jesus? Will we confess Him as Savior, Healer, baptizer, King, Lord, and God before men?
- And what we will do with ourselves? Will we take up our cross and follow Him?

The first application in taking up your cross to follow Jesus is this: You must publicly confess Him as God. Do you? All hell will try to silence you, and the devil does not have to hurt you if he can shut you up. It's critical that we confess Jesus as God.

IT'S CRITICAL THAT WE DIE TO SELF

It's critical that we live a cruciform life. A. B. Simpson wrote:

> The very test of consecration is our willingness not only to surrender the things that are wrong, but to surrender our rights... When God begins to subdue a soul, he often requires us to yield the things that are of little importance in themselves, and thus break our neck and subdue our spirit.[41]

No Christian worker can ever be used of God until the proud self-will is broken and the heart is ready to yield to God's every touch, no matter through whom it may come. To carry a cross means an unavoidable march to crucifixion. The unfortunate reality is that we can't crucify ourselves. Who can actually self-crucify in his or her own strength, without horrifically bungling the operation? Can you really pound a nail through your own ankles? Let's say by some surge of adrenalin you did. Could you then hold a nail to your own wrist and pound it in with your other hand? Let's say by some extraordinary effort you did. You have one hand left—who nails that to your cross?

"The origin," said Bonhoeffer, "and goal of our distress—is God!" God does not send the devil to do His dirty work. God is responsible for our crucifixion. God orchestrates the events that help us die. God is intricately involved in the suffering of each of our lives. God calls us to the cross. God ordains that others help us suffer indignity, scorn, mocking, and worse. My friend Butch Frey says that if he had to choose any one to design his suffering, he'd prefer it be the One who suffered and pressed through to glory. You see, Jesus uses friends to crucify us. Jesus uses colleagues to pound the nails in. Jesus uses spouses and children, parents and leaders to help us die. And to die to self is not to curse the ones who pound the nails at excruciating cost to both you (and often them), but to love, thank, honor, and bless them for doing what you could not do for yourself. It's not twisted to thank those who crucify us, for something glorious happens when we suffer and die, when we lose our life for His sake (Matt. 10:39).

Kenneth Bailey points out that the Old Testament word for glory— *khavod*—has to do with weight. The essential biblical understanding of glory is the weight of the presence of God as when we refer to someone as a "weighty individual in society" or a "weighty opinion." We mean they are to be reckoned with and respected. Gerhard von Rad notes that *khavod* is something weighty or impressive, a gravitas. The glory, the gravitas of God, the strong presence of the Lord upon us comes from two places—one that I will address in a moment and the other through the suffering and the crucifying of the flesh.

> *But rejoice to the extent that you partake of Christ's sufferings, that when His glory is revealed, you may also be glad with exceeding joy. If you are*

reproached for the name of Christ, blessed are you, for the Spirit of glory and of God rests upon you. (1 Peter 4:14)

But may the God of all grace, who called us to His eternal glory by Christ Jesus, after you have suffered a while, perfect, establish, strengthen, and settle you. (1 Peter 5:10)

For our light affliction...is working for us a far more exceeding and eternal weight of glory. (2 Cor. 4:17)

Biblical glory is weight and wisdom wrought by the presence of Jesus and His sufferings. Biblical glory for the believer is not earthly power and wealth; the true glory of God shines forth through the glory, weakness and suffering of the cross. Certainly God is glorified when His servants suffer well, but when we die to self daily, the glory of God shines just as brightly from us. Bailey says that the glory/presence/gravitas of God dwelt uniquely in the temple. Jesus was the new temple, and the disciples saw the glory of God shining through His suffering. Through baptism and faith they were united with Jesus, and the life of Jesus produced in them the power to reprocess their suffering into glory—the gravitas of God.

Why does Jesus ask us to carry our cross? Why does loving Jesus call for division from family? Why does the God of all comfort march us daily to dying? Why does God ordain that His beloved children suffer? Why does Bonhoeffer say God is the origin and goal of our distress? Not to punish or shame us, but in order to share His glory with us! And God shares His glory with us so that we can share His presence in the world.

I remember the time I walked by a demon possessed man and felt the evil emanating from him. In my spirit I sensed darkness, and it sent shudders down my spine. Lillian Harvey writes, "Evil men immediately bring with them an unwholesome atmosphere wherever they go, but if evil can be felt, how much more can righteousness be radiated?"[42] What did that demoniac sense of me as I walked by him? Did righteousness radiate? Did the peace of God allure Him? Did the glory of God on me attract him? Was there any glow on my physical being, any fire of love from my spirit that he could feel?

Did he shudder with longing, hope, or even godly fear? Did that demoniac see or feel anything of the glory of God from me? It's not magic. It's not forced. It is the instrumentality of human vessels, of jars of clay so full of the glory of Jesus that He spills out wherever we are.

Which begs the question again—what is spilling out of you and out of me? What presence and what glory emanates from us when we walk into the classroom, store, restaurant, office, or prayer meeting? Is there a gravitas of God? Is there a glory that can be felt? If tragically and all too commonly not, then why? How can we grow up into this glorious life of being so close to Jesus that His very presence in us changes the atmosphere of a room? How does your presence change the atmosphere? Not without carrying a cross and without dying to self. It is divine power using dire distress to make us weighty, to give us the gravitas of glory. This, then, is the beauty and the majesty and the purpose of the call to die.

IT'S CRITICAL THAT WE LIVE DEAD

Live Dead's mission is to walk the crucified self to the peoples who do not yet know the crucified Lord, and to live that crucified life before them with such joy that they long to become disciples of Jesus, willing to joyfully take up their own cross and follow Him.

Live Dead in one way applies to all Christians everywhere. All are to carry their cross. "When God calls a man," said Bonhoeffer, "He bids him come and die." Live Dead is not new in the general sense, and it's not new in the mission sense either. Live Dead is simply this—the crucified life in a missions context determined to bring the church to unreached peoples through multi-national teams. The values of Live Dead are to abide in Jesus, apostle the gospel, and abandon all, to make intimacy with Jesus our first priority and method, to proclaim Jesus where He is not glorified, and to give it all up for Jesus and the gospel's sake.

Henry Martyn died when he was only 31. He was brilliant. Before he died, after only four years on the field, he worked on translations of the Bible in Urdu, Arabic, and Farsi. Henry was an academic: the top of his class at Cambridge, first in the mathematics division, earned the title of "Senior

Wrangler." He was known as the student who "never lost an hour." His trajectory was a life in the Academy where he thrived and was admired. The university was his natural habitat. Lauded by all, certain to thrive and excel in his chosen profession, until he heard a sermon on this theme: seekest thou great things for thyself? Seek them not…saith the Lord. "The Lord," says Lillian Harvey, "changed ascent to descent."[43] Martyn records the struggle of the descent in his diary, a descent to live dead for Jesus among Muslims. In the struggle he wrote, "Pride shows itself every hour of every day; what long and undisturbed possession does self complacency hold in my heart! What plans, and dreams, and visions of futurity fill my imagination, in which self is the prominent object."[44]

Why is there such a dearth of men in missions? Is it because they are too proud to raise support, or too fearful? Is it because their mind is full of plans, dreams, and visions of their own futurity? Is it because they love to be the "Senior Wrangler" in the firm, business, academy, or stadium? Why do the nations rage? Why do the peoples perish? Because men, strong men, top of their class men, refuse to die to self and live that death in pioneer fields? This is not new. Martyn continues, "I determined on entire devotedness though with trembling, for the flesh dreads crucifixion, but should I fear pain, when Christ was so agonized for me? No, come what will, I am determined, to be a fellow worker with Christ."

And what became of Henry Martyn? Leaving the woman he loved in England, spending four years to translate the Bible into Urdu, Arabic, and Farsi, traveling to Arabia and Iran to test the translation, debating with mullahs about the deity of Jesus and being told they would burn out his tongue if he kept proclaiming Jesus as God, and dying in a lonely Turkish village, vainly trying to recover from ill health at 31. Martyn, the first, modern, evangelical missionary to Muslims, the translator of the Scriptures into three major Muslim languages, the fearless proclaimer of the deity of Christ, and in the end a wrangler of darkness and deceit, a man's man, a godly man. Where are the Henry Martyns of today?

Edward Payson said,

It occurred to me…that most of my sins and sufferings were occasioned by an unwillingness to be the nothing which I am, and, by consequent struggles, to be something. I saw that if I would but cease struggling and consent to be anything or nothing, just as God pleases, I might be happy. Since I have lost my will, I have found happiness. There can be no such thing as disappointment to me, for I have no desires but that God's will may be accomplished.[45]

"Take up thy cross and follow me," I hear the blessed Savior call. How can I make a lesser sacrifice when Jesus gave His all?[46]

WHAT NEXT?

Make a recommitment to live the crucified life now, here, right where you are, every day. The beginning of that self-denial is actually a positive. Abide in Jesus and lavish time on Him in His presence.

Make a commitment to find one Muslim in your world and pursue them, serve them, love them, befriend them, pray for them, invite them into your life and home, live the joyous Jesus life in front of them, and open your mouth and proclaim the gospel to them.

Make a commitment to advocate for unreached people by starting a prayer band of three or more people who pray for the unreached. Resources for that prayer band can be accessed through the Live Dead website (livedead.org).

Consider your willingness to come live with us among the dead. Come die to self with others who are stumbling in that direction and join a church planting team among the unreached.

But most immediate, pray quietly and reverently. Tell Jesus "yes" before you know the question or where He asks you to go. I specifically challenge the men. It's time for men to step up into their missions' destiny.

Surrendered

MATTHEW 24:14

Now as He sat on the Mount of Olives, the disciples came to Him privately, saying, "Tell us, when will these things be? And what will be the sign of Your coming, and of the end of the age?"

And Jesus answered and said to them: "Take heed that no one deceives you. For many will come in My name, saying, 'I am the Christ,' and will deceive many. And you will hear of wars and rumors of wars. See that you are not troubled; for all these things must come to pass, but the end is not yet. For nation will rise against nation, and kingdom against kingdom. And there will be famines, pestilences, and earthquakes in various places. All these are the beginning of sorrows.

"Then they will deliver you up to tribulation and kill you, and you will be hated by all nations for My name's sake. And then many will be offended, will betray one another, and will hate one another. Then many false prophets will rise up and deceive many. And because lawlessness will abound, the love of many will grow cold. But he who endures to the end shall be saved. And this gospel of the kingdom will be preached in all the world as a witness to all the nations, and then the end will come.
(Matt. 24:3–14)

I went to boarding school when I was 7 years old. Cry no tears for me, for my best friends, my fondest memories, and my growth in Jesus all came from those blessed years. Nevertheless, as a 7-year-old, I longed for term to end. I longed to go home. There were many things to enjoy at school—sports, music, drama, friends, and more. But my little heart knew that school was not home and that loving teachers were not my precious mother and father.

A winding dirt road led to the front of that school. At term's end, I perched with my sisters on the stone steps, and we fixed our eyes on the turn of that road. It was the late 1970s, and my father had a white 504 Peugeot Saloon with mandatory roof rack. This was the ubiquitous missionary vehicle of choice during that era in Africa. We sat and stared as other cars made that turn, and with each passing moment, I grew more excited and more anxious. My heart yearned, my pulse quickened, and my eyes fixed. I never left my post. I had one desire, one blessed hope, and one longing — I wanted to go home! Suddenly around the bend came the white Peugeot with the trumpeted horn and license plate KVF703. I still remember it. The clouds parted and allowed the sun to shine. My father had come for us! Joy in my soul! Life in my bones! Troubles forgotten! School passed away! It was time to go home!

Enlightenment had brought darkness. Industry manufactured weapons of war. Education ushered in arrogance. Commerce fueled slavery. Every advance of man corrupted. Every promise became a nightmare. The world was not improving. All the wisdom, might, and effort of humanity proved incapable of bringing peace, hope, joy, or love. But a longing grew and burst in the hearts of men and women: "This world is not our home. We're just passing through."

Missions history refers to the 1800s as the "Great Century." Building on William Carey's foundation to reach the coastlands, men like Hudson Taylor, C. T. Studd, and John Patton went to inland China, inland Africa, and the islands of the sea. They searched for the peoples and places beyond. Then something happened in the 1900s, now referred to as the "Pentecostal Century," something wonderful, something prophesied. That something was the growth of the church exploding around the world, and it was birthed by a collective desperation for the heavenly home.

This school of earth has some shiny attractions, to be sure, but ultimately our souls long for our heavenly home. This is not where we belong. We cannot redeem the earth, for we bear the cause of its demise. We are part of the problem. *Oh, Lord, come and deal with fallen man and restore fallen creation. Oh, Lord, take us home!*

God's people of the century past perched on the stone steps of fallen Eden and fixed their eyes on the bend of history with one hope and one prayer alone: Jesus, would You come? Jesus, please take us home. As they waited to go home, their attention was drawn to the indicator that Scripture gives about timing: "And this gospel of the kingdom will be preached in all the world as a witness to all the nations, and then the end will come" (Matt. 24:14). There were other indicators — earthquakes, famines, signs in heaven above, the beginning of sorrows — but the clearest indication and requirement for the end game is the global declaration to every ethno-linguistic people that Jesus alone is Savior, that Jesus alone is Lord of every people, and that in Jesus' return alone is the ultimate redemption of all things.

Our fathers and mothers in the faith believed in imminence — that Jesus could come at any moment — and they also believed in obedience to the Scriptures: Go make disciples, preach the gospel to every ethnic group, and then the end will come. These beliefs were complimentary in their minds and linked in mutual fulfillment. Therefore, dependent on Christ's return for final liberation, agreeing that Jesus could return at any moment, conscious of the requirement that every ethnic group hear the gospel, our fathers and mothers asked the obvious question: How? How on earth can the gospel be preached to every ethne so that Jesus comes and we all go home? The heavenly answer was spirit empowerment. To be Pentecostal is to be dependent on the Holy Spirit. It is to be dependent on the Spirit to preach the gospel in every nation among every *ethne*, compelled by love for the glory of God in obedience to the Great Commission that Jesus comes and we all go home.

We now stand on the edge of a new millennium. We are not the first to dream of closure, yet the Scripture is not changed, nor is its mandate fulfilled. We have seen more war, bondage, injustice, economic oppression, racial divides, abuses of human dignity, perversion of culture, violation of creation, and corruption of institutions than ever before. More sobering and troubling yet, we all still struggle with indwelling sin. There yet remains one blessed hope. There is still one precious and priceless priority. There is yet the promise of empowerment, and all these are in the context of "the gospel of the kingdom will be preached in all the world as a witness to all the nations, and then the end will come." Our theme tonight is surrender. In order for the gospel to be preached among every people, in order for the end to come, we must surrender.

NOTHING OTHER THAN PREACHING

We must surrender the idea that the peoples of this world will be won by anything other than preaching. The verb "preached" comes from the Greek word *kerysso*. It means the verbal announcing, the spoken proclamation, and the audible hearing of a message.

In Acts 6, the apostles said, "It is not right that we should give up preaching the word of God to serve tables.... But we will devote ourselves to prayer and the ministry of the word" (vv. 2, 4). Stephen is chosen, and as a result "the word of God continued to increase, and the number of disciples multiplied.... Stephen, full of grace and power, was doing great wonders and signs among the people...but they could not withstand the wisdom and the Spirit with which he was speaking...and they set up false witnesses saying, 'This man never ceases to speak...for we heard him say...'" (vv. 7–8, 10, 13).

It is academic to us that super apostles, leaders, luminaries, pastors, and clergy devote themselves to prayer and proclamation. But note what pedestrian Stephen, the table waiter, did — he opened his mouth and spoke. Grace, power, signs, and wonders accompanying, Stephen did not shut up. His spoken wisdom — controversial as it was — could not be countermanded. We know nothing of the tables that Stephen served, but we have 53 verses in Acts 7 of Stephen's proclaimed sermon.

"Words, words, words," saya Eliza Doolittle. "I am so sick of words."[47] She has a point because the words of man are pompous, hypocritical, and self-serving. Humanity is sick of the empty words of the do-littles and do-nothings of the world. The cure is not to overcompensate and say little. The cure is to open our mouths, die to our silence, and proclaim the unsearchable riches of Christ because faith still comes by hearing and hearing by the Word of God. And how will they hear unless we preach (Rom. 10:14)?

The forces of your age seek to muzzle you. The siren song of respectability urges moderation. Powers within, powers without, and powers from below make it their one ambition to silence the compelling, consistent verbalized presentation of the gospel. You are pressured not to offend. You are persuaded not to inflame. You are badgered towards suffocating tolerance. Impress on your thinking anew, Jesus' words brought division. He came to bring not peace, but a sword. The words of John the Baptist brought his beheading. Stephen's steady sermons summoned stones down on his head. Yes, in the kingdom we attack injustice wherever we find it, but you want a justice issue? Let us not waver from the greatest of them all! Not all are poor, not all are trafficked, not all are illiterate, not all lack clean water, and not all have AIDS, *but* all have sinned and fallen short of the glory of God (Rom. 3:23). Sin is the universal malady. You want a justice issue? Men and women, boys and girls, young and old, rich and poor, *they perish*. They die eternally. They suffer. They march in their legions towards damnable hell, not because of the excesses or hypocrisy of our fathers, but because of our thundering silence!

Our prayers, our finances, our mission, and our action must prioritize the proclamation of the gospel among the unreached. Entire people groups are damned and rumble towards incalculable horror because the church will not proclaim in power. The unparalleled injustice of our day is simply this: 6,500 unreached people groups — or two billion people — have not heard the gospel. And yes, faith comes by hearing. The unreached are blind because the church is mute and because of our self-protecting silence. God have mercy on us all! We must surrender our words, and our lack of them, for this gospel must be preached to every people and then the end will come.

NOT FROM A POSITION OF SECURITY

We must surrender the idea that the gospel can be preached from a position of security.

A friend sent me a Helen Keller quote: "Life is either a daring adventure or nothing. Security does not exist in nature, nor do the children of men as a whole experience it. Avoiding danger is no safer in the long run than exposure. The fearful are caught as often as the bold."[48]

Our text reminds us just how the gospel must be preached. Let me juxtapose verse 14 with its context in chapter 24: And this gospel, wars and famine, of the kingdom, earthquake and pain, will be preached, trials and death, throughout the whole world, hatred and falling, as a testimony, betrayal and falsehood, to all nations, astray and cold, and when we have endured in so proclaiming Christ, under such pressure, then the end will come.

One of my closet friends was imprisoned in Sudan for 58 days. He was released three weeks ago. He demanded a Bible and after one week received one. He memorized the whole books of James and Romans. For 52 days, he was in solitary confinement with no comfort of human interaction. He stood hour after hour at the window of his cell, reading the Scriptures at the top of his voice into the prison courtyard. He continued to read even after the guards insisted that he stop because the gospel has always been preached under pressure. The best sermons in Acts took place in prisons or at trials. The most powerful testimonies of our day come from the mouths of those who suffer and die for their witness, after giving up their demands for security.

I live in Cairo, and the daily existence of our team reminds me that we cannot wait for peace. We cannot wait for Pax Americana, for stability in the Arab world, for a guarantee against danger, abuse, rape, prison, pain, or death. We cannot wait for assurances of non-violence. The gospel speaks loudest when its message of hope is contrary to the times. The uncertainties and instability of our day are no excuses not to be spent for the gospel. The dangers that are real and that rush upon us do not remove our preaching mandate.

We must embrace ongoing insecurity. Instability is the new normal. Suffering and persecution must increase as the end draws nigh. The Word will soften some; it will harden others. Missionaries will increasingly be imprisoned and suffer and die. We will deploy to war zones. We will remain in contexts of famine, destruction, and death. We will lose some of our finest and replace them with you, our ruddy youth. Preach from the prison! Preach from the pit! This is our new privilege. This is our destiny. This is the Live Dead joy. There is no "safe" time to preach the gospel. We must surrender the idea that the gospel can be preached from a position of security, for the gospel has ever gone forth and must now again be preached under pressure.

NOT IN SELECT PARTS OF THE WORLD

We must surrender the idea that the gospel can be preached only in select parts of the world. Our text is very clear. The gospel must be preached among every people. The Greek word for "nation" in our text is ethnesi. From it we derive the word "ethnic," and it refers to specific language and cultural peoples or what we call ethno-linguistic groups.

This has ever been the understanding of the Assemblies of God. The gospel must go to every people group. This is why we plant indigenous churches, so that they can reach their own people and the peoples beyond them. This is why we train national leaders, so that they may rise up apostolically and go to the regions beyond. This is why we touch with compassion, so that we might access those peoples who have never heard the gospel. The goal is not (and never has been) planting churches or training leaders. The goal is not (and never has been) compassion toward the hurting. All of these are valuable, but none are salvific by intent. All are a means to an end and all work towards the ultimate goal of mission. Why do we plant churches? So the gospel can be preached to every people group and the end come. Why do we train ministers and leaders? So the gospel can be preached to every people group and the end come. Why do we touch with compassion? So the gospel can be preached to every people group and the end come. The goal is the glory of God and the imminent return of Christ. The motive is love, and the means is the preaching of the gospel among every people group, for then and only then will the end come.

William Carey admonished us that we should pray with an open Bible and an open map. Author Alan Johnson reminds us that we cannot pretend not to know what we know. In some places among some peoples of the world, the gospel has been preached. Hallelujah! The church is planted, and the people are capable of reaching their own. We dare not build on another man's foundation (Rom. 15:20), and we dare not confuse geo-politics with the strategy of the Spirit. Somalis flood into Minneapolis. Indonesia is outside the 10-40 Window. Many of Europe's peoples are less than one percent evangelical and inoculated against the gospel by the traditional church. The borderless church is not bound by the politics or nation-states of man. The strategy of the Holy Spirit has always been the glory of God for the joy of all peoples. Missionaries in Africa will catalyze the African church for the unreached. Missionaries in Europe will model frontier missions to the lethargic. Missionaries in Latin America will function apostolically and raise up new armies of those who will live and die among unreached people. In all places among all people, the priority of God's people will once again resound: Preach the gospel among every people and then the end will come.

In our world today are 6,500 unreached peoples. This is the priority of Scripture. This is the purpose for the filling of the Holy Spirit. This is the reason for mission. We must surrender the idea that the gospel be preached only in certain places of the world. Though none of us would ever admit to thinking that way, we collectively act that way. We must now be resolute, for the Spirit demands and the corporate calling of the Assemblies of God insists that we will ever prioritize the regions beyond; that we will ever focus on neglected peoples; and that we will ever preach the gospel among the peoples where it has not been preached. This is our requested obedience. This was our beginning, and this will be our culmination. The gospel will be preached among every people and then the end will come.

NOT IN OUR OWN POWER

We must surrender the idea that the gospel can be preached in our own power. There are three spirits that plague humanity and hinder the mission of God: I know. I can. I am. These spirits must be strangled out of us, and in their place, we must desperately, frantically seek the Holy Spirit. For even the circumstantial exposure to the realities of mission impresses the sobering reality upon us that indeed *I know not, I cannot, and I am not.*

I am Pentecostal by necessity, not by choice. From sheer desperation, I daily seek the baptism of the Holy Spirit to be filled and refilled. The continual refilling of the Spirit is the lifeline of the weak. I have nothing to give. I have nothing to offer. We have no solutions or sources. We know not, we cannot, and we are not. Our spirits are sour wine. Prone to wander, Lord, we feel it. Our spirits betray us. We are prone to leave the God we love. And unless the Father sends the Spirit, all is lost.

The cardinal doctrine of Pentecost can be summed up in one word: more. In Acts 2:4, the disciples are filled. In Acts 4:31, this same group prays again, is shaken again, and is filled again. I don't have enough of the Father. I need more of You, Abba. I don't have enough of the Son. I need more of You, Jesus. I don't have enough of the Spirit. I need more of You, wonderful Counselor. And like D. L. Moody says, what I do have leaks out. Jesus, baptize me again in Your Holy Spirit today! Jesus, fill me afresh. Jesus, give me more of Yourself. Because if You don't, I will dry and die. Jesus, I need more of You. My spirit is so small and the unreached world is so big.

"Jesus," the Christian repeatedly cries. "Jesus," the missionary constantly pleads. "Help me! Fill me, Jesus, or I perish."

Earlier this year I was at a conference. Late one night I sat with three friends. Alan works in Thailand, Jason in China, and David in Lebanon. We talked of the many times that the Spirit led us to pray for healing for Muslims and nothing happened. The week after the conference, one friend wrote the following to us in an email:

> I think God gets a different kind of glory when His servants pray and nothing happens. And pray again and nothing happens. And believe and nothing happens. And trust and look foolish. And step out in faith and are not rewarded. And their spirit persists. And they pray and pray and pray and pray, and nothing happens. And their spirit endures, and their spirit remains, and their spirit believes, and their spirit trusts. And they pray again and nothing happens. They pray again and nothing happens. They pray again and nothing happens. And they pray and pray and pray and pray and pray. And the heavens are as brass, and the answer does not come. And they believe again and trust again and depend again and pray again, and nothing happens. And when the spirit of man is subject to God under such duress and disappointment, God elbows the devil in the ribs and says, "Do you have anyone like that, devil? Do you have anyone like that? Do you have anyone so surrendered, devil? Do you have anyone whose spirit is so soft? Do you have anyone like that, devil? Do you have anyone who trusts you so unshakably? Do you have anyone with a surrendered spirit like that? Devil, do you have anyone like that?"

Nothing strikes fear into the heart of that old serpent like the spirit of one completely surrendered to Jesus. For a surrendered spirit doesn't have to know why. A surrendered spirit doesn't have to be known. A surrendered spirit doesn't have to be able. A surrendered spirit doesn't have to be the center. A surrendered spirit doesn't have to succeed. Yet, a surrendered spirit can be trusted with power from on high, for a surrendered spirit is unlimited and unstoppable.

We must surrender the idea that this gospel can be preached to every nation in our own strength, for it is to the desperate that Jesus sends more of His Spirit.

GOD DOES NOT NEED YOU

Disabuse yourself of the notion that God needs you. China, Afghanistan, and Libya do not need you. The Middle East, the Orient, the islands of the sea, Somali pirates, Thai Buddhists, Saudi princes, European atheists, they don't need you. They don't need your smallness, weakness, baggage, or sin. You need Cairo more than Cairo needs you. You need Syria, Mauritania, Turkey, Myanmar, Indonesia, and Spain to reveal your smallness, to break you, to cast you in fragments upon the Mighty Rock.

You were not providentially brought to this summit[49] because you are needed. We don't need you. The nations don't need you. Jesus doesn't need you. He doesn't need your words, deeds, or ideas. He doesn't need your puny security measures. He doesn't need your strategy or individual preference about where you should go. He certainly doesn't need your ridiculous strength or undisciplined spirit.

We are not needed, but we are invited. The God of glory invites us. The Lord of all peoples instructs us to preach the gospel among all the ethne, and His surprising condition of invitation is surrender. Jesus doesn't stand before us begging. He never has and never will negotiate. These are the terms of Jesus' invitation to you:

1.   We must surrender the idea that the peoples of this world will be won by anything other than preaching.
2.   We must surrender the idea that the gospel can be preached from a position of security.
3.   We must surrender the idea that the gospel can be preached only in select parts of the world.
4.   We must surrender the idea that the gospel can be preached in our own power.

If on these sacred understandings you are willing to take up the invitation of God and join Him in His grand, precious priority of the gospel being preached among every people group and then the end coming, would you surrender all?

You are the Christ

MARK 8

Mark 8:27-29 says: "Now Jesus and His disciples went out to the towns of Caesarea Philippi; and on the road He asked His disciples, saying to them, 'Who do men say that I am?' So they answered, 'John the Baptist; but some say, Elijah; and others, one of the prophets.' He said to them, 'But who do you say that I am?' Peter answered and said to Him, 'You are the Christ.'"

Today we sang, worshiped and lifted our hands. But what saves us from the hypocrisy of hollow praise? What moves us to the depths of costly, beautiful surrender?

We live in a culture that promotes self. We indulge a form of Christianity that champions ease. What lifts us from the narcissism of our selfish spirituality and plants us in the heavenly reality of death that leads to life? What liberates us from the folly of indulgent living? What teaches us to hide behind the cross? What compels us to magnify Christ? What empowers us to love a diminished role so that Jesus will rise and be glorified, that Jesus alone is exalted in that day?

Who will rescue us from these bodies of death? Who will liberate us from the chains of safety? Who will so grip our hearts that we lose our fears? Who has the power to transform our weak, broken, carnal flesh into agents of life, health, liberty and justice? Who can take these stammering tongues and make us oracles of God? Who can take the tragedies of our past to win triumphs for eternity?

Who can take shame and make it glorious? Who can take folly and make it wisdom? Who can take weakness and manufacture strength? Who can raise us from the death we choose and plant us as indestructible, immortal? Who can take death and make it live? Who is sufficient for these things? Who but the Christ! Who indeed, but the Christ!

"You are the Christ!" Peter said. "I heard you call me from my nets. I felt you, Jesus, I felt you make me a fisher of men. I was there, Jesus, I was there when you cast out the unclean spirit. You spoke with authority and my heart burned. You raised my mother-in-law and she stood to serve. You healed the sick at the door. You are the Christ!

"When they broke through the roof, I heard you forgive sin. I saw the paralyzed get up and walk. I shook the withered hand that grew. I was in the boat when the storm turned. I saw Legion freed from demons. I watched the pigs plunge into the sea. I saw the widow who doctors couldn't help cry for joy. I heard Jairus sob when his daughter died, and I held him up when his daughter rose. You are the Christ!"

"You sent me out and I healed the sick. You gave me power and demons fled. You fed the crowd; I shared their bread. Jesus, You are the Christ! I saw you walk on water. I saw you raise the dead. I saw you heal the mute. I saw the people fed."

"My heart inside me burns. My Spirit for You yearns. You are the Lord, the Son of God. Jesus, You are the Christ!"

Peter would one day die for Jesus. But first he had to live with Him. Love Him. Be loved by Him. Peter walked with Jesus, laughed with him, worked with him and cried with him. Peter saw Jesus heal. His heart burned within him when Jesus spoke. Peter swam and sank with Christ. Peter and Jesus communicated without words. Peter was so intimate with Jesus that one knowing look from Christ devastated him.

We cannot die for Christ if we have not lived with Him. We cannot dream of changing the nations if our spirits have not been yanked inside out by Jesus himself. You cannot live dead if you do not live with Jesus!

What does it mean to live Dead? Well, first of all it means to live. It means health, joy, vitality, vibrancy and strength in the Holy Spirit. The profile of the one who lives dead is not boring, sanctimonious, stuffy, judgmental, religious, and dry.

No, to live dead is to live! It is the life of Christ flowing in our mortal bodies. It is to rejoice in the created world. It is to laugh with the Savior and to run fast and sing loud. It is to work hard and sleep deeply; it is to live and move and have our being in Him. It is to rise to the challenges with a leap and a whistle and to charge the giants giggling. It is freedom from sin, bondage and self. It is to embrace the arts—to dance, to share, to inspire. To live dead is to love, embrace and delight. To live dead is. . .

Raindrops on roses and whiskers on kittens
Bright copper kettles and warm woolen mittens...
Doorbells and sleigh bells and schnitzel with noodles
Wild geese that fly with the moon on their wings...

Silver white winters that melt into springs...[50]

Jesus is the Christ, the source of all that is beautiful! He is the fount of life and the reason for being. He is the Alpha and the Omega. He is all that thrills my soul. He is seated in the heavenly places. Jesus is far above all principalities, power, might, and dominion, and every name that is named. All things are under His feet. He is head over all things; He is the fullness of Him who fills all in all. Jesus is the Christ. He made us alive, we who once were dead in trespasses and sins! He is rich in mercy because of His great love with which He has loved us. Even when we were dead in trespasses, He made us alive together with Him (Eph. 1:21–2:1, 4–5). In Jesus Christ, all the fullness dwells. Jesus is the Christ, pre-eminent in all things. He is very God of very God. He is the Christ!

And with Peter we live dead by living unto Jesus! We declare that Jesus is Lord to the glory of God the Father.

Jesus is the goal, the prize, the destination, the fuel, the reward and the center. Jesus is my all in all. Jesus, is my Christ! Buried with Him in baptism, I am raised with Him in glory. Christ in me, the hope of glory. To live is Christ. I live for Christ, by Christ, with Christ and in Christ.

When I run, I feel the pleasure of Christ. When I paint, every stroke is for His fame. When I hit a jump shot, I may not be LeBron, but my Spirit says, "For You, O Christ, for you!" When I teach, it is for Christ. When I study, it is for His glory among the nations. When I drive and when I dance, it is for Christ! In my work, in my play, in all things, everywhere are for Christ. In Christ, I live and move and have my being!

"You are the Christ!" Peter declared. Well done, Peter! You got it right.

Do you have it right today? Do you know the Christ? Do you live for the supremacy of Jesus in all things? Have you laid down your will to take up His? Will you give up your dreams and carefully planned future to take up His summons, whatever that means, wherever faith takes you? Do you know the Christ? Is Jesus your all in all?

If you are here living a nominal, lazy Christian life, if you are backslidden, if you are marginal, inward, selfish and carnal, you are a fool and an idiot. Why? Because there is so much life in Christ!

Mark 8:31-33 says, "And He began to teach them that the Son of Man must suffer many things, and be rejected by the elders and chief priests and scribes, and be killed, and after three days rise again. He spoke this word openly. Then Peter took Him aside and began to rebuke Him. But when He had turned around and looked at His disciples, He rebuked Peter, saying, 'Get behind Me, Satan! For you are not mindful of the things of God, but the things of men.'"

Is it shocking to you that the devil spoke through an apostle? One of the reasons Peter got it so wrong was because he got it so right. Jesus is the Christ. Jesus is God. Jesus is power, life, truth, and strength. Christ is victor and King of Kings. Jesus is Lord of Lords. Jesus is everything.

And a Christ doesn't suffer; a Christ isn't rejected; and a Christ isn't killed. But "God called Jesus to what seemed unmitigated disaster," says Oswald Chambers.[51] Poverty, scorn, abuse, rejection, suffering, torture, shame, naked on a cross and death. "When Christ calls a man," writes Dietrich Bonhoeffer, "He bids him come and die."[52]

What does it mean to live dead? It means many things, but let's take three from the text of Mark 8:31. Living dead means joyfully following Jesus to suffering, rejection, and death.

LIVING DEAD THROUGH SUFFERING MANY THINGS

"I don't go to religion to make me happy," wrote C.S. Lewis. "I always know a bottle of port would do that. If you want a religion to make you really feel comfortable, I certainly don't recommend Christianity."[53]

There is a beauty in suffering. There is a strength that comes from loss. Suffering is the privilege of all who follow Christ. Suffering is the great gift we continually refuse to open. Scripture says:

> *For to you it has been granted on behalf of Christ, not only to believe in Him, but also to suffer for His sake.* (Phil. 1:29)

> *Yes, and all who desire to live godly in Christ Jesus will suffer persecution.* (2 Tim. 3:12)

So they departed from the presence of the council, rejoicing that they were counted worthy to suffer shame for His name. (Acts 5:41)

We dread suffering, but we should welcome it. The most loving gift God could give the American church is a large dollop of suffering. Oh, that you and I would be worthy of the sweetness of suffering.

You can tell when someone has not suffered. When a man or woman stands and pontificates on some aspect of God's Word, you can tell whether those truths are memorized or if they are seared into the soul by fire. I asked a dear saint, now in heaven, about her new pastor. "Oh, he is nice enough," she said, "but you can tell he has never suffered."

In mission to Muslims, every time the gospel breaks out, there is a suffering catalyst. Every time there is internal violence, when Muslim majority ethnic groups kill Muslim minorities, it leads to thousands of Muslims rejecting Islam and accepting the Christ. This happened in the 1960s in Indonesia, in the 1970s in East Pakistan (now called Bangladesh), in the 1980s in Iran and Iraq, in the 1990s in Algeria among the Kabaile and more recently in Darfur, Sudan. Suffering is part and parcel of the gospel.

To live dead is not self-flagellation. It is to follow Jesus to the cross. It is to endure great sorrow for the joy set before us, to be crushed so that perfume comes out, to suffer many things. David Mathis writes:

> Suffering is not only the consequence of completing the [Great] Commission, but it is God's appointed means by which He will show the superior worth of His Son to all peoples…. Just as it was fitting that… He should make the founder of [our] salvation perfect through suffering [Heb. 2:10], so it is fitting that God save a people from all peoples from eternal suffering through the redemptive suffering of Jesus displayed in the temporal suffering of His missionaries…. What is lacking in Jesus' sufferings is not their redemptive value, but their personal presentation to the peoples He died to save.

For Jesus and the Apostles, this primarily meant physical torture. It means the same around the world today. More followers of Jesus have been martyred in the 20th century than the previous 19 combined. Every 24 hours, 480 believers are martyred for their faith. In the hour we spend in these reflections, somewhere around the world 20 of our brothers and sisters will die for Jesus. May they die well.

It will ultimately be the same here in America one day.

And God does not stand aloof from the pain of His people. God suffers. He is a God outside of time in eternal agony when His children are bruised. Jesus suffered at cost to the Father. We learn obedience by the things we suffer; we fill up what is lacking in the sufferings of Christ.

Our suffering does not save. There is one Christ and His work on the cross is done. But God has designed that we know the fellowship of His sufferings, and that we are like Him in His death. In some eternal way, our suffering serves to help people come to Jesus.

Let us settle it forever then—to live dead is to suffer many things. Not even knowing what that means, not daring to define it, let us be done forever with the notion of ease, safety, health, wealth and prosperity. Let us reach for the piercing thorns and embrace the rugged cross. Let us count trials all joy.

We need not look for suffering or not imagine it by our own means. We will not provoke trouble for trouble's sake. We will simply follow Jesus—just cling to Him, forsaking all others. The suffering He ordains will find us and cause Him to be glorified.

LIVING DEAD THROUGH REJECTION BY THE ELDERS, CHIEF PRIESTS, AND SCRIBES

In the fourth century, when the Christian faith was preached in its power in Egypt, a young brother sought out the great Macarius. "Father," said he, "what is the meaning of being dead and buried with Christ?"

"My son," answered Macarius, "you remember our dear brother who died and was buried a short time since? Go now to his grave and tell him all the unkind things that you ever heard of him, and that we are glad he is dead, and thankful to be rid of him, for he was such a worry to us and caused so much discomfort in the church. Go, my son, and say that, and hear what he will answer."

The young man was surprised and doubted whether he really understood; but Macarius only said, "Do as I bid you, my son, and come and tell me what our departed brother says."

The young man did as he was commanded and returned.

"Well, and what did our brother say?" asked Macarius.

"Say, father!" he exclaimed. "How could he say anything? He is dead."

"Go now again, my son, and repeat every kind and flattering thing you have ever heard of him; tell him how much we miss him; how great a saint he was; what noble work he did; how the whole church depended upon him; and come again and tell me what he says."

The young man began to see the lesson Macarius would teach him. He went again to the grave and said many flattering things to the dead man, then returned to Macarius.

"He answers nothing, father; he is dead and buried."

"You know now, my son," said the old father, "what it is to be dead with Christ. Praise and blame equally are nothing to him who is really dead and buried with Christ."

Jesus was rejected by the cultural and religious leaders of His day. The elders, chief priests and scribes all rejected Jesus. Cultural architects, futurists, reporters, bloggers, talking heads, magazine editorials, public radio, Twitter and social media, we are ready for their scorn. We know that every perversion will be tolerated in the secular world. We understand that a score of athletes can publicly pray, but it is the one who consistently and winsomely exalts Jesus as the only Savior that gets crucified. We understand that secular humanists and radical Muslims—with antithetical views on homosexuality, abortion, modesty, alcohol and human rights—will link arms against anyone who proclaims a divine Christ. We are ready for their scorn.

But that is the easy part about living dead. What about when your Christian friends reject you? What about when mentors criticize? What about when pastors in the community and ministers on the campus work against you? What about when district officials don't recognize your labor? What about when godly people don't seem to care? What about those who don't believe in you? What about the ones who leave your church, critique your leadership and transfer to the thriving ministry? What do you do when your vision is doubted, your motives questioned, and cold water poured on your dreams by your leaders?

What about when everyone forsakes you? What about when you are betrayed? What about when all men doubt you and the truth you've spoken becomes "twisted by knaves to make a trap for fools?"[55] What about when you are slandered by co-workers? What about when you are taken advantage of and abused?

What about when God gives you a message that annoys everyone and bruises some? What about when God gives you a method that doesn't work? What about when God's will for you is to have the smallest, most insignificant ministry ever seen? What about when you are wrongly accused? Jesus was. What about when you are misunderstood? Jesus was. What about when you are blamed? What about a life that no one praises?

"You know now, my son," said the old father, "what it is to be dead with Christ. Praise and blame equally are nothing to him who is really dead and buried with Christ."[54]

LIVING DEAD THROUGH BEING KILLED AND AFTER THREE DAYS RISING AGAIN

> *"When He had called the people to Himself, with His disciples also, He said to them, 'Whoever desires to come after Me, let him deny himself, and take up his cross, and follow Me'"* (Mark 8:34).

It has never been an unusual thing to die for Jesus—literally. Dying for Jesus used to be the way Christians lived. Elisabeth Elliot writes of her slain husband Jim:

> He and the other men with him who died were hailed as heroes, "martyrs." I do not approve. Nor would they have approved. Is the distinction between living for Christ and dying for Him, after all, so great? Is not the second the logical conclusion of the first? Furthermore, to live for God IS to die, "daily," as the apostle Paul put it. It is to lose everything that we may gain Christ. It is in thus laying down our lives that we find them.[56]

In Roman coliseums, in Arabian deserts, in Communist jails or on the islands of the Pacific, for 2,000 years men and women, old and young, have shed their blood for Jesus. "One Christian in India," writes David Platt, "while being skinned alive, looked at his persecutors and said: 'I thank you for this. Tear off my old garment, for soon I will put on Christ's garment of righteousness.'"[57]

Platt retells the story of Christopher Love, who preparing to be executed wrote a note to his wife, saying: "'Today they will sever me from my physical head, but they cannot sever me from my spiritual head, Christ.' As [Love] walked to his death, his wife applauded while he sang of glory!"[58]

Joseph Tson, Romanian Pastor while being tortured said: "Your supreme weapon is killing. My supreme weapon is dying."

If you were standing in Hawaii, John Piper explains, and drew a straight line to Australia, somewhere in the middle of that line would be a group of islands. They used to be called the New Hebrides—now called Vanuatu. In the mid 1800s a ship took two missionaries to the New Hebrides. The missionaries went ashore and while the crew of the boat watched, they were captured by cannibals and eaten.

Twelve years later in England, a man named John Patton felt the call of God to take the gospel to the New Hebrides. An elderly gentleman in the church rebuked him. "You can't go to the New Hebrides," he said, "you'll be eaten by cannibals!"

"Mr. Dixon," Patton replied, "your own prospect is soon to be laid in the grave there to be eaten by worms. What does it matter then if you are eaten by worms and I by cannibals. For in the day of resurrection, mine will be much more glorious!"

And if you know the story, Patton went to Vanuatu and through a series of adventures led many on that island to Christ. The point is this: Should Jesus tarry, we will all die. What does it matter how? Martyrdom is not to be sought; neither is it to be feared. And those who die for Christ should really not be considered heroic or foolish. It is merely following Jesus. "If anyone serves Me, let him follow Me; and where I am, there My servant will be also" (John 12:26).

C. S. Lewis said that our bodies and spirits are so closely connected that they catch each other's diseases.[59] The same is true for life and death in God's majestic design. Life comes from death and we don't start living until we die. You know where carrying a cross takes you? Ultimately to abundant life. Death is just a rest stop on the way.

We were all born into the "Shadowlands." This life is a vapor with eternity behind us and 80 brief years here if we are lucky. Then immortality beyond. In the light of forever, what's a little death, a little trouble, a little shame, a little rejection? In the light of heaven, what are torture, rape, prison, hunger and abuse? Horrific as those things are—and I do not mitigate their pain—yet they are temporary. What's a little temporary death in the light of everlasting life? Oh yes, it is death that is momentary—not the other way around! And we must die if we are to rise again.

IF YOU ARE WILLING

"For whoever desires to save his life will lose it, but whoever loses his life for My sake and the gospel's will save it. For what will it profit a man if he gains the whole world, and loses his own soul? Or what will a man give in exchange for his soul? For whoever is ashamed of Me and My words in this adulterous and sinful generation, of him the Son of Man also will be ashamed when He comes in the glory of His Father with the holy angels" (Mark 8:35–38).

Let us not be the fools who only see the limitations of this shadowy life. Jesus is coming in glory. What's a little shame, a little rejection, and a little death in the now, compared to joy in the beloved forever?

As you look out over your world, what do you see? Do you see a world that is broken? Do you see a culture reeling towards self-destruction? Do you see lies growing stronger than truth? Do you see darkness choking out the light? Do you see 300 million Arab Muslims? Do you see that 6,300 of them die every day? Do you see 6,500 ethno-linguistic peoples unreached? Do you see two billion people who have never met a Christian? This is what I see with my natural eyes.

But when I close my eyes of flesh, when I lift my eyes to Jesus, when I see the Christ, another vision is unveiled. I see broken men restored and battered women rescued. I see mercy triumphing over judgment. I see God enthroned in glory. I see the gospel proclaimed everywhere and I see every tribe and tongue in worship around His throne. I see nations reclaimed. I see Saudis, Libyans, Syrians and Iraqis aflame for Christ. I see glory, justice, peace and wonder forever!

I also see that the path from our reality to God's destiny goes through the valley of the shadow of death. All who traverse it, all who will live dead must suffer and be rejected and die.

Today, if you are willing to follow Jesus, to lay down your will and take up His, if you are willing for Christ in all things to have the supremacy, if you are willing to live dead, to suffer, to be rejected, to die, that Jesus might bring life and life abundantly whatever that means, wherever that takes you and whatever the cost, take time to pray right now.

Unless They Are Sent Surrendered

MARK 10

This is my paraphrase of Mark 10:23–31:

> Then Jesus looked around and said to His disciples. "How hard it is for those who have riches to do missions." And the Latinos were greatly astonished at His words. But Jesus answered again and said to them, "Children, how hard it is for those who trust in riches to do missions." And they were greatly astonished, saying among themselves, "How then can the nations be saved?" But Jesus looked at them and said, "With Americans it is impossible, but not with God: for with God all types of mission are possible." Then Pedro began to say to Him, "See, we have left all and followed You." So Jesus answered and said, "Assuredly I say to you, there is no one who has left house or brothers or sisters or father or mother or wife of children or lands, for My sake and the gospel's, who shall not receive a hundredfold now in this time—houses and brothers and sisters and mothers and children and lands, with persecutions—and in the age to come, eternal life. But many who are the first will be last, and the last first."

Today four of my multi-national team members help me share on surrender, for no matter what culture we come from, we all surrender something. No matter what the Lord restores to us—be it "houses, brothers, sisters, mothers, children, and lands"—we cannot escape the strange phrase in Mark 23 that all things restored come "with persecutions." We cannot ignore the reality that often the pain comes from our brothers.

WE MUST SURRENDER OUR PRIDE (FIDEL MONZON)

Fidel Monzon is from the Philippines. He is a medical doctor, as is his wife. He left his house for Jesus' sake. Every man is king of his own castle, but when you go to the field, you have no house and you are often under the authority of another from a different culture. If the nations are to be reached, we must surrender our pride.

King David said, "Behold, how good and pleasant it is when brothers dwell in unity" (Psalm 133:1 ESV)! Another King, our Lord Jesus said, "Every kingdom divided against itself is laid waste, and no city or house divided against itself will stand" (Matt. 12:25). One king highlighted the fruit of unity while the other the danger of division. Unity will bless a kingdom; division will destroy that same kingdom. And often what destroys unity is pride.

On the field, one of my greatest challenges was surrendering my pride.

There was a time our field leader from a different country confronted me. In a missionary gathering he asked to speak with me in a separate room, and he requested another missionary from his country join the meeting. In the meeting, he asked my opinion regarding a particular issue. My opinion differed from his. He said I was wrong in my understanding and accused me of not knowing how to submit to leadership. The other missionary with us in the room was silent.

I responded to his accusation, explaining I would gladly submit to leadership, however the issue at stake was not of submission to leadership but of understanding proper protocol. He was irritated with me and was sure I was at fault. We then agreed to wait for our area leader to explain what should be done. (The area leader was from the same country as our field leader.)

A few weeks passed until the area leader arrived. He clarified that my understanding of the situation should be followed. By then the other missionary with us in the room realized I was correct. The field leader who accused me was not present at that time due to a meeting outside the country. I was relieved that the area leader saw the bigger picture and agreed with my position, but I was also hurt because our field leader never apologized.

I could have responded by no longer wanting to work with the team. I could have allowed my pride to prevent me from fellowshipping and praying with them. But I realized that in God's Kingdom, what's more important than my pride is His will and His work. In order for me to move on and be an effective worker in His kingdom, I have to surrender my pride and allow His love to prevail in my heart.

God's work is massive—it is impossible for only a few to accomplish His work. I believe this is why Jesus Himself exhorted us to pray for laborers. He said, "The harvest is plentiful, but the laborers are few."

The truth is these laborers will come from different cultures and from different backgrounds with different preferences. If I come with my pride, I will never be able to unite and work with others for the harvest. If I don't surrender my pride, I will always be offended. I will always be frustrated because they don't think like I do, they don't dress like I do, they don't eat like I do. For God's kingdom to come upon the different unreached regions, nations, and tribes, for the harvest to happen, there can be no room for division—God's people have to unite.

To unite, I have to surrender my pride.

WE MUST SURRENDER OUR CHILDREN (MAAJID BENJAMIN)

Majid Benjamin is from the Arab Republic of the Sudan. He is married to the daughter of a chief. He knows the emotion of leaving family and losing children. Majid knows that if the nations are to be reached, we must surrender our children.

Our family had a small group of believers from a Muslim background meeting in our home. One young lady in her 20s came to Christ and started attending our house group meeting. Her family discovered that she was Christian and they started to beat her mercilessly.

We talked her into going back home and succeeded twice, but the third time she insisted that she run away. She knew a Catholic family who would help her leave the country, and they were willing to hide her until she left. We didn't ask which family or where they lived. We gave her some money to help her.

Soon she disappeared, but her family knew about our church and our home. They started coming and asking about her. We told them what happened but that we didn't know her whereabouts. They didn't believe us. We started receiving phone calls telling us that because they lost their daughter, we would soon lose our kids.

One day, the school bus was an hour and half late. We called the driver (who was a church member and worship leader), but we couldn't get through. I quickly forgot all the sermons and lessons I gave on Abraham's love and commitment to God and his readiness to offer his only son as a sacrifice. Shortly thereafter, the kids arrived home safely. The bus had been stuck in a traffic jam.

The whole situation caused me to think about the story of Abraham and Isaac. I wept and repented before the Lord who willingly gave His only Son for me. I wish I could tell you that I have full victory over the fear that something might happen to my kids because of the tough area where we serve God, but I'm sorry, I can't.

Turns out, the Sudanese church thought the bus driver was a government informant who reported a lot of information about the church and different ministries in the country. It seems God's plan was to protect my kids at that time—and He did.

WE MUST SURRENDER OUR POSSESSIONS (ALBERTO SOSA)

Alberto Sosa is from Paraguay. He, too, is married to the daughter of a chief. Alberto has now been kicked out of two countries in the Arab world. He and his family have lost everything. Alberto knows that if the nations are to be reached, we must surrender our possessions.

Working on multi-national teams I have learned to surrender many things. I have surrendered my language. As a Latino, we communicate everything in our second language with our team and in our third language with the national community.

I have also, come to the place where I surrender my possessions and say, "Jesus, my stuff is your stuff." After working hard to make my small business successful, I quit it all to follow what Jesus called me to do. Later, in a different surrender in North Africa, where we lived for a year, we received police orders to leave the country in 48 hours.

In the process of leaving, we lost a lot of money. We tried to sell stuff from our house but still found ourselves in a very tight economic situation. It became worse when we discovered that to carry more weight in our baggage we needed to pay $30 for every extra kilo—we did not have that kind of money. There was no way to carry our stuff to the next country.

The most difficult part was the conversation we needed to have with our daughter Zoe. I tried my best to explain to her that we didn't have the space in our luggage for much of our stuff including her dolls and princess dresses. It was hard for my little girl to grasp at first but finally she understood and said, "Dad, I understand now. If I give up my toys, Jesus will provide me with more."

Very quickly, I went to my bedroom to have a serious conversation with Jesus about Zoe and my wife's broken heart. I asked Him, "Why do they have to suffer like this? I know I don't have any money to pay for their stuff. I lost almost 60 percent of everything and I don't have enough money to pay for anything!" After sharing my complaint with Him for a few minutes, I gave up and I prayed, "Jesus, I give you everything because You called me to do that." The Lord was quiet.

No angel in my room.

No messages on the wall.

No nothing, but Zoe and my wife, and they were very confident with the next step without any thoughts about their lost stuff.

We arrived to our new field, new life, and new team. Nobody knew our economic situation, but a few days in, our team leader Dick said, "In the team's storage you'll find some things that another family left there just a week ago. Anything that you guys need, you can take it for your new home."

We went to the storage room and there was a lot of stuff for our new home. I said, "Look at this, Diana! It is a miracle!" Zoe disappeared among the furniture and home furnishings until I heard her call me. "Dad, Dad, look what I found!" It was a big pink bag with what things inside? Yes, with new dolls and new princess dresses and toys. That was a joy like nothing else.

I learned something that we now apply in our family: When we surrender our stuff, our skills, our chances, our human possibilities, our decisions, our jobs, Jesus can do everything that is good for His glory and our needs as well! Just ask my daughter Zoe.

WE MUST SURRENDER OUR FEAR OF FAILURE (MILWARD MWAMVANI)

Milward Mwamvani is from Malawi. He has been my right hand and most of my brain for more than a decade. We have laughed together and cried together. We have fought, we have prayed, and we have played. Milward and I have some successes and many failures.

Milward knows that if the nations are to be reached, we must surrender our fear of failure.

I could share numerous things that have required surrender to the Lord. I could talk about surrendering my family for daily provisions when I had nothing, or surrendering my will to that of the Lord's when things were uncertain and I was fearful of life itself. But I would like to share my surrender of my fear of failure.

Working in missions sets high expectations from those that send you. They would like to hear news of the work's progress, and knowing the areas where we have been, instant results are far from reality. The excitement of being in the field serving the Lord waned quickly in the early months as reality set in that this was going to be a long journey. By the end of the first year, I realized that I needed to surrender my fear of disappointing my senders to the Lord, and it gave me peace.

On the field, a major fear that constantly bothered me was that of failing in my responsibilities in a multi-national team. Being the only differently colored person coming from a little known country, I felt I needed to "perform" in order for me to be accepted by the others who seemed to naturally fit into the team. I feared that if I did not perform, then I would be regarded as a lesser member of the team and bring shame upon myself and my people.

However, an accepting and non-segregating team leader and a realization that this work was for the Lord were two freeing experiences. Surrendering my fear of failure to the Lord and realizing that I am accepted just as I am both by the Lord and by my co-workers set me free and helped me to serve for many years alongside others of like mind.

I am thankful that the Lord took control of my ministry life and let me minister without fear of failure—fully accepted.

WE MUST SURRENDER OUR BROTHERS (DICK BROGDEN)

Not only must we surrender our pride. Not only must we surrender our children. Not only must we surrender our possessions. Not only must we surrender our fear of failure. We must also surrender our brothers.

Brotherhood is stronger than friendship. We choose our friends; God chooses our brothers. These men who shared are my brothers and I love them with all my heart. I am their leader, but I am not embarrassed to confess that they have led me.

- Fidel from the Philippines has taught me what it looks like to be humble. He knows more about submission and authority than I do.

- Maajid from Sudan has taught me what it means to overcome fear. He knows more about Islam and ministry to Muslims than all of us combined.

- Alberto from Paraguay has taught me about joy, humor, and grace. He knows more about the joy of the Lord and mother-in-law jokes than I do.

- Milward has taught me how to fail to the glory of God. He knows more about endurance than the saints of Hebrews 11.

These men are my brothers, and with them I am armed for war. I fear no battle; I fear no foe. With God as our captain and these men at my side, we are able to go up and take the country!

I have learned, however, that I cannot protect them all the time. I have learned that I must surrender my brothers. The last six months of my life have been the most painful in some respects, for I have had to send my brothers to war. And when they have been wounded, I have had to send them back. I have had to tell my brothers and their families difficult news. I have had to watch some of them suffer, some of them bleed, and some of them die. Gladly, I would suffer in their place. It is much more painful to watch helplessly as your brothers suffer than it is to suffer yourself. Yet, it is sometimes necessary to send your brothers to battle, to the fields where they must bleed and die. And then to send them back again

We must surrender our desire to protect one another from harm. We cannot win this battle and we cannot win the nations unless we are willing for our brothers to suffer. When our brothers suffer, God's primary plan is not their escape.

First, God is concerned with His glory. God must be glorified in our suffering, in our pain, in our trial, in our prison, in our death.

Second, God is concerned with the defense of the gospel. Is the gospel true or not? Is Jesus worth it or not? Is heaven real or not? Are the things we have taught sure or not? Muslim background believers are watching. They will have to suffer. Can they learn to suffer from us? Muslims are watching. Will our suffering call them to Jesus?

Third, God is concerned with the character of the one suffering. Suffering can make us like Jesus. God uses suffering to remove sin and self and let His image shine.

Only after all these priorities are considered, does God want to deliver us from suffering. And God's deliverance is sometimes escape—He takes us out. It is sometimes endurance—He takes us through. And it is sometimes eternity—He takes us home.

I am learning I must surrender my brothers to suffering.

RECONCILED TO SUFFERING

My brothers and I, we are reconciled to suffering. We know it is coming. And while we wonder if we will be found faithful in our time of testing, we are more worried about you. What will our fathers and mothers do?

Will you surrender us? Will you surrender our little brothers and sisters?

When missionaries are raped, when missionaries are beaten, when missionaries are imprisoned, when missionaries are killed, when grieving family members beat on your office door and take you to court, when the press blames you for inciting Muslims to violence, when the culture shouts at you to be cautious, when your own emotions demand that you protect your sheep from pain, when your intellect advises that the cost is not worth it, when you stand around the caskets of your children, when you watch them shot or beheaded on Al Jazeerah TV, when they do not come home and there are widows and orphans that return from the field weeping, what will you do then? Will you surrender more?

What will our fathers and mothers do when the children they send to the field, are eaten by lions, beheaded by emperors, crucified by angry mobs, and stoned by religious zealots? Yes, they must be sent surrendered, but those who send must surrender—surrender more of your children when your firstborns fall.

Only this level of surrender, the surrender of the sent and the surrender of the senders, will propel us to the end—God's great glory among every people.

Three Martyrdoms

JOHN 12:20-26

A God-ward direction in life depends on the right perspective. The issue is not really "How much do I love Jesus?" but how much He loves me!

> *In this is love, not that we loved God, but that He loved us and sent His Son to be the propitiation for our sins.* (1 John 4:10)

The question is not "How significant will I be?" but "How famous has Jesus become?"

> *The kingdoms of this world have become the kingdoms of our Lord and of His Christ and He shall reign forever and forever.* (Rev. 11:15)

The question is not "how big is my church?" But "where does the Church not exist, and what am I going to do about it?"

> *And this gospel of the kingdom will be preached in all the world as a witness to all the nations, and then the end will come.* (Matt. 24:14)

And this gospel will be preached at great cost. Live Dead is church planting in teams among unreached people groups, among the 40 percent of the world untouched by the gospel.

The Hebrew word for glory, *khavod*, means "heavy." The sense of the presence of God is so tangible that it can be felt. It has weight. God—supreme, holy, love, pure, powerful, majestic, creator, sustainer—so real to us, so awesome, that we fall with prophets and kings and say, "I am undone! Nothing on earth compares to the weight of the presence of God. I am spoiled for anything else, anything less."

Missions must start with the question of glory. God is dedicated to His own glory, to making himself famous. And this is not megalomania, writes David Mathis.

> If knowing Jesus were anything less than the greatest of enjoyments, then his pursuit would be unloving. But he IS the most valuable reality in the universe...Therefore it is profoundly loving for Jesus to exalt

himself. He cannot love the nations without putting himself on display because it is only him that truly satisfies the human soul. This makes God's heart for God the deepest foundation for missions.[60]

Yet, God is not glorified as He should be—not in me, not in His Church, not in the earth. "Mission exists," John Piper says, "because worship doesn't."[61] Does God have enough glory in my life? Does God have enough glory in the church? Does God have enough glory in the earth? Does it honor God that there are people groups who do not worship Him? Is God exalted as He should be when there are people and places that have never been exposed to the weight of His presence? Is God praised when He is not yet famous to every person, lauded by every tongue? Is God magnified when 1.5 billion Muslims deny His Christhood and mitigate His deity? *Ich-khavod*, the Glory has departed. God's glory is not known by unreached peoples.

Let's look at John 12:20–26.

> *Now there were certain Greeks among those who came up to worship at the feast. Then they came to Philip, who was from Bethsaida of Galilee, and asked him, saying, "Sir, we wish to see Jesus." Philip came and told Andrew, and in turn Andrew and Philip told Jesus. But Jesus answered them, saying, "The hour has come that the Son of Man should be glorified. Most assuredly, I say to you, unless a grain of wheat falls into the ground and dies, it remains alone; but if it dies, it produces much grain. He who loves his life will lose it, and he who hates his life in this world will keep it for eternal life. If anyone serves Me, let him follow Me; and where I am, there My servant will be also. If anyone serves Me, him My Father will honor."*

"We want to see Jesus!" the Greeks said. "If anyone serves Me, let him follow Me," Jesus answered, "and where I am, there My servant will be also." What was Jesus talking about? Where was Jesus that we might follow Him?

The context of our passage helps us. It was Passion Week. Jesus was a few days away from Calvary and he knew "that His hour has come" (John 13:1). Jesus said to the Greeks, and to you and me, "You want to see me? You want to serve me? You are welcome. But you should know, I am going to the cross, and anyone who follows me, must go there, too." Any who want to serve Jesus must end up crucified.

If we are going to reach the ethno-linguistic peoples that remain—more than 6,000 people groups that are less than two percent Christian—if they are going to glorify God, someone is going to have to live dead.

I would like us to reflect on three martyrdoms, and how God wants us to live them. Three deaths God wants us to die: The Red, the Green and the White.

THE RED MARTYRDOM

The Red Martyrdom is the most famous and the least common. We call it "Red" because it refers to literally dying for Jesus, to your blood being spilt for your faith.

Church history tells us that Peter died in Rome. According to one legend, persecution was so fierce that Christians were fleeing from Rome. Peter had moved to Rome and pastored a flock there. He, too, tried to flee Rome and the unspeakable persecution. On the way out, Peter encountered Jesus. Jesus was going against the flow, heading back into Rome. Peter, surprised, asked him, "Quo vadis, Dominae?" "Where are you going, Lord?"

"Back into the city to die again for the flock that you desert," Jesus said. Peter, ashamed, turned on his heel and returned to Rome and witnessed in Red to Jesus, by being crucified upside down. Upside down, according to tradition, because he did not feel worthy to be crucified in the same manner as Christ.

Greeks and disciples through the centuries have asked the same question: "Quo vadis, Dominae? Quo vadis?" Where are you going, Lord? Where are you going? Jesus' answer has not changed. He is still going to the cross, and if we are His servants, we must follow Him there. Quo vadis, Dominae? Jesus is still going to Libya. Jesus is still going to Afghanistan. Jesus is still going to Somalia. Jesus is still going to Yemen, Syria and Oman. Jesus is still going to the Muslim people in your city.

If as a church, as a Christian, you want to go where Jesus is going, it is back into the cities of death and destruction, of oppression and war, to the unreached, to the Pashtum and the Bedouin Arabs.

Where are you going, Lord? Quo vadis, Dominae? I am going to my death. I am going to die in an effort to save others. I am going where everyone else is fleeing, and where no one else wants to go. It has never been an unusual thing to die for Jesus, literally. It has happened all through history. It started with Paul killing others and in an ironic twist he, too, died a Red death.

Dying for Jesus used to be the way Christians lived. Elisabeth Elliot noted that her slain husband Jim and the other men with him were hailed as martyrs, but that she did not approve. She wondered if the distinction between living for Jesus and dying for Him was so great because to live for God is to die daily.

In Roman coliseums, in Arabian deserts, in Communist jails or islands of the Pacific, for 2,000 years men and women, old and young, have shed their blood for Jesus.

The point is this: should Jesus tarry, we all die, what does it matter how? Many through history have shed their blood for Muslims. Four hundred eighty believers in Christ will die today because of their faith. Twenty followers of Jesus in the course of this sermon will be tortured and killed for Christ. Why should the American Church be exempt from dying for Jesus?

The Red Martyrdom is not to be sought; neither is it to be feared. And those who die for Christ should really not be considered heroic or foolish. It is merely following Jesus. "If anyone serves Me, let him follow Me; and where I am, there My servant will be also."

I have a friend taking his wife and three small children to Somalia to be missionaries. I asked his wife, "do you know what this means? Do you realize that your husband might die for Jesus? Do you realize you are looking at a distinct possibility of a Red Martyrdom?" This was her reply:

In prayer, I cry with Jesus over these matters—over the ramifications on our children, on my husband, on me, on our marriage, on the work. We cry together. Jesus speaks to me comfortingly, "all die." I know that these words may not comfort all, but they comfort me. They mean so much to me, these two words. They give me such peace. They humble me. They bring me clarity. They ground me with perspective for living well.

Death is so normal. Death touches all. Death often comes unannounced. I cannot control it nor will I be ruled by some irrational fear of it. What fools who do! I most likely won't know it is coming. It could come today or tomorrow. Harm, the same.

I do hope God isn't leading us to die in Somalia at the hands of hatred. But I will not be ruled by that possibility, and I would be a fool to think that my life anywhere is free from death. I see it as a terrible (meaning huge and strong) privilege to serve God among these lost. And I surrender with great joy to His plan, trusting however He intends to sow our lives.

All die. Death is so normal. One life to live, one death to die. If by Red Martyrdom we can glorify Christ, why not? It is how he died. It is where and how He went. Would it not be an honor if He allows us to go the same way, if in death our witness is Red, as we live dead among the unreached peoples of the world?

On November 17, 1957, at Dexter Avenue Baptist Church in Montgomery, Alabama, Martin Luther King, Jr. preached a sermon entitled, "Loving Your Enemies." This is what he said:

To our most bitter opponents we say, "we shall match your capacity to inflict suffering by our capacity to endure suffering. We shall meet your physical force with soul force. Do to us what you will, and we shall continue to love you… Throw us in jail and we shall still love you. Bomb our homes and threaten our children, and we shall still love you. Send your hooded perpetrators of violence into our community at the midnight hour and beat us and leave us half dead, and we shall still love you. But be ye assured that we will wear you down by our capacity to suffer. One day we shall win freedom but not only for ourselves. We shall so appeal to your heart and conscience that we shall win you in the process and our victory will be a double victory."

Jesus wants His Church to not only turn the other cheek but to lay down our lives for precious unreached peoples. He wants us to die for them. He wants us to take our turn in a long line of others who have been Red martyrs to follow Him to the cross, to sacrificial death.

God is calling His Church. God is calling Christians to the Red Martyrdom—to wear down Islam by our capacity to suffer, to live dead and to walk to our executions while our spouses clap and we sing glory.

THE GREEN MARTYRDOM

Around 350 AD, a young Romanized English boy was stolen from his country. Irish pirates threw him into a leather-covered boat, bundled him across the water and made him a slave in Ireland. Some years later Patrick escaped, and through a process of time returned to Ireland as a missionary. By this time Patrick was elderly (some think he was 72) and he gave the rest of his life to evangelize the Irish, understanding the Irish as few before or since.

By the time Patrick died, much of Ireland was Christian. Patrick and his team had done such an exceptional job of preaching the gospel that Christians almost lamented that they could not die for Jesus. There was little opportunity for Red Martyrdom among the fifth century Celts.

So the Irish, being the Irish, innovated. There is a delightful little book by Thomas Cahill from which I draw some of my material called, *How the Irish Saved Civilization*. The basic premise is this: The Goths sacked Rome in the fifth century, and much of the learning of the Romans and Greeks was lost as Europe plunged into the Dark Ages. The Irish, by copying the writings of the classical period, preserved them, and thus we have a record of the scriptures, philosophy, history and more.

How did the Irish do this? It was through what they called the Green Martyrdom. The Irish established missional monasteries wherever they went. These monasteries were not like the Egyptian monasteries of the desert fathers who tried to get away from the world. These monasteries were established to take the gospel to the world.

Here's how they worked: Patrick and his band would go to a new location. They would settle in and build houses in a ring. These houses would have a fence around them. Inside the fence and in the middle of the houses were public buildings. There was a chapel, a workshop, dining hall and guesthouse or lodge. There was also a scriptorium, a place where the monks would copy the Scriptures. And these Irish monks were characters, inserting little jokes and poems around the manuscripts. The Irish monks drove the Roman monks crazy with their informality, and the Irish were the friendliest of folk. They planted flowers and gardens, built roads and bridges, brewed ale and shared it. Their highs were high and their lows were low, and they celebrated life with all.

A monk would station himself at the gate of the monastery and wait for travelers or guests. As soon as a traveler arrived, the monk would greet him, smile and welcome him, and take the traveler right to the Abbot. The Abbot would welcome him, pray for him, inquire of his news and needs, and then assign him to another monk. This monk would take him to the dining hall, feed him and find him a bed in the guesthouse. Then he would bring the traveler to prayers, and before the guest knew what was happening, he was sucked into the life of the community. He ate their food, sang their songs, slept in their houses and shared their chores. The visitors felt like they belonged!

And they did belong! For this was the genius of Patrick and the Irish. They welcomed the lost to belong—before they asked for a change in belief

The Romans and most of us today do it the other way. We present propositional truth and ask Muslims to agree to it, but we make no provision for community or create any space for belonging. For example, Maajid Benjamin, a Christian Arab and one of my best friends, tells me that of the hundreds of Muslims who have come to Christ at his church over the years, only a handful remain as there was no relevant place for them to belong. The Celtic way of evangelism put belonging ahead of believing, and in so doing, Christianity spread joyously among the peoples of Ireland and Scotland.

There is an underlying tension here then. The picture I painted sounds kind of rosy—or at least green. Why call it martyrdom? Was the Green Martyrdom or the Green Witness all joy and celebration? No. It is called martyrdom because it still involved death. But this death was a death to self within community.

The theory of team, of missionary team, of the body of Christ working together, sounds wonderful. Everybody today wants to be part of a community, a team, a family—and rightly so. But it does not take you very long in a team or community to realize that theory and practice are two very different things. Missionary teams, like Paul and Barnabas, splinter. Churches split. Countries divorce, like my beloved Sudan in 2011. Marriages struggle. If the Red Martyrdom involves laying down your life for Jesus, the Green Martyrdom requires the laying down of your will for one another. And I think the Green Martyrdom is so much harder.

Let's look at an application that starts with the white American church is not going to reach the world. It will take multi-national teams, like a multi-faceted diamond. It looks like this: American Westerner goes to the government office while the African goes to purchase in the market and the Latino goes to cast out demons.

Very few of us will be Red martyrs, but God is calling us to go Green. As we look towards the challenge of unreached peoples, let's allow the Holy Spirit to reveal His control of us by how often we are willing to cede our will and our culture to others for the glory of God among all peoples.

THE WHITE MARTYRDOM

Over time something began to gnaw at the spirits of the Green Martyrs in Ireland. The monasteries boomed and bloomed. Ireland is like central Africa—everything grows. Drop your mobile phone in the Rwandan ground and a cell phone tower will grow.

In Ireland, life was good, food was plentiful, and friends abounded, but something was missing. To be contented, satiated and surrounded by friends and family was strangely not enough. There had to be something more in the world. There had to be higher purpose than living well, than raising and educating one's children so they could live well and do the same for their children. There had to be greater meaning in life.

And of course, there was—and there is even for us. Because the Good Shepherd is not content to stay with the 99 who are safe if even one is lost. The missing witness was a witness of Christ to the whole world.

Columcille was a disciple of Patrick and his heir apparent, his best. He was commissioned to take the gospel to Northern England. He would do so by establishing a missional monastery at the cross-section of the sea. He would leave Ireland and sail in his leather-covered boat to the Isle of Iona. Thomas Cahill writes:

> As he [Columcille] sailed off that morning, he was doing the hardest thing an Irishman could do, a much harder thing than giving up his life: he was leaving Ireland. If the Green Martyrdom had failed, here was a martyrdom that was surely equal of the Red; and henceforth, all who followed Columcille's lead were called to the White Martyrdom, they who sailed into the white sky of morning, into the unknown, never to return.[62]

We can witness to Jesus by giving our physical lives. We must witness to Christ by following Him with surrendered wills. But there is another witness he demands of us—the White Martyrdom of taking His gospel to the ends of the earth to the inconvenient lost

And here is my plea. I urge you to send your best. Don't send your castoffs to sail into the white sky of morning. You get into the boat and lead the way. Send your professionals. Send the pastors of your best churches. Send the leaders and the influencers. Send your richest and your most educated. Send the ones you cannot afford to send. We send sons and daughters to die for flag and freedom in Iraq and Afghanistan, from the halls of Montezuma to the shores of Tripoli, but will we release them to live and die for Jesus among unreached peoples?

Don't hoard the best resources to your overfed selves and cast the crumbs of the marginal to the nations. You lead the way! You walk away from prestige and become a nothing that Jesus might become everything to one Muslim. You. Yes, you! Walk away from everything comfortable and live dead on a church planting team in Tripoli, Jeddah or Mogadishu!

Jesus asks His church for the White Martyrdom, the white death of sending our best. Adoniram Judson entered Burma (now known as Myanmar) in July 1813. He went to India first where William Carey told him not to go. It was too dangerous. There was war with Siam (now Thailand), raids, rebellion and no religious freedom. All the missionaries had died or left.

Judson went anyway. He was 24; his wife was 23. Their first three children died—the first stillborn on the boat between India and Burma; the second died after 17 months; the third died at two, only six months after her mother died. Judson lost three children and his wife in his first years in Burma.

He was thrown in prison. His legs fettered. At night a bamboo pole was inserted in his leg chains and lifted up, so that all night long, his feet were in the air and only his head and shoulders could touch the ground. He slept this way every night for 17 months. He was marched through the jungle barefoot, emaciated, sick and weak.

He remarried and his second wife died. He remarried and his third wife also died. His brother died. His father died. Another child died. Judson knew great suffering and was bruised by much death. After 10 years, there were only 18 converts in the church. Judson was a grain of wheat that fell to the ground and died.

In 2000, because of Judson's work to preach the gospel and translate the Scriptures, because of his White Martyrdom, the Baptist convention in Myanmar consisted of 3,700 churches, 617,781 members, and 1,900,000 affiliates.

In a riveting sermon on Judson entitled "How Few There Are, Who Die So Hard" after some of Judson's last words, John Piper summarized the reality and necessity of Red, Green and White Martyrdoms, of living dead:

> Life is fleeting. In a very short time, we will all give an account before Jesus Christ, not only as to how well we have fulfilled our vocations, but how well we have obeyed the command to make disciples of all nations.
>
> Many of the peoples of the world are without any indigenous Christian movement today. Christ is not enthroned there, his grace is unknown there, and people are perishing with no access to the gospel. Most of these hopeless peoples do not want followers of Jesus to come.
>
> At least they think they don't. They are hostile to Christian missions. Today this is the final frontier. And the Lord still says,

"Behold, I am sending you out as sheep in the midst of wolves." ". . . [S]ome of you they will put to death. You will be hated by all for my name's sake..." (Matthew 10:16; Luke 21:16–18). **Are you sure that God wants you to keep doing what you are doing?** For most of you, he probably does. Your calling is radical obedience for the glory of Christ right where you are. But for many of you, God wants to loosen your roots and plant you in another place.[63]

Rise up, O men of God! Have done with lesser things.
Give heart and soul and mind and strength—to serve King of kings.

Rise up, O men of God. The Church for you doth wait.
Her strength unequal to her task, rise up, and make her great.

Lift high the cross of Christ. Tread where His feet have trod:
As brothers of the Son of Man, rise up, O men of God.[64]

BECAUSE JESUS IS WORTH IT

We will all follow Jesus. We will all live dead. The Church of Christ will once again be consumed with His passion: Who has not heard? Where is there no church? Where has the gospel not gone? We will live dead—not because we are noble or courageous, not because we are morbid or cavalier, not because we are worthy, but because Jesus is worth it. Jesus is worth everything.

> *But Jesus answered them, saying, "The hour has come that the Son of Man should be glorified. Most assuredly, I say to you, unless a grain of wheat falls into the ground and dies, it remains alone; but if it dies, it produces much grain. He who loves his life will lose it, and he who hates his life in this world will keep it for eternal life. If anyone serves Me, let him follow Me; and where I am, there My servant will be also."*
> (John 12: 23-26)

If you will follow Jesus, should He so call, and work with a church planting team among unreached people, would you now kneel wherever you are now and pray? If you will live dead, to witness in Red, Green or White, should Jesus require it, would you pray?

Jesus is Worthy

JOHN 12:23-28

But Jesus answered them, saying, "The hour has come that the Son of Man should be glorified. Most assuredly, I say to you, unless a grain of wheat falls into the ground anddies, it remains alone; but if it dies, it produces much grain. He who loves his life will lose it, and he who hates his life in this world will keep it for eternal life. If anyone serves Me, let him follow Me; and where I am, there My servant will be also. If anyone serves Me, him My Father will honor. Now My soul is troubled, and what shall I say? 'Father, save Me from this hour?' But for this purpose I came to this hour. Father, glorify Your name." (John 12:23-28)

It can be somewhat pompous to claim to "live dead." If the message is, I am more consecrated than you; I am more sanctified than my brother; I am more adventurous, sacrificial, intelligent, devoted or daring; I am greater, purer or wiser than my sister or my colleague, then the point has been missed and we who espouse such a message live very much in delusion and darkness.

But if the heart song is Jesus—Jesus, worthy of glory, worthy of living, worthy of dying—if the message is Jesus then our prayer must be. . .

Your name is great; Your glory is supreme; the nations are yet rebellious, the ethne are still lost; my strength is so pitiful, if You do not live, speak, touch and raise me through, then Jesus, the giants are too strong and I am very much a grasshopper.

Jesus, kill that within me which hinders you; quench that within me that envies your unique glory; crucify the flesh in me that longs and strives to be known; rise, the woman's conquering seed; and bruise in us the serpent's head. Jesus, "life" us with resurrection power; illumine our minds; empower our speech; make me dead to sin, flesh, fear and devils; make me alive to You and Your worth.

If that is the message and if we like Richard Baxter say, "Preach as never sure to preach again and as a dying man to dying men,"[65] then we very well might be on to something. For Jesus is worthy of glory, worthy of live and worthy of dying.

JESUS IS WORTHY OF GLORY

> *The hour has come that the Son of Man should be glorified.* (John 12:23)

Jesus is worthy of glory by me, by you and by every people.

C. S. Lewis points out in *The Four Loves*, that when a friend dies, those that remain have less of each other not more. Take three close friends, lifelong soul mates. One of them passes away, and the remaining two might think they have more time for each other and that their relationship will be fuller. But the converse is true, for the missing friend draws out of each of them what they cannot mine for themselves. When the body is missing a member, all are disadvantaged.

Jesus has sheep not of our fold (i.e., kind, ilk, color, culture). In order to know and worship Jesus better, we need other perspectives. Others illustrate and illuminate parts of Jesus for me that I am blind to. This is a vital aspect of mission that is so little understood. We don't have the fullness of Jesus until the fullness of the nations has Him. As long as there are unreached peoples, the bride is still disfigured. Every time a new believer joins the fold, a new perspective of God is released into the Christian corpus.

Think of it! Every time a people group is reached, a massive fresh revelation of God's glory is unleashed and revealed to the world. The progression of the gospel across the peoples is the progressive unveiling of majestic God to me! I benefit from the spread of the gospel. I am enriched when the kingdom is advanced. Jesus is revealed to me when He is embraced by others. And the further the gospel spreads, the greater our God is known! And as the nations are reached, so the glory of God is unleashed. And it is in the worship of every tongue that Jesus is further revealed to us. So missions becomes heavenly hedonistic—for the greater the spread of God's glory, the more He is revealed to my limited perspective and the purer my worship. The fuller our corporate praise, the greater His glory!

Jesus is worthy of the glory of all the nations. The growth of the body of Christ is my growth in the knowledge of God. As the kingdom expands, my heart and mind are lifted out of the parochial mud and I ascend the vistas of a unified, glorified city of God. The joy of the nations in worship is my personal joy, for as the nations come to Jesus, Jesus comes to me. I, therefore, must be pro-peoples reached with the gospel—as the nations are reached by Jesus, Jesus reaches further into me!

This is why multi-national teams are a must! Where would we be without the Germans and the Africans? When Filipinos are gone, we are missing the Asians—and missing the Asians we are missing a part of God. This is why we must embrace the African, Arab and Latino—not for their sake alone, but for ours. Without them we are without the fullness of God. Without them Jesus does not have fully orbed human worship—and Jesus is worthy of all that glory.

The absent worship of the Arabs will not be tolerated by God, and it must not be tolerated by us. Jesus is worthy of glory from Saudi, Syria and Libya. From Iraq, Qatar, Oman and Yemen. Jesus is worthy of glory from the West Bank. If Jesus was born in Bethlehem and wise men purposely bowed in worship, don't you think Muslims in that now Arab city should also bend their knees and lift their hands in praise. The worship ascending to the eternal throne from the Arab world is pitifully small, and the time has come that the Son of Man be glorified! Jesus is worthy of glorious worship from the Arabs.

JESUS IS WORTHY OF LIVING

> *He who loves his life will lose it, and he who hates his life in this world will keep it for eternal life.* (John 12:25)

You are going to die. All people do. Is your death worth living for? "So live your life," Tecumseh instructed, "that the fear of death can never enter your heart."[66] When it comes your time to die, be not like those whose hearts are filled with the fear of death, so that when their time comes they weep and pray for a little more time to live their lives over again in a different way. Sing your death song and die like a hero going home.

All people perish. You are going to die. The Assemblies of God is going to die; no denomination is vibrant forever and no man is intrinsically eternal. Daily we progress towards death. We all—should Jesus tarry—are going to die, and upon your death, what will it be said you lived for?

"Men, think of the world," A. W. Tozer wrote, "not as a battleground but as a playground. We are not here to fight, we are here to frolic. We are not in a foreign land, we are at home. We are not getting ready to live, we are already living and the best we can do is to rid ourselves of our inhibitions and our frustrations and live life to the full."[67]

This is the blatant poppycock philosophy of the world and the tacit reality of millions in the church who think they live (but because they live unto themselves are only dying). When the record of history is released, when your life is reviewed before the all-seeing Judge, what will it show your life stood for? And to what end did you die? To live dead means that your life was lived and your death given as extravagant worship to a worthy Jesus!

They call him the "Angel in Ebony"; we know him as Samuel Morris. As a child, Samuel would speak at Sunday schools and the Spirit would fall. He would speak at churches and revival would fall. He went to study at Taylor University in Indiana, and so many funds poured in to help him, there was enough to buy a new campus in Upland, Indiana (where the school is today). News of revivals that Samuel preached spread, and people from near and far would come to see him. This 21-year-old uneducated, simple child always kept the focus on Jesus. He got sick and died in May 1893 at 21-years-old.

Samuel was an African born in the Ivory Coast, the son of a prince. He was given to a neighboring tribe as security—which happened several times and included torture. One day he was strapped to a log and whipped to a pulp. Honey was poured in his mouth and he was left to die as ants would come to eat him. He saw a light and heard a voice telling him to run. He freed himself from his bonds and escaped in the jungle. He lived on fruits and berries and made his way to Liberia. He attended a Methodist church service and heard a missionary speak on Paul and the Damascus road experience.

"That's what happened to me!" The missionaries baptized him and gave him the name Samuel Morris.

Little Samuel was ravenous for Jesus. One night in the bunkhouse he had a glorious experience with Him. He experienced a filling of the Holy

Spirit and woke everyone by shouting. They thought he was crazy. He asked the missionaries about the Holy Spirit and they could not answer his questions (this was circa 1882). The missionary, a Miss Knolls, who named him after an American banker and donor, told him all she knew about the Holy Spirit that she learned from her pastor Stephen Merritt in New York.

So little Samuel decided he would go to New York. He begged and begged a ship captain, was treated badly by a Malaysian giant, prayed healing over the crew, led the crew and captain and Malaysian giant to the Lord, got off the boat in New York and said to the first person he saw, "Where can I find Stephen Merritt?" That person happened to be an old hobo who knew Pastor Merritt. He took little Samuel to Pastor Merritt, and Samuel said, "I am Samuel Morris. I have come from Africa to talk with you about the Holy Spirit!" The Pastor told him to wait a second, ran an errand and when he returned, 17 grown men were on their knees crying, repenting of their sin because of the preaching of little Samuel.

Pastor Stephen took Samuel home and put him in the Bishop's Room. The next day he took Samuel with him to a funeral. Two other pastors came along and it was obvious that they did not want a little black boy in the carriage with them. Pastor Stephen tried to cover the awkwardness by pointing out all the sights of New York City. All of a sudden, Samuel interrupted Pastor Stephen and said, "have you ever prayed in a carriage?" No one had. "We will pray," said the lad and, as Pastor Merritt stopped the horses and knelt, Sammy talked to God. "Father, I wanted to see Stephen Merritt," he prayed, "so I could talk to him about the Holy Ghost. He shows me the harbor, the churches, the banks and other large buildings, but says nothing to me about this Spirit I want to know more about. Fill him with Thyself, so that he will not think, talk, write or preach about anything else."[68]

Let us not talk of buildings and banks, harbors and monuments. Let's not waste our time talking about how much we gave to missions. Let's not waste God's time showing off the edifices and projects of men. Let's not waste our lives just existing and living so our children can live after us. Let's stop the carriage of an empty life. Let's get down on our knees. Let us ask again the Father what is our right—more of Jesus. Jesus is worthy of our desire. Worthy of our life! Let us plead again to be filled and possessed of His Holy

Spirit that we might live for the glory of God among the nations.

We all know the pull of addiction. I awake and email seduces me. My computer embraces me and will not let me go. There is a compulsion in my being to awake and rush into the arms of my betrayer. I live for task, I live to be important, I live to be the answer, the deliverer. I lust to be included, essential, depended on. Why do I not thus desire Jesus?

In Luke 22:15, Jesus says, "With fervent desire I have desired to eat this Passover with you." The Greek word is *epithumia*. It means passionate longing, lust, desire. "It is not that our desires are too strong," says my friend Eli Gautreaux. "They are too weak; they are weak for they are so easily satisfied by what is temporal, by what is wicked. But where is our raging desire, our *epithumia*, our sanctified lust for Him?"[69]

Why do I not awake with raging desire for Jesus? Why do I not turn from my slumber shaking in eagerness to be with my Savior? Why do I not rush to my abiding place, rush to the arms, the presence of Jesus? Is Jesus not worthy of my life? Is Jesus not worthy of my affection? Is Jesus not worthy of our desire?

If I do not desire Jesus, how do I expect my Muslim neighbor to hunger for Him? If Jesus is not my desire, why should a wayward Arab world forsake her abusive lovers for Him? If Jesus is not the desire of His church, how can we possibly believe He will be the desire of all nations?

Stop the carriage!

Let us not talk of numbers, of structures or strategies of man. Let us not talk of programs, of methods, or of others. Let us most certainly cease talking endlessly about ourselves. Let us hate what we have been deluded into calling life. Let us live a life that desires Him!

Oh, for men and women sick of pretenses and show! Oh, for sons and daughters disgusted by shallowness and self-promotion! Oh, for churches devastated at the lostness of humanity and willing to pay any price and live any life for the worth of Jesus.

God doesn't want bribes. How dare we think the Lord of Heaven can be bought? How dare we think that sin, flesh and immorality can be atoned by an annual missions' project? How dare we think that missions' giving—or missions' going—removes the responsibility of a crucified life? How dare we parade ourselves, trample on the blood of Jesus, preen and perform on platforms, then think that God's disgust is assuaged and His wrath appeased by the size of our pledge?

God does not want your money—not if it is a putrid and laughable effort to cover sin. He wants your life. He wants it all. Jesus is worthy of our living!

JESUS IS WORTHY OF DYING

> *If anyone serves Me, let him follow Me [to the Cross]; and where I am [the cross], there My servant will be also. If anyone serves Me, him My Father will honor. "Now My soul is troubled, and what shall I say? 'Father, save Me from this hour?' [Save me from the cross?] But for this purpose [the cross] I came to this hour. Father, glorify Your name.* (John 12:26–28)

Hebrews tells us that Christ's body is the veil. The tearing apart of incarnate God on the cross establishes the means for the unleashed presence of God among the nations. The torn veil connected forever the torn flesh of Jesus and the Spirit unleashed on the world. "The nations must have their Calvary before they have their Pentecost," said Samuel Zwemer.[70] As must we.

Jesus is worthy of our dying. For when our God-dwelt bodies are poured out like drink offerings, when our God dwelt temples are torn apart, the fragrance of Jesus is re-released in the world. Something in suffering releases the tangible presence of Jesus. Jesus is worthy of suffering, worthy of death. Suffering elevates and elucidates the realization of His worth.

It sounds repetitive; it is actually ascending. Suffering releases the presence of Jesus. Suffering establishes His worth. And because a fallen world is in rebellion, a worthy Jesus is persecuted further, and further persecution releases further fragrance and further worth. And the more the body of Christ suffers, the more Jesus is lifted up. Thus, Jesus is worthy of our suffering over and over again!

Suffering is not a one and done. We are not to have one traumatic experience, get our persecution badge, write a book and join the lecture circuit. No! The worth of Jesus calls us to a lifestyle of suffering. We are invited into an ongoing fellowship!

What shall we say then when we enter suffering and death? Father, save us from this trial? No! But for this purpose we come to this hour. Father, glorify Thy name! Nik Ripkin in his book *The Insanity of God*, tells the story of a man named Dmitri. Dmitri started a house church in Russia in the Soviet era. ."[71]

Security accosted him. "You have started an illegal church!"

"How can you say that?" he argued. "All we are doing is reading and talking about the Bible, singing, praying, and sometimes sharing what money we have to help out a poor neighbor. How can you call that a church?"

"We don't care what you call it," they replied. "It looks like a church to us, and if you don't stop it, bad things are going to happen."

The church grew to 50 people. Dmitri was fired from his job. His wife was fired from her job. Their kids were expelled from school. "Little things like that," Dmitri said. The church grew to 75 villagers packed in the house, standing around the windows outside. And the officials stormed in and slammed Dmitri against the wall, rhythmically slapping him back and forth across the face.

"We warned you and warned you. If you do not stop, this is the least of what will happen," they said.

One grandmother then accosted security saying, "You have laid your hands on a man of God, and you will not survive."

This was on a Tuesday; that Thursday the official dropped dead of a heart attack. The next house church meeting had 150 people. The authorities could not let this happen—so Dmitri went to jail for 17 years.

For 17 years in prison, every morning at daybreak, Dmitri would stand at attention by his bed. He faced the east, raised his arms in praise to God, and then he sang his heart song to Jesus. The reaction of the other prisoners was predictable—laughter, cursing, jeers, metal cups banging, food and human waste thrown.

Dmitri foraged in the prison for scraps of paper. With charcoal or a stubby pencil, he wrote out all the verses and songs he could think of. Defiantly he stuck them to the wet pillar in the corner of the room. Guards found them and tore them down and beat him. But again he wrote and posted the Word of God again—full of scripture, full of praise.

Security told him his wife was murdered and his children taken by the state. "You win," he admitted to the guards. "I will sign any paper you want." God appeared to him that night in his despair and let him see a vision of his wife and children praying for him. He physically heard their voices as they prayed. So he refused to sign the paper and continued to sing his heart song morning by morning.

One day he found a whole sheet of paper and a pencil by it. He rushed back to his cell. "I know it was probably foolish," Dmitri admitted, "but I couldn't help myself. I filled both sides of the paper with as much of the Bible as I could. I reached up and stuck the entire sheet of paper on that wet concrete pillar. Then I stood and looked at it: to me it seemed like the greatest offering I could give Jesus from my prison cell. Of course my jailor saw it. I was beaten and punished. I was threatened with execution."

Dmitri was dragged from his cell, and as he was hauled down the corridor, the strangest thing happened. Before they reached the door leading to the courtyard of execution, 1,500 hardened criminals jumped to their feet and stood at attention by their beds. They faced east. And they began to sing. Dmitri said it sounded like the greatest choir in human history. There, 1,500 criminals raised their arms to the heavens and began to sing the heart song they had heard Dmitri sing to Jesus every morning for 17 years.

Dmitri's jailers released their hold on him in horror and stepped away from him. "Who are you?" they asked.

Dmitri straightened his back and stood as tall and proud as he could. "I am a son of the Living God, and Jesus is His name," he answered. Dmitri's life sang, "Jesus is worth dying for."

The last six months have not been easy in the Arab world. Our friends have been imprisoned in Jordan. Our colleagues have been abused in Yemen. Young men I discipled have been tortured in Sudan. A brother in the work was killed in Libya. Christians have been murdered in Egypt. And all—every one—would say if they were standing here today, "Jesus is worthy of dying."

IT WILL BE OUR DEATHS

It will not be my death that reaches the Arab Muslim world. It will be yours. It will be ours. Only a martyred church will exhibit enough of Christ's worth to see the Arabs rise from the dead.

A man named John Woolman is an unheralded saint who did more to abolish slavery than any other human being. More than Wilberforce, more than Lincoln. One hundred years before the American Civil War, Woolman helped turn the Quakers against slavery to their own cost and economic hurt. The wheels of justice were set in motion to slowly grind ever fine. Woolman writes,

> In a time of sickness, a little more than two and a half years ago, I was brought so near to the gates of death that I forgot my name…. In this state I remained several hours. I then heard a soft melodious voice, more pure and harmonious than any I had heard with my ears before; I believed it was the voice of an angel who spoke to the other angels. The words were: "John Woolman is dead…. As I lay still for a time, I at length felt a Divine power prepare my mouth that I could speak, and then I said, "I am crucified with Christ, nevertheless I live; yet not I, but Christ liveth in me… Then…I perceived there was joy in Heaven over a sinner who had repented, and that the language, "John Woolman is dead," meant no more than the death of my own will.[72]

Jesus is worthy of glory from all nations. Jesus is worthy of living, worthy of all our desire. Jesus is worthy of dying, and there is great joy in heaven when we come to the end of our own will. It is a sweet heavenly voice that bids us die, that lets us know we are dead. If Woolman was willing to die to self that slaves be free, what are you willing to do that Arabs might live?

Samuel Zwemer landed in Cairo, the heart of the Arab world in September 1912—one hundred years to the month before the start of the Live Dead Cairo team. What we are doing is not new. Many have walked this path before us. Many have lived a crucified life. Zwemer candidly put it this way: "Does it really matter how many die or how much money is spent in opening closed doors if we really believe that missions are warfare and the King's glory is at stake?"[73]

Now [our world] is troubled, and what shall [we] say? Father, save [us] from this hour? But for this purpose [we] came to this hour. Father, glorify Your name (John 12:28).

every Christian Dies

JOHN 12:23-28

In the mid-1870s, Henry Morton Stanley ("Dr. Livingstone, I presume") traveled through Uganda. Appalled at the spread of Islam by way of the Arab-led slave trade, he appealed for missionaries to go to Uganda. A man named Mackay responded to the call and entered Uganda from the south through the slave route that ended in Zanzibar. In 1885, Bishop James Hannington, the first Bishop for Equatorial East Africa and Mackay's leader, entered Uganda from the north via Kenya. He wanted to see what Mackay was doing in the ministry.

Mujasi was the Muslim captain of Ugandan King Mtesa's bodyguard. He hated Christians and arrested missionary Mackay (later, Bishop himself) and some of his young Ugandan students who had decided to follow Jesus. The boys were seized on the pretext that Hannington invaded from the north and that these youth joined the white men against the king. Six students were arrested, and three survived to tell the tale.

The three Ugandan students who died were tortured. Their arms cut off, they were bound to scaffolding under which a fire was lit. Armless, they slowly burned to death. As they hung in protracted agony over the flames, Mujasi and his men stood around jeering: "Pray now to Isa Al-Massiya [Arabic for Jesus Christ] if you think He can do anything to help you." The spirit of the martyrs entered these lads and together they raised their voices and praised Jesus in the fire.

Daily, daily sing to Jesus
Sing my soul, His praises due
All He does deserves our praises
And our deep devotion too
For in deep humiliation
He for us did live below
Died on Calvary's cross of torture
Rose to save our souls from woe

The students sang until their shriveled tongues refused to form a sound.[74]

EVERY CHRISTIAN DIES

In the natural, life is first ending in death. In the spiritual, death is first ending in life. "Death ever precedes life in the spiritual realm," wrote author Lillian Harvey, "and the worker who insists upon the life of the Holy Spirit must always be delivered to death if the Life of Jesus is to be made manifest."[75] She is commenting on 2 Corinthians 4:10: "Always bearing about in the body the dying of the Lord Jesus that the life of Jesus might be made manifest in our mortal body."

George Matheson explains: "The dying of the Lord Jesus was not passing from earth to Heaven; it was passing from Heaven to Earth. *Every step of His dying was a step downward.* He took the servant's form. He took the human likeness. He took the fleeting fashion of a man. He took the image of the humblest man. He went down deeper than humility... He became one with the poor, the outcast, the erring. He felt the pains that dwelt in other bodies, the griefs that lived in other souls, the sins that slept in other hearts" (italics mine).[76]

If we are to have the life of Jesus manifest through our mortal bodies in missional impact of the nations, we are going to have to die. We are going to have to lose our life. We are going—Jesus said—to have to hate our life. Godly hate is to be so passionately against something that you determine to destroy it.

What within are we going to have to destroy? What within must die if we are to see Jesus glorified among the unreached?

First, every Christian has to die to the terrorizing reign of self.

Our culture has been cruel to us. American culture has taught us self-gratification from the cradle. Toddler tyrants now rule America. Children are the new idols. Parents bow and worship their progeny. We are bombarded with the message that indulgence is harmless, that safety is preferred to risk, and that glory is found in success and popularity rather than in shame and suffering. This is not unique to this age or our generation. It's exacerbated perhaps in these last days, but not new. Every generation has had to stare down the mortal enemy of self.

A great missionary to Africa, Morris Williams said, "Self-denial is the first requisite for the man or woman God would use. We're taught not to deny ourselves, but the man or the woman who would rise...whom God can really use must come to the place where they say: 'Lord, I will deny myself and I'll go without. I'll do whatever is necessary...to bring deliverance to the people of this world.'"[77]

I heard author Heath Adamson once say, "Are you ready to say yes to Jesus even before He asks the question?" You want to be a life-giving missionary? It starts with dying, giving up what you thought it would be like and perhaps giving up where you would like to go, and certainly giving up what you pre-determined to do. Are you willing to say, "Yes, Lord, I die to my own ideas of mission. Lord, I say yes before I even know the question."

Nothing is as tragic as the Live Dead missionary who does not live dead. Live Dead is just a new way to state the old reality of the crucified call. Live Dead, generally speaking, is every Christian, everywhere, taking up the cross daily and following Jesus. Live Dead in its mission focus is church planting to unreached people groups in teams.

Let no one attempt to be a missionary who has not first committed to march to the cross daily. The lost of the world don't need your putrid, un-crucified self. The unreached don't need your tyrannical nature leading the way. The lost need the sweet fragrance of a crushed will, a broken heart, and a contrite spirit. The Lord is near to the crucified; He hung among them and very far indeed from those who sit on self-made thrones.

Every believer who would say yes to Jesus and yes to mission must be radically committed to not getting their way. We must delight in God's rule over us as evidenced by our submission to others. Others have to crucify me; I can't crucify myself. I must hand my roommate, my leader, or my spouse the hammer and urge them to pound away no matter my protests. Listen not to the screams and wails of my flesh. Love me enough to nail all my limbs to the splintered cross. Love me enough to let me hang there in misery. Cut not my cocoon. Rescue me not from my Calvary. Friend, help me die for self is a poisonous monster, and I have too long suffered under my own tyranny.

"Did you ever hear of a man so mad as to rush upon the sword's point to avoid the scratch of a pin? Or run upon a roaring cannon rather than endanger getting wet feet? Why this is the best wisdom of the distracted world who will sin rather than suffer?" writes 17th century English pastor Joseph Alleine.[78] Rather than die to self, we indulge ourselves and do more injury to both self and Savior than if we would take up our cross and suffer.

Do you want to be a missionary? Do you want to reach the unreached? Before you can conquer the world, you must conquer the selfish tyrant within.

Second, every Christian has to die to the crippling intimidation of fear.

Missionary Morris Williams says: "God can't use the normal Christian. He's looking around for people who will say: 'Lord, I don't care what people think. The only thing I care about is doing your will and seeing Your job done. If it means being different or laughed at, I'm willing Lord. It doesn't matter that other people aren't doing it. If it takes more consecration, more time, more money, I'm willing to do it Lord, because it needs to be done, and I'm not going to look around to see what others are doing."[79]

We can't be afraid of man — neither the ones that scorn nor the ones that strike. And we have no need to fear death, for death has no terror when we believe in resurrection. "By removing eternal risk, Christ calls His people to continual temporal risk. For followers of Jesus, the final risk is gone," says pastor and *Desiring God* author John Piper.[80] You can't kill the dead, and when we are dead to fear, the devil doesn't know what to do to us for faith has robbed him of his main weapon.

Bob Blincoe, Frontiers USA president, shares the story of Roland and Becca, missionaries to Lebanon. "Roland was a dedicated evangelist. He made it his practice to open his Arabic Bible and speak of Jesus Christ to Muslims every day. Then the region descended into chaos; months of lawlessness disturbed their city when Muslim factions began blowing up cars. During those days, when Roland would leave the house in the morning, Becca would walk with him to his car. She would say, 'I love you.' While she sat in the passenger seat, Roland would put the key in the ignition and turn on the car. If nothing happened [if the car did not explode and kill them both], that was the 'all clear.' Then Becca would open the car door and return to their home, while Roland drove to his appointment."[81]

Let me be clear: Jesus does not want us dead. Jesus came to bring life

— and life abundantly. Live Dead is not about suicide bombers. It's not about being an "Eeyore" pessimist. It's not about darkness, gloom, doom, and despair. It's not about martyrdom. It's not about graves, tombs, skulls, or bravado. The desire to physically die is a demonic twist. Suicide is a cowardly suggestion of the devil. Waste and foolishness have no place in the heart of God. There is no crown for stupidity. Live Dead is about life. We die to self so the life of Jesus can be manifest.

Jesus is the Prince of life! Life will reign in our mortal body. Death is the last enemy. We advance toward eternal life with no curse, no tears, no pain, and no death. The world moves from life to death — and is endlessly depressed. We move from death to life — and are eternally at joy!

Live Dead cannot be misconstrued to be sinister. Perhaps we should say Live Dead Live, for the goal is life — joyous, abundant, eternal life — both for the messenger and the one who receives the message. To live dead means to live, fully, completely, freely, that others may live likewise. To live dead means death has neither attraction nor power over us.

> *It is no longer I who live, but Christ lives in me; and the life which I now live in the flesh, I live by faith in the Son of God, who loved me and gave Himself for me.* (Gal. 2:20)

> *O Death, where is your sting? O Hades, where is your victory... Thanks be to God, who gives us the victory through our Lord Jesus Christ.* (1 Cor. 15:55, 57)

> *[Jesus is] the resurrection and the life. He who believes in Me, though he may die, he shall live.* (John 11:25)

> *I live, I live because He has risen; I live, I live with power over sin.*[82]

Friends, we die to death. We embrace life with all its glories. We read, we dance, we run, we savor, we laugh, we delight, we love, we grow, we rejoice, we bless, we smile, we affirm, we drink deeply of the water of life, and we spray it everywhere we go. We die to self that we might overcome fear. We overcome fear with the joy of eternal life. The joy of eternal life is our core invitation.

Come, oh Arab, out of the grave! Rise, oh Somali, out of your tomb! Come forth, oh Lazarus, the Turk! Arise and shine, oh Tuareg! Leap to life, you Pashtun, Bengali, and Kashmir! Awake! Die to fear of man and death that life might reign!

Third, every Christian has to die to the notion that mission will happen quickly or will happen without prudent missiology.

Yes, the task is urgent. Yes, we run to battle. But untold damage has been done to the cause of Christ when we misunderstand the difference between short-term trips and lasting biblical mission.

Real mission learns language. Real mission is antithetical to mission tourism. You are not called to the nations. You are called to one nation — to live there, to learn there, to sweat there, to toil there, to make friends and enemies. "Woe to you," Jesus says, "when all men speak well of you" (Luke 6:26). You may suffer and die or get kicked out or plant the church and move on, but none of this happens due to haste. Mission incarnates and puts down roots until the Master leads us on.

I would not be saying all of this if I did not believe that God can use this generation to reach the unreached! Like Samuel Pollard, you will have your thousands.[83] But I also stand here in the clear light of Scripture and on the sober rock of experience. No soul is won quickly or thoughtlessly. No great work of God is easy. Haste does not make disciples. Rush does not plant the church.

In this age of instant media, instant gratification, and instant results, every student will have to die to haste, and if this world is to be reached, you must commit to a long, painful, stubborn fight in one place, in one direction. Never losing a sense of urgency, you must die to the idea of haste. You must die to the crippling chain of fear. You must die to the tyrannizing rule of self.

The defining characteristic of the missionary is falling to the ground and dying, taking up the cross for the long, splinters-in-your-bloody-back march. Are you ready for a long, slow death that others might forever live?

Every Christian is called to die to the tyranny of self. Every Christian is called to die to fear and rise through faith. Every Christian is called to die to haste and ease and commit to a long, determined cross-bound march. And when we die these noble deaths, when we live dead, no matter where or who we are, something beautiful happens.

EVERY CHRISTIAN GLORIFIES

What was true of Jesus will be true of us. His glory followed His dying. It is the dead missionary, the dead Christian that truly lives. It is the disciple dead to self who shines with the glory of Jesus.

> *But Jesus answered them, saying, "The hour has come that the Son of Man should be glorified. Most assuredly, I say to you, unless a grain of wheat falls into the ground and dies, it remains alone; but if it dies, it produces much grain. He who loves his life will lose it, and he who hates his life in this world will keep it for eternal life. If anyone serves Me, let him follow Me; and where I am, there My servant will be also. If anyone serves Me, him My Father will honor. Now My soul is troubled, and what shall I say? 'Father, save Me from this hour'? But for this purpose, I came to this hour. Father, glorify Your name."* (John 12:23–28)

Unless we fall to the ground and die, we remain alone. If we die, we produce much grain, much glory. If we love our life, we lose it. If we hate our life, we keep it. When Jesus said these words to His disciples, He was a couple days away from the cross. He has been anointed at Bethany, crucifixion soon to follow. Listen again to the text in that light.

If anyone serves Me, let him follow Me [to the cross]; and where I am [the cross], there My servant will be also. If anyone serves Me, him My Father will honor. Now My soul is troubled, and what shall I say? "Father, save Me from this hour" [Save me from the cross]? But for this purpose [the cross] I came to this hour. Father, glorify Your name [by the cross].

"Every Christian," said Stephen Neil about the early church, "knew that sooner or later he might have to testify to his faith at the cost of his life."[84]

This is true. Still today, following Jesus is going to cost your life. You can't reap in death what you do not sow in life. Death only amplifies a life; it does not recreate it. Death can't build on what life has not birthed.

For a missionary death to be glorious, it must be merely the final act of a life lived well. It's not actually how we die that glorifies Jesus. What glorifies Jesus is if we live in Christ-exalting self-denial, if we live dead. Ironically, dying to self for the sake of the gospel is all about how we gloriously live!

Anna Hampton writes about the myth of suffering in mission always glorifying God. Her corrective point is: "Living faithfully *wherever we are* is what always glorifies God" (italics mine).[85]

Nothing spiritually magical happens when you cross an ocean. If you are selfish here, you will be selfish there. If you don't glorify God when things go well, you won't mystically start glorifying Him when things are tragic.

Do you want to glorify God among the nations? You can't! Unless you learn to glorify Him right here, right now in your broken home, in your messed-up school, in your rundown city, in your imperfect church, under your flawed leader. The glory of God is not geographical and external; it is heart and obedience based. It is indelibly linked to dying to self.

The glory of God is also indelibly linked to being with and like Jesus. Thomas Chalmers, Scotland's greatest 19th century church leader, preached a sermon entitled, "The Expulsive Power of a New Affection." In it he said, "The love of the world cannot be expunged by a mere demonstration of the world's worthlessness. But may it not be supplanted by the love of that which is more worthy of itself."[86] He meant, of course, that lower joys can only be pushed out by higher ones.

It is the love of Jesus and the love of Jesus alone that gives us the capacity to live dead, to die to self in a way that is not twisted or ironically self-exalting.

Do you remember the story of Moses coming down from the mountain? His face was so bright he had to veil it. The people could see God shining from him.

Do you remember the story of Peter's shadow healing someone as he walked by? He was obviously so full of the power of Jesus that his presence brought healing.

Some time ago, I passed a demon-possessed man on the street. I did not know him, but I knew he was possessed. I could feel it. I could see it in the wildness of his eyes. I could smell it in the filth of his body. I could sense it in the evil emanating from his being. I shuddered as I walked by, for I could tangibly feel and sense the power of evil upon him. But what did he sense of me? What effect did my passing shadow have? What light did he see shining from my face? What I felt for evil, did he feel for righteousness? What I felt of darkness, did he sense of light? I shuddered and recoiled at the filth on him. Was there anything about my spirit that wooed him to Christ?

When you walk into a room, can others sense something changing in the atmosphere? When you join a conversation, does the tone shift inexorably toward what is pure? Is there something indelible, something unmovable, something commanding of the presence of Jesus from within and emanating out of you? Does your life drip with the glory of God? Is there a gravitas about you, a weight of the presence of Jesus, something that can be felt and sensed, that shines from your eyes and radiates from your being, that when you open your mouth to speak, the listener leans in eager, for their imagination is already captivated?

No?

There are two certain probabilities: First, you are still living under the tyrannical rule of self, fear, and haste, or second, you are not abiding in Jesus, lavishing extravagant time in His presence. Do you long for the Moses and Peter effect? Do you desire that God's authority and presence be so strong upon you that your face shines and your presence attacks evil?

There is no other way but to live dead and to abide in the presence of Jesus. The glory of God is evident upon us when we fall to the ground and die and when we rise in obedience, cherishing the presence of Jesus.

BACK TO THE UGANDAN YOUTH

Let me conclude by returning to the Ugandan youth of 1885. Remember the students sang until their shriveled tongues refused to form the sound:

Daily, daily sing to Jesus
Sing my soul, His praises due
All He does deserves our praises
And our deep devotion too
For in deep humiliation

He for us did live below
Died on Calvary's cross of torture
Rose to save our souls from woe[87]

Their lives, deaths and song are the essence of John 12. Now is the time for the Father to be glorified among all nations. The means is our death. We are going to have to die to our self and live for Jesus. It's the daily dying that leads to glorious living. The true glory of man is the gravitas of God, gained only from the wisdom and weakness of suffering and extravagant time abiding in Jesus. Everything, every day for Jesus' sake.

Here are some immediate practical applications:

1. A recommitment to live the crucified life — now, here, right where you are, every day. The beginning of that self-denial is actually a positive: Abiding in Jesus and lavishing time on Him in His presence.
2. A commitment to find one Muslim friend in your world and pursue them, serve them, love them, befriend them, pray for them, invite them into your life and home, live the joyous Jesus life in front of them, open your mouth and proclaim the gospel to them.
3. A commitment to advocate for unreached people by starting a Pray Band—three people that pray for the unreached. Sign up at livedead. org/pray.
4. A willingness to come live with us among the dead. Come die to self with others who are stumbling in that direction. Join a church planting team among the unreached. For those in college, once you finish, come give a year and pray about giving your life. Start the conversation with a worker on the ground at livedead.org/go.
5. Most immediate, make an altar now to pray quietly and reverently. Tell Jesus "yes" even before you know what the question is or where He is asking you to go.

Three Branches

JOHN 15

The Apostle John wrote his Gospel to believers. He writes to Christians to exhort them to super-exalt Jesus and to follow His command to make disciples of Jesus of all peoples, everywhere.

By the time we read John 15, we have reached the night of betrayal during which Jesus gave His last instructions to His disciples. Some think Jesus spoke while He walking (because John 14:31 says, "Arise, let us go from here," and the direction of John 18:1 is vague). Perhaps he passed a vineyard. Perhaps he passed the Temple and its "Golden Vine," a gilded image of Israel as God's vine on the Temple mount. Perhaps he was still inside thinking about the Maccabean coins, one of which had an image of an engraved vine. But for whatever reason, the metaphor of vine was on His mind.

There are many false vines, but "I am the *true* vine," Jesus said. Life is not found through religion or in politics or money. Jesus is life; He is the vine.

You realize, of course, that mission work is a false fuel? The lostness of man as our cause can only take us so far. If our lives are derived from missions (preaching, evangelism, and church planting), that is a false vine. Ministry is a thing of earth. It will grow strangely dim. There is no ministry or mission in heaven. If our identities are established by church planting or pioneering or being on the front lines, what happens when that is taken away? Capacity takes us far, but not far enough. It gives us focus and external results, but not divine life.

Jesus is the true vine. Only Jesus can "life" these mortal bodies.

I abide from sheer desperation! I abide because my experience has painfully taught me that without Jesus I can do nothing. Without Jesus all my labor crumbles, disappears, blows away. Without Jesus I can sweat, toil and build a castle of cards, but divine transformation and disciples that make disciples cannot be done unless Jesus does it.

Five years ago, we began to see an increase in disciples—Muslim background believers, Christian background believers, teams—all were growing numerically and spiritually. House churches began to form. At the same time, we began to face spiritual attacks at a heightened level. For me, it was my dreams. I have not slept well in almost three years. I have the most demonic, horrific dreams. I wrestle and agonize and struggle all night long, and though I am sleeping, I am not resting. Many mornings I wake up exhausted (emotionally, spiritually, physically). There is only one thing that sustains me. I drag myself out of bed, and I go to Jesus. Jesus puts me back together again. I sit with Him. He talks to me, and I talk to Him. I sing, I read, I pray and I write. I abide in Jesus out of sheer desperation. I feel like Humpty Dumpty, only my reality means I am broken every night, and Jesus has to put me back together every morning. Sometimes it is so bad, that even though I am weary, I don't want to go to bed because I know the battle awaits me.

This is my progression:

DESPERATION – DISCIPLINE – DESIRE – DELIGHT

I am desperate for Jesus. If I do not abide in Him, I have absolutely nothing to offer. So out of desperation, I discipline myself. From sustained discipline, God in His sweet mercy gives me a desire for Himself and from the combination of desperation, discipline and desire comes the sweet fruit of delight in the presence of Jesus.

Today, I simply want to point you to what Jesus says about being a branch that abides. Before we look at the various branches, let me simply state that in this passage, John uses the word "fruit" to refer to disciples, and when John says "bear fruit," he means "make disciples." By "abiding" John means two things: (1) daily, disciplined, extended time in the presence of Jesus through prayer and His Word and (2) all-day communion with Jesus. With these definitions as a base,[88] let's look at the branches in the text. Most people think there are two branches in the text, but there are indeed three. At the end of the message, I am going to ask you to reflect on which branch you are.

THE FIRST BRANCH

> *Every branch in Me that does not bear fruit He takes away.*
> (John 15:2)

The word "take away" comes from the Greek word *aero*. Take away is an unfortunate translation, for *aero* literally means "I lift up."

Viticulture, the cultivation of grapes, helps us get a sense of what this means, for when the shoot of a vine falters, it often sinks to the mud. At other times, other branches take up so much sun that the smaller, weaker, newer branch needs help to get exposure, so the vinedresser, both in the Middle East in the time of Jesus and today in modern methods, lifts up that branch—out of the mud or into the sun—and lovingly ties it to the trestle. He gives it an opportunity to be revived that it may bear fruit.

Note the text. It says "branch *in* Me." This is the missionary in Jesus who is not making disciples. I am not naïve to the difficulties of pioneer work. I live it. I love to read about the pioneers in mission, and I'm sobered and humbled by my own failings in this regard. What is the mind of Jesus? What is the heart of Jesus towards the many of you who are legitimately in Him, loved by Him, loving Him, working your tails off, learning language, integrated in community, and laying down your life but not seeing disciples made? What is the intention of Jesus over you?

The intention of Jesus is *not* to take you away or ignore you or abandon you. Jesus will not discard you. Jesus will not throw you away. You know what He will do? He will teach you to abide. He will lift you to Himself and make provision for you to get out of the mud and into the sun.

Jesus commissioned us to make disciples anywhere and everywhere. Jesus promises: "If you abide, you will make disciples." Jesus does not commission us for that which He will not enable us. He does not promise what He will not deliver. It is God's intention and purpose that you make disciples. How many and of what color are up to Him, but *all* of us are commissioned towards this task, no matter the challenges or complexities of our context.

So, what is our recourse if it is not happening? What if you are that branch here today who is not bearing fruit, if you are not making disciples? The answer is so simple if you will have ears to receive it. Jesus wants you to abide in Him!

If you don't, especially in mission, most especially in frontier mission, you will not make it. You will wilt. You will not survive. You will certainly not thrive. And you definitely won't make disciples that make disciples.

It happens to the best of us. Hudson Taylor returned to the UK after his first stint in China, exhausted and burnt out. He had not learned to abide. He spent five years as a nobody, five difficult years, but in them he learned to abide in Jesus. When he returned to China, a colleague name Judd, said this about him:

> He was a joyous man now, a bright happy Christian. He had been a toiling, burdened one before, and latterly not much rest of soul. He was resting in Jesus now, and letting Him do the work, which made all the difference.
>
> Whenever he spoke in meetings after that, a new power seemed to flow from him, and in the practical things of life, a new peace possessed him. Trouble did not worry him as before.
>
> He cast everything on God in a new way and gave more time to prayer. Instead of working late at night, he began to go to bed earlier. Rising at 5 a.m. to give time to Bible study and prayer (often two hours) before the work of the day began. It was the exchanged life that had come to him, the life that is indeed "No longer I."[89]

Abide in me, and I in you. It is a reciprocal indwelling—Jesus in us as we are in Him. In it is exchanged strength. "Those who wait [abide] on the Lord shall renew [exchange] their strength" (Isa. 40:31).

Missionaries and friends in Christ who are weary and wilted, missionaries who are not making disciples, what does the Spirit say to you today? Jesus wants to lift you into the sunshine of abiding with Him. Jesus delights to give you the exchanged life—His impossible strength for your pitiful effort. Let us not be the fools who break down because we never heeded Christ's provision to be lifted to Himself!

THE SECOND BRANCH

> *Every branch that bears fruit He prunes, that it may bear more fruit.*
> (John 15:2)

The intention of the vinedresser is to glorify Himself. By this is the Father glorified, when His disciples make many disciples (John 15:8). In order to self-glorify, God prunes His missionaries; those that are making disciples get pruned so they can make more.

The Greek here is *kathairo*. It is the washing of suffering. It is the removing from our natures of all that limits growth. It is the pinching off, even of some good things, that others might benefit. But make no mistake— pruning hurts. It is the washing of God's ordained affliction that prepares us to make more disciples. This painful washing is a gift. It has been granted to us on behalf of Christ, not only to believe on His name, but also to suffer for His name (Phil. 1:29).

We know and preach that believers ransomed from Islam will suffer. Has it sunk into our spirits that we are to suffer for our disciples? Paul writing to the disciples in Ephesus: "Therefore I ask that you do not lose heart at my tribulations for you" (Eph. 3:13).

When was the last time you suffered on behalf of a non-Christian? The Lord guarantees when we embrace that type of suffering, it is redemptive, and it bears fruit. One mystery of suffering is that it brings people to Jesus, for when we lay down our lives for others, they can walk over our backs to the risen Lord!

Be encouraged, oh beloved branch. Those of you who are making disciples, be encouraged. Jesus is going to wash you through suffering. If you will submit to it, you will bear more disciples. "That I may know Him [Christ] and the power of His resurrection, and the fellowship of His sufferings, being conformed to His death" (Phil. 3:10). "Unless a grain of wheat [a seed] falls into the ground and dies, it remains alone, but if it dies, it bears much grain [fruit]" (John 12:24).

Temple Gairdner was an amazing CMS[90] missionary in Cairo 100 years ago. His best friend was Douglas Thornton. They did everything together. They worked together and played together. When Thornton fell sick, Gairdner experienced the presence of God in the room with other Egyptian believers as he died. "I learned that joy and sorrow are not opposites," he wrote of that experience.[91] It brings words from William Blake to mind:

It is right it should be so:
Man was made for joy and woe;
And when this we rightly know
Through the world we safely go.
Joy and woe are woven fine,
A clothing for the soul divine.
Under every grief and pine
Runs a joy with silken twine.[92]

THE THIRD BRANCH

> *If anyone does not abide in Me, he is cast out as a branch and is withered;*
> *and they gather them and throw them into the fire, and they are burned.*
> (John 15:6)

Branches are disciples, and this verse reveals it is possible to be a disciple and not abide in Jesus. The Greek word *ballo* has been translated "cast out." It can also mean to "let fall." Jesus does not force us to abide. He woos us, He invites us, He desires to linger with us, but we have a part to play.

When missionaries or Christians do not abide in Jesus, they dry up. They wither on the vine. They fall, and they are marginalized. They are good for nothing but to be gathered and discarded. But make no mistake— they fall of their own accord. They dry up and are "let fall" into uselessness because they did not abide.

Please understand, you could survive in the Muslim world. You could make it functionally for years in Sudan or Saudi Arabia or Oman or Syria. You can serve doggedly at administration for decades. You can labor in Morocco or Mozambique, Comoros or China, but if you are not abiding, you will have no divine life! No power to make disciples. No authority in the Word or in the Spirit. Your disciples will be sterile. Your house of cards will blow away in the wind immediately once you leave. You will not glorify God, and you will be no use to the Master. You will whittle away your time, wasting your life, and in the end, be cast to the side and marginalized—all because you did not learn to abide. Don't be fooled by the external appearance of success. If you have not learned to abide, you have built with wood, hay, and stubble. It will disappear at the first wolf puff of resistance. There will be no depth, no lasting church, and no disciples making disciples that know how to abide in Jesus.

Beloved, do not be the branch that due to your own folly dries up, is marginalized, and exists but with no divine life, no disciples and no eternal legacy.

APPLICATION

I have some application questions for you. First, which branch are you?

- The wilted one? Jesus invites you to abide.

- The fruitful one? Jesus promises you joy and woe—and more fruit.

- The one who will not abide? You are headed for disaster, the disaster of a powerless and marginalized life.

Some resent the perceived legalism of a daily abiding time. They claim to always be in the presence of Jesus, but as author John Dalrymple rightly says: "The truth is we only learn to pray all the time everywhere after we have resolutely set about praying some of the time somewhere."[93] I learned this from my parents. They called it their 8-10. Every morning at 8 they took their Bibles, journals, and cups of coffee out to the garden. They ignored the phone and the gate and spent extravagant time with Jesus. The fruit? Disciples that I run into all over the world—Kenyans, Europeans, Japanese, and Americans.

Perhaps you're like me. I love my abiding time in the morning, and as I mentioned before, I cannot live without it. But equally important is the other aspect of abiding, and that is where I struggle—all-day communion with Jesus. From about the fourth to sixteenth centuries, breath prayers were normal. Breath prayers are one sentence of seven syllables. The prayer is the deep cry of your heart, a personalized address to the Lord, voiced all day. For example, my breath prayer is "be near me Lord Jesus." It comes from Psalm 34:18 (ESV): "The Lord is near to the brokenhearted and saves the crushed in spirit." I use this breath prayer in my all-day communion with Jesus.

So which branch are you? Not making disciples, making disciples and going through pruning, or not abiding? Will you pay the price necessary to make disciples—to abide and to suffer? In which aspect of abiding are you stronger? Do you have a breath prayer? If not, spend some time to reflect (possibly journal) on what the cry of your heart is. What do you long for in your walk with Jesus? Develop a breath prayer, and allow it to lead you into the aspect of abiding that involves communing with Jesus all day long.

Jesus Calls Me

GALATIANS 2

I have three points to make today:

1. Jesus calls me to Himself.

2. Jesus calls me to die to self.

3. Jesus calls me to glorify Him in the most difficult places and among the most difficult people of earth.

JESUS CALLS ME TO HIMSELF

Moses spent extravagant time with Jesus. His face so bright, he had to veil it. His people could see God shining from him (Exodus 34:29–35). Peter's shadow healed as he walked by (Acts 5:14–15), obviously so full of the power of Jesus that his presence brought healing. Jesus commanded us to make disciples in Matthew 28, then tells us how in John 15, by abiding in Him, by spending a lot of time with Him (John 15:5).

Some time ago, I passed a demon-possessed person. I have often passed a demon- possessed person on the street. I did not know him, but I knew he was possessed—I could feel it. I could see it in the wildness of His eyes. I could smell it in the filth of his body. I could sense it in the evil emanating from his being. I shuddered as I walked by, for I could tangibly feel and sense the power of evil upon him. And I felt the Holy Spirit prompt this question: "You felt the evil emanating from him. What did he feel from you?" But what did he sense of me? What effect did my passing shadow have? What light did he see shining from my face? What I felt for evil, did he feel for righteousness? What I felt of darkness, did he sense of light? I shuddered and recoiled at the filth on him. Was there anything about my spirit that wooed him to Christ?

When you walk into a room, can others sense something has changed in the atmosphere? When you join a conversation, does the tone shift inexorably toward what is pure? Is there something indelible, something unmovable, something commanding of the presence of Jesus from within and emanating from you? Does your life drip with the glory of God? Is there a gravitas about you, a weight of the presence of Jesus, something that is felt and sensed, something that shines from your eyes and radiates from your being, that when you open your mouth to speak, the listener leans in eagerly, for their imagination is already captivated.

Helen Ewan was a simple British girl born in 1910. She died at 22. James A. Stewart, a well-known evangelist of that time, wrote: "The manifestation of His glory [on Helen] astonished us all. Hers was only a common life, but it was lit up with the glory of God. I only wondered how she could stand so much glory in her fragile, Earthenware, container Being full of the Holy Spirit. She was full of Christ."[94]

Helen woke up at 5 a.m. to abide with Jesus. In the winter, she did not turn the heat on in her little room, feeling she could be more alert in the cold. And besides, she was praying for missionaries, and they lived with discomfort. She prayed daily for the lost by name until they were saved. "Her yearnings after salvation of the lost were awful to behold."[95] Helen was an incredible personal soul winner—out on cold nights rescuing prostitutes and witnessing to drunks, and walking miles to university each day so she could give tracts out all along the way. But it was not her personal evangelism that marked her:

> Her body was a walking temple of the Holy Spirit. Thus, wherever she went, the power of God was manifested. When she entered into any service, immediately the atmosphere was charged with His power. I have known her to slip quietly into a prayer meeting which had already begun and sit on the back seat. Yet everyone of us knew that she had arrived because of the mighty sense of God manifested in our midst. Evangelists often sought after her service. It was not that she could sing or speak in public. I don't think she ever sang a solo or gave a public testimony in any of their campaigns. All she did was sit quietly in the meetings and pray. Yet these evangelists knew that if they could only have Helen attend their services, there would be sure to be a mighty anointing upon the meetings.[96]

At university prayer meetings, they could always tell if Helen was present, whether she prayed aloud or not. They could tell when she entered the room without seeing or hearing her because they sensed the presence of

God in their midst. Stewart ends the story of Helen Ewan with this anecdote:

> One night we were all having a special evening together. Young people rejoicing in the Lord and having a good time when my wife said, "Is that Helen Ewan's photograph on the mantelpiece?" Suddenly there was a dead silence, and she said, "Jim, have I said anything wrong?" All the laughing ceased, and one by one, without anybody saying a word, we dropped down on our knees and began to pray.[97]

Think of it! Long after she was dead, even the memory of her glorious and godly life drew people to Jesus. Stewart closes, "I believe that this spiritual life is for every child of God."[98]

This is the glory of God! This is the shining face of Moses! This is the shadow of Peter healing the sick! It's not magic. It's not forced. It is the instrumentality of human vessels, jars of clay, so full of the glory of Jesus that He spills out wherever we are.

Some time ago, a Muslim from Yemen went to Sweden and found the Lord. He joined a radio ministry named IBRA based in Cyprus that produces Arabic programming for Yemen and other Muslim countries. The IBRA team went to Istanbul for a conference. This believer from a Muslim background (BMB) felt led to stay in Istanbul for a week after the conference looking for Yemeni people to whom he could minister. Not much happens, so one day he goes into the mosque. It's between noon and 3 p.m., so he just sits on the floor and reads his Bible. After an hour, nothing happens. He tries to get up but can't stand. He grows afraid and wonders if demonic powers are holding him or if God is punishing him for going to the mosque. He sits there for an hour, unable to move. Then a young 22-year-old man approaches him. "I am from Yemen, and my wife and I fled to Turkey. Can you come with me to the women's section as my wife (who is 15-years-old) wants to hear as well. We are disillusioned with Islam as in Yemen, Muslims are killing Muslims. We had a dream of this mosque and a man sitting on the ground. Light was coming from heaven to him, and the light came from him to use. So we decided that my wife would come to this mosque and wait for that person to appear. She has been coming for two months. Today, she saw you. You are the man in the dream, but you started to leave so she prayed, 'God, don't let that man leave until my husband comes!' She called me, and I ran down here. Please tells us what the dream means." So the Yemeni BMB began to speak to them in Arabic, and the young man said, "It's a miracle! This Turk can speak my dialect." The BMB was in tears and explained that he was Yemeni and that the light they saw in the area was the life of God, not anything in him. They met the next day and spent from 6 p.m. to the next morning talking about the gospel. The man and his wife came to Jesus in the fellowship of Syrian believers in Istanbul!

This story then begs the question: What is in your shadow? What shines form your face? What beams out your back? What light, joy, radiance, blessing, and peace shoots from your body and being? So that before you open your mouth (because we must open our mouth as we are essentially messengers and faith *still* comes by hearing and hearing by the Word of God)[99], those in your presence *sense* the presence of God and so lean in, front foot, to hear what you have to say. Do you change the atmosphere? Is there something so magnificent of Jesus upon you and in you that others can feel it, even before you open your mouth?

How do we get there? By abiding in Jesus! By spending extravagant time daily in the presence of Jesus. It is a discipline of regular times with Jesus, in the Word and in the Spirit through prayer, and it is a state, walking in communion and obedience to Jesus all day long. Moses was with Jesus, and the people could tell. Peter had been with Jesus, filled with the Spirit multiple times, and the people could tell. Can anyone tell that you've been with Jesus? Jesus is calling you to Himself! Will you answer?

JESUS CALLS ME TO DIE TO SELF

You are perhaps familiar with the Bonhoeffer quote: "When Christ calls a man, He bids him come and die."[100] The term "live dead" is based in Galatians 2:20: "I have been crucified with Christ; it is no longer I who live, but Christ lives in me; and the life which I now live in the flesh I live by faith in the Son of God, who loved me and gave Himself for me." It is what we have called "the crucified life" or dying to self, and it's nothing new.

Our culture has been cruel to us. Western culture has taught us self-gratification from our cradle. We are now ruled by toddler tyrants or petulant presidents. We are bombarded with the message that indulgence is harmless, that safety is preferred to risk, and that glory is found in success and popularity, rather than the Biblical understanding that glory is found in shame and suffering.

This is not unique to this age or our generation. Exacerbated perhaps in these last days, but not new. Every generation has to stare down the mortal enemy of self. Morris Williams, a great missionary to Africa, said: "Self-denial is the first requisite for the man or woman God would use. We're taught not to deny ourselves, but the man or the woman who would rise, whom God can really use, must come to the place where they say: 'Lord, I will deny myself and I'll go without. I'll do whatever is necessary to bring deliverance to the people of this world.'" [101]

You want to be a life-giving Christian? It starts with dying. Giving up what you thought it would be like. Perhaps giving up where you would like to go and certainly giving what you have pre-determined to do. Are you willing today to say, "Yes, Lord, I die to my own ideas of life and mission. Lord, I say 'yes' before I even know the question." Nothing is as tragic as Christian or missionary who does not live dead. Let no one attempt to be a missionary who has not first committed to march to the cross daily. The lost of the world don't need our putrid, un-crucified selves. The unreached don't need our tyrannical nature leading the way. The lost need the sweet fragrance of a crushed will, a broken heart, and a contrite spirit. The Lord is near to the crucified—He hung among them and very far indeed from those who sit on self-made thrones.

Every Christian who would say "yes" to Jesus and "yes" to mission must be radically committed to not getting their way. We must "die daily" with Paul. We must delight in God's rule over us as evidenced by our submission to others. You who have declared: "King of my life, I crown Thee now. Thine shall the glory be, lest I forget thy throne crowned brow lead me to calvary."[102] You who have declared "I want the cross," are you not tired of trying to crucify yourself? Are you not ashamed of the partial crucifixion? Are you not wounded by self-mutilation? Are you not exhausted by the pride of life and lust of the flesh? Are you not embarrassed of failing in your own wisdom and strength? What did you think crucifixion would feel like? Who did you think would crucify you? Why did you think that crucifixion, dying daily would be gentle? It's not just if we are crucified—it's how! Do you want to be a global Christian? Do you want to change the world? Do you want to reach the unreached? You must answer the call of Jesus to die.

In the physical world, first we live and then we die. But in the spiritual world, we die in order that we might life. Let me be clear. Jesus does not want us dead. Jesus came to bring life—and life abundantly. I'm not talking about suicide. This is not about being an "Eeyore" pessimist. It's not about darkness, gloom and doom, or despair. It's not about martyrdom. It's not about graves, tombs, skulls, or bravado. Waste and foolishness have no place in the heart of God. There is no crown for stupidity. To die to self is about life! We die to what "deaths" us. We die to self so the life of Jesus can be manifest. Jesus is the Prince of life! Life will reign in our mortal body. Death is the last enemy. We advance toward eternal life with no curse, no tears, no pain and no death. To die to self means death has neither attraction nor power over us. The world moves from life to death—and is endlessly depressed. We move from death to life—and are eternally at joy! We die to self that we might overcome fear. We overcome fear with the joy of eternal life. The joy of eternal life is our core invitation to those who live where Satan has his throne.

Come, oh Arab, out of the grave!
Rise, oh Somali, out of your tomb!
Come forth, oh Lazarus the Turk!
Arise and shine, oh Tuareg!
Leap to life you Pashtun, Bengali, and Kashmiri.

Jesus calls me to die to self that through me He might call the unreached to life!

So, Jesus calls me to Himself; Jesus calls me to die; and...

JESUS CALLS ME TO THE DIFFICULT PLACES

It's never been easy to spread the gospel. The spread of the gospel has never waited for a smooth path. God has never been dependent on Roman roads or a trade language.

Are you not glad that the Father did not wait until it was safe to send His Son? "Now, just wait a minute, Jesus. Romans are restless. If I send you now, Herod will kill thousands of babies, and You will have to flee to Egypt. Just wait a minute, Son. It is too unstable. It is too unsafe to send you as a missionary now." Are you not glad that was NOT the discourse of heaven? Are you not glad the Father sent His son to a dangerous place *knowing* He would die?

You ask on what authority, by what audacity, I dare to stand before you and ask you to send your own sons and daughters to places like Yemen, Libya, and Somalia, where they might suffer and die? It is not daring or courageous; it's not even foolishness. It is merely obedience. We send our children to suffer and die because that is what God did with His only Son— and aren't you glad He did?

And so, we send our best, our children to dangerous places to join Paul in filling up the sufferings of Christ, not in a salvific way, but by testimony and by the glad song of the martyrs that says Jesus is worthy of it all, that says eternal life is worth temporary death.

Jesus calls us to the hard places because He already came to one and He simply asks us to follow in His steps. The Arab world was 13 percent Christian in 1900. Today, it is 4 percent and declining. There were 2.5 million Christians in Iraq five years ago. Today, there are less than 230,000. Ninety percent of Iraqi Christians have fled, been killed, or recanted their faith. Syria was 19 percent Christian before this recent war. Now with more than 60 percent of their population displaced, it could very well be down to 5 percent or less. Egypt lost a million Christians in the revolutions and over one million Muslims are born in Egypt every year. We would need to lead 1,000,001 Muslims to Jesus annually just to gain an inch of ground. Never before in history, since the launch of the church 2,000 years ago, has the Middle East been less Christian. Who comes to lift the cross instead?[103] Jesus is still calling to the difficult places. Who takes the standard from the dead?[104] We have a Live Dead team in the area of radical Muslims. One Muslim came to Jesus and works in partnership with our team. Recently he met with a fanatic, long bearded Muslim, and immediately afterward, the secret police arrested him. They covered his head with a sack and treated him roughly. He was told to stop that activity and leave the city. In fear he left, but felt convicted, so he returned to the city and the militant Muslim contracted him again. The Muslim asked to meet again but in a village south of the city. Again, fear entered the believer's heart, but he prayed and felt led to go. He entered the villa and to his surprise found a whole room of militant Muslims. They were all long bearded radicals, and again, fear mounted up within him. Then the Holy Spirit came upon this man, and he began to preach. For two hours, he preached the gospel to those radicals, and they sat in stunned silence listening to every word. When he left the villa, the radical that brought him said: "I want to tell you something that you should not repeat. I am actually not a Muslim. I work for the secret police. My job is to infiltrate all the radical Muslim groups in the area. This group brought you down here to kill you, but what you shared astonished them! I have never heard anything like that in my life. It is the only hope for this area. I want you to come with me to the other radical cells I have infiltrated and share the same message with them. Furthermore, I am a powerful person. I know your activities. I know the names of the missionaries you are working with. I know where you meet and when, and if you ever have any trouble, call me and I will help."

Friends, our security is not in the safe places. Our security is not in our silence. If this man would have stayed silent, he would have been killed by the radicals. If this man stayed silent, the whole team would have been considered sympathizers with radicals and would have been thrown out. Because this believer went to a dangerous place with a dangerous message, not only is he alive today, not only is the team still there proclaiming, but whole radical Muslim groups will now hear the gospel!

Jesus is calling us to difficult places.

Samuel Pollard, a missionary to China, had seen no fruit after several years of language and culture learning. He became desperate. He began to seek Jesus and to be filled and empowered by the Holy Spirit. After a week of prayer and fasting, he writes:

> I shall never forget it. Our room was filled with glory, and I had a manifestation such as I had never realized before. The glory came down and so filled me that I felt the Holy Ghost from my head to the soles of my feet. It was about as much as I could stand and for a minute I thought I should faint or die... I had the promise at that meeting that we are going to have thousands of souls... I believe that from the bottom of my heart. Some folks may say: "He's a fool." Let them. we'll have our thousands. "He's gone mad." So be it, but we'll have our thousands. "He's young and enthusiastic." Yes, glory be to God, I am; and we'll have our thousands.[105]

I would not be here if I did not believe God can use the African church to reach the difficult places and peoples. Yes, Jesus is calling us to the hard places, but He is not calling us to futility. You will have your thousands. Yet, I stand here in the clear light of Scripture and on the sober rock of experience. No soul is won quickly or thoughtlessly. No great work of God is easy. Haste does not make disciples. Rush does not plant the Church. In this age of instant media, instant gratification, and instant results, missionaries will have to accept difficult processes in difficult places, and if this world is to be reached, we must commit to a long, painful, and stubborn fight.

Pollard's biographer goes on to say: "When a soul yields himself completely to his Master, then He (the Master) undertakes to give the grueling training necessary to make him His yielded servant." Pollard had his thousands, but this is how they came. He endured seven more years of weary toil before he could baptize his first two converts, and then nine more years of weary toil—sixteen years after believing for the thousands— and the Holy Spirit broke through. The Lord began to move among the Miao, a remote people group, and numbers swelled to 100. They invaded his home and slept on his floor. He tried to escape them and lock himself in his upstairs bedroom. Ten of them climbed the wall outside and in his bedroom window; they sat all around him on his bed and listened to him teach, pleased that they had the missionary all to themselves. The movement grew into the thousands. Sixteen years after the promise, sixteen years of diligent, resident, linguistically fluent, culturally relevant, back-breaking work, sixteen years of oppression, resistance, trouble, and difficulty, sixteen years of being called to a difficult place, and then the breakthrough came.

Hudson Taylor wrote: "China is not to be won for Christ by quiet ease-loving men and women...The stamp of men and women we need is such as will put Jesus, China and souls first and foremost in everything and at every time—even life itself must be secondary... Of such men and such women, do not fear to send us too many. They are more precious than rubies."[106]

Recently I was teaching in Egypt. I was encouraging believers to not only evangelize Muslims but to teach those new believers to evangelize their families. Some Christian Arab women disagreed: "It does not work." They told the story of a Christian background believer (CBB) who led a Muslim woman to the Lord and discipled her to share. This new believer's family killed her and the CBB had a nervous breakdown. I responded, hopefully in the Holy Spirit passion, "A woman is with Jesus forever, and a family heard the gospel and has a chance at eternal life. Hallelujah!"

Yes, Jesus calls us to dangerous places, and we may or may not come back. But the point is not our survival, comfort, freedom or health, the point is another Muslim woman in heaven.

JESUS CALLS ME. JESUS CALLS US.

Jesus calls us to Himself. Jesus calls us to die to self. Jesus calls us to glorify Him in the difficult places and peoples. If you are willing to say "yes" to the call of Jesus, before you even know the specifics of the question, will you make an altar wherever you are right now and pray?

the
Blessing
of being like
Jesus

My parent's generation used to sing a simple chorus:

To be like Jesus
To be like Jesus
All I ask, is to be like Him
All through life's journey
From earth to glory
All I ask is to be like Him[107]

Do you want to be like Jesus? Is there something deep within you that longs to be like Him?

I'm going to pray an extended prayer over you right now. It is a prayer of blessing, though it may not seem so. It is a prayer that the Lord bless you by making you like Him.

May the Lord bless you with hunger.
May the Lord bless you with limitations.
May the Lord bless you with unanswered prayer.
May the Lord bless you with fatigue.
May the Lord bless you with poverty.
May the Lord bless you with simplicity.
May the Lord bless you with suffering and death.
Out of the riches of His great mercy with which He has loved you, amen.

MAY THE LORD BLESS YOU WITH HUNGER

> *Then Jesus was led up by the Spirit into the wilderness…and…he was hungry.* (Matt. 4:1–2)

I once heard an Ethiopian minister speak on hunger in Canada. With a gentle smile he said, "It is not easy for a North American to understand hunger."

What can one know of spiritual hunger who has never involuntarily missed a meal? What can one with full pantries and public drinking fountains know of hungering and thirsting for righteousness? What can one who eats out once a week, and overeats continually, what can that one know of holy dissatisfaction?

Oh, God, who opened the windows of heaven, who spread a table in the wilderness, oh God of all supply, would You not have mercy on Your people? Would You not love us enough to lead us like Jesus by the Spirit into the wilderness? Will You not, oh Lord, bless us with hunger? Lord, grant us the honor of an empty cupboard. God, give us the blessing of not being able to afford to eat out. Savior, do not deny us involuntarily lack and longing. Faithful One, be faithful to us in this: Bless us by leading us to hunger. Give us food that we know not of.

I pray over you the blessing of hunger—to not have, to not be able to provide for yourself, to be unsatisfied—that your body may teach your spirit, as a servant will on occasion teach its master, that man does not live on bread alone.

Jesus, make us hungry for You. Give us a longing and desperation for more of You. May our spirits be in pain, and our hearts restricted. May nothing else satisfy us and may nothing else matter. Because we are starving for more of Jesus, oh Lord, bless us with hunger.

MAY THE LORD BLESS YOU WITH POVERTY

> *Foxes have holes and birds of the air have nests, but the Son of Man has nowhere to lay His head.*
> (Matt. 8:20)

Jesus was poor. At his dedication, Joseph and Mary offered two turtle doves because Leviticus 12:8 says that when a woman sacrifices after childbirth, "If she is not able to bring a lamb, then she may bring two turtledoves or two young pigeons." At what point do ten pairs of shoes become a liability? At what point do fifteen shirts, five pairs of jeans, club memberships, three-bathroom homes, and double mortgages become crippling? At what point do the conveniences of life blind us to the realities of eternity?

Jesus was poor. You want to be like Jesus? Empty your closet. Give away your golf clubs. Downsize your house.

This is not mandatory. This is a blessing. It is hard for the rich to enter the kingdom. Affluence inoculates us. We have insurance and assurance and stock and travel points. We have air conditioning and form-fitting mattresses and disposable income and disposable cameras and disposable marriages. We have so much that we have nothing.

May God bless us with poverty. May God show us how much we can live without. May Jesus show us that joy is not found in the abundance of possessions. May Jesus take away our jobs, deny our promotions, and reduce our incomes. May He strip away our comforts. May He replace money with time, and treasure with peace. May God rescue us from self-sufficiency and endow us with dependency on Him!

Oh, may the God of all comforts grant us this great gift: May He strip away all the insulation that wealth provides. May He slap us, stir us, wake us, and force us to realize that mammon is a cruel, tyrannical master. May God make us vulnerable, dependent, simple, and poor that we might revel in the unsearchable riches of Christ. O God of the cattle on thousands of hills, have mercy on us and bless us with poverty.

MAY THE LORD BLESS YOU WITH LIMITATIONS

> *Christ Jesus, who, though he was in the form of God, did not count equality with God a thing to be grasped, but emptied himself.*
> (Phil. 2:5–7, ESV)

Jesus did not do everything He could have done. Jesus limited himself. He only did what the Father wanted. This self-limitation of Jesus is called kenosis in Greek. Limits are blessings. Prisons are benefits. Paul wrote the above text from jail. If Paul had not been confined to a cell, much of the New Testament would not have been written.

May God bless you with prisons, handicaps, and restrictions. May God favor you with chains, restraints, fences, hedges, and walls. May the Spirit of liberty bless you with His boundaries.

May you be unable in your own strength. May you be slowed and stopped, diverted and redirected.

May you be confined and constrained and locked up. May your words be few and your opinions throttled.

May your limitations bring life. May your restriction bring liberty. May your confinement announce release. May your captivity ransom.

May you be blessed by incapacity. May you be rewarded by being pruned. May you be trusted with removal. May you be diminished, weakened, overlooked, and blocked. May you be born blind and become blind, for if you are blind, you have no guilt. And we are blind, and we are limited, not because we or our fathers sinned, but that the glory of God might be revealed!

Bless God for crutches. Praise Him for terminal diseases. Thank God for hospital stays, days being shut-in, and unexpected denials. May God take away and strip down. Jesus limited himself. O God, bless us with limitations.

MAY THE LORD BLESS YOU WITH UNANSWERED PRAYER

> *He went a little farther and fell on His face, and prayed, saying, "O My Father, if it be possible, let this cup pass from Me."*
> (Matt. 26:39)

And the Father said no.

I was in Palermo, Sicily, and late one night I was talking with my friends Alan, Jason, and David. Alan serves in Thailand, Jason in China, and David in Lebanon. We were talking about prayer. We were talking about praying for miracles and healings among Muslims and about how often God does not answer our prayers.

A few days later Jason wrote to us all. "I think," he said, "that while God is glorified when prayers are answered, He gets a different kind of glory when His servants pray and nothing happens, and pray again, and nothing happens, and look foolish and pray again and nothing happens, and pray yet again and nothing happens."

When God's servants trust Him so much, when they care so little about their reputation that they pray and pray and pray and pray again, and God elbows the devil in the ribs and says, "Hey, boy, Look at that! You have anybody like that? You have anybody that loves you and trusts you so much that unanswered prayer is a joy, that loss of face is gain. You got anyone like that devil? You have any one like that?"

May the Lord bless you by denying your petitions. May the Lord bless you by saying "no" to your requests. May the Lord bless you by imposing His will on yours, and may you find His will sweeter! May you rise again and pray again and be denied again. May you ask, seek, and knock and not find, and do it again and do it again. In your importunity may you gladden the heart of God. "Look at my servant Job," He will cry. "Look at my daughter. Look at my son. Look how they love me. Look how they trust. Look how they embrace what I decree! You have anyone like that devil? You have anyone like that!"

MAY THE LORD BLESS YOU WITH FATIGUE

> *[Jesus said,] "I must work the works of Him who sent Me while it is day; the night is coming when no one can work."*
> (John 9:4)

William Whiting Borden was the son of a wealthy businessman. Rejecting inherited wealth, he answered God's call to be a missionary. Arriving in Cairo, he fell sick and died. In his Bible they found these words: "No retreat, no regrets, no reserves."

How many reserves did Jesus have at the end? How much strength did He take with Him to heaven? How much money did Jesus leave for His followers? What cabins on the lake were recorded in His will?

Let's die tired. Let's get to heaven spent. Let's run so hard we have to crawl the last few meters. May the Lord bless us with lives used up for the gospel. You work so hard to leave a legacy of comfort for your children. Why not leave them nothing? Why not spend it all for the gospel? Why not die with no reserves? Why not go to heaven with nothing in the bank, nothing on the lake? Nothing under the mattress, and no ounce of energy left. May God bless you with fatigue. May God bless you with exhausted reserves. May God bring you to the end with everything spent on Him.

Break your alabaster boxes. The poor will always be with us. Bequeath your children the dignity of labor. Lavish your savings on Jesus. Retire in Mecca or Mogadishu or Damascus. Go out fighting; go down swinging. Go preach your own funeral with Raymond Lull in Algeria. Leave your children the legacy of a life consumed by toil for Jesus. Your progeny don't need your accumulated wealth. Give them the gift of dying tired, dying spent. No reserves! May the Lord bless you with a life exhausted on Him.

MAY THE LORD BLESS YOU WITH SIMPLICITY

> *[Jesus] steadfastly set His face to go to Jerusalem.*
> (Luke 9:51)

Jesus resisted the siren song of power. Jesus rebuffed other people's ideas for His life. Because His face was set to die for others, Jesus lived for one big idea: "I must get to the cross! I must die for others."

So many causes—even Christian ones—compete for our attention and our affections. May the Lord bless you with one simple ambition. May God make you narrow.

I contend there is only one big idea worth living for—dying to save others. "Greater love has no man than this, that a man lay down his life for his friends." Jesus simplified His life so that nothing would distract Him from the cross. Nothing would stop Jesus from dying for others. Everything Jesus did propelled Him to a sacrificial death.

You want to be like Jesus? Live and die to save others. It is a simple goal, a simple focus. Set your face to go to the cross.

I pray that your life would be this simple: That you are blessed with a life that frames every decision—who you marry, what you study, where you live, who your friends are, how you spend your money, what church you attend—on these simple questions:

- Who does not know Jesus?
- What peoples have no access to the gospel?
- What am I going to do about it?

It does not have to be complicated. May Jesus bless you with simplicity.

MAY THE LORD BLESS YOU WITH SUFFERING AND DEATH

> *I count everything as loss because of the surpassing worth of knowing Christ Jesus my Lord. For his sake I have suffered the loss of all things and count them as rubbish, in order that I may gain Christ...that I may know him and the power of his resurrection, and may share his sufferings, becoming like him in his death.*
> (Phil. 3:8, 10 ESV)

Robert Stewart was a missionary martyred in China. He said, *"Agonia* is the measure of success. Christ suffered in agony: so must we. Christ died: so perhaps may we. Our life must be hard, cruel, wearisome, unknown. So was His."[108]

North American culture has not been good for Christians. We have been fed the poison of prosperity, and we have swallowed it. Our geographical isolation from and material elevation above the rest of the world has betrayed us. We live life confused—full of possessions but empty in spirit. Abounding in opportunity, but accomplishing nothing of eternal value, we cannot understand why having so much we possess so little. We are bewildered at how our unrestrained freedoms have bound us. We have been presented with and accepted a distorted Jesus.

Do you want to be like Jesus?

Is this all you ask?

Jesus was hungry. He lived under limitations. His prayers were sometimes denied.

Jesus was tired, poor, lived with one simple aim, disappointed everyone, was thought crazy by His family, was abandoned, lonely and ridiculed. He suffered and died in a way no one expected.

Do you want to be like Jesus?

Oh, precious children, so wise in the world, so foolish in the Spirit, the things you long for can only be gained by dying.

Satisfaction comes from hunger.

Freedom comes from limitations.

Access comes from denial.

Strength comes from weakness.

Riches come from poverty.

Purpose comes from simplicity.

Life comes from suffering and death.

Jesus understood this. If we will understand Him, if we will be like Jesus—hungry, limited, denied, tired, poor, simple, suffering, dying—the Father will bestow on us life everlasting.

the
Will of
God

COLOSSIANS I

Knowing God's will. In the big themes, it is easy for the Scripture tells us plainly:

> *For this is the will of God, your sanctification....* (1 Thess. 4:3)

> *In everything give thanks; for this is the will of God in Christ Jesus for you.* (1 Thess. 5:18)

> *For this is the will of God, that by doing good you may put to silence the ignorance of foolish men.* (1 Peter 2:15)

> *God willed to make known what are the riches of the glory of this mystery among the Gentiles: which is Christ in you, the hope of glory.* (Col. 1:27)

The Scripture is very plain on the big picture of God's will, both positively and negatively.

> *The Lord is not slack concerning His promise, as some count slackness, but is longsuffering toward us, not willing that any should perish but that all should come to repentance.* (2 Peter 3:9)

Our sanctification is God's will. In everything, give thanks is God's will. Do good to silence the accusers is God's will. Making the mystery of Christ in you known is God's will. All coming to repentance is God's will. Mission to unreached people, obviously, is God's will.

We understand these things, but what about the other decisions of life? What about whether you should go to Valley Forge University as a student? What about if you should leave? Should you go to Libya and pioneer with a church planting team after graduation? Should you go to Somalia or Afghanistan? Should you stay here and send others? How do you know?

We attempt to discern God's will for many different issues. For example, in relationships and marriage, how do you know to whom you should commit? When I was trying to determine if my wife Jennifer was the one for me, I added all kinds of tests. I wanted to see what she was made of. I took her to Rainbow Foods in Minneapolis, made her get into the trunk, and drove all the way back to the college with her locked in the trunk. I took her to the top of a multistory building, put a chair on the edge overhanging a drop to the death, and made her sit on it. I wanted to see her mad; I wanted to see what she would do if pushed. (I don't advise you to do anything like what I did!)

When my father proposed to my mother, she was afraid of marrying a man with false teeth. So before she said yes, she insisted on pulling on his upper and lower teeth. When they remained in his mouth, she agreed to marry him.

Discerning the will of God requires more than external observation. Discerning the will of God requires more than first impressions and human wisdom, because sometimes the will of God is not conventional. Sometimes the will of God is to build an ark with Noah or to prophesy naked with Isaiah or to unpatriotically recommend surrender with Jeremiah or to go to the cross.

Let's take a look at a marvelous passage of Scripture in Colossians 1. This is a passage that gives us hope—hope that we can not only know God's will but we can be filled with that knowledge.

A WONDERFULLY BALANCED STATEMENT

> *For this reason we also, since the day we heard it, do not cease to pray for you, and to ask that you may be filled with the knowledge of His will in all wisdom and spiritual understanding….*
> (Col. 1:9)

The filling of the knowledge of God's will is through wisdom and spiritual understanding. This is a wonderfully balanced statement.

Is it God's will to poke yourself in the eye, cut off your foot, or engage in destructive behavior? Is it God's will to be rude, undisciplined, lazy, or needlessly offensive? Is it God's will to take unnecessary risks, to be foolish or cowardly, arrogant or insecure? No.

Common wisdom sets the initial parameters for God's will. God's will does not include stupidity. If someone tells you to do something stupid, like throw yourself off the top of the temple or give them $1,000 so God will give you a Mercedes, is that God's will? No, of course not. It's not even faith; it's stupidity.

God's will is not stupid. God's will is wise. In discerning God's will, God gave you a brain—use it. God gave you wise friends and counselors—consult them. God works through history—refer to it. Common sense wisdom is almost always in harmony with God's will.

The balance to the statement is found in the "spiritual understanding" phrase. Some things seem foolish, but are actually wise. Things like arks and crosses, things like giving up what you cannot keep to gain what you cannot lose, things like sailing off into the white sky of morning, never to return.

Spiritual wisdom is different than practical wisdom because spiritual wisdom has a God component. There is a revelation, a wisdom that comes directly from God, something only He knows. A little warning in your spirit. A nudging in your soul. Something that may not be rational, defensible, explainable, or logical. As Christians, however, we must be very selective, very careful about when we play the God card. You know what I mean, don't you? "God told me this, and God told me that." Many times, we discredit God by using Him as an excuse for our will or our opinion. That is not spiritual understanding, and it is not the will of God.

More often spiritual understanding is a quickening of your natural intellect. Sure, sometimes God gives you facts straight from the heavens. Like Ananias, "Go to a street called Straight." But more often, it is just a sharpening of natural wisdom, an anointing for clear thinking.

Most often it is not detailed, factual data. Rarely is it: "Go to Cairo and look for a man in a pink robe who is 400 pounds. He will be 5-feet-tall and blind in one eye. His shoes will be white, and he will be holding a cane. His name is Bubba Muhammad and his brother just died. I want you to hit him on the head with your Greek New Testament, and this will cure him from the hiccups. Then lead him to Christ."

Usually it is: Go into the all the world and preach the gospel. And when we obey the general leading, it is little promptings that lead us to the specific will of God.

THE INDICATORS

> *...that you may walk worthy of the Lord, fully pleasing Him, being fruitful in every good work and increasing in the knowledge of God; strengthened with all might, according to His glorious power, for all patience and longsuffering with joy....*
> (Col. 1:10–11)

The fullness of the knowledge of God's will has concrete purpose. We are filled with the knowledge of His will so that:

- We walk worthy of the Lord, fully pleasing Him.

- We are fruitful in every good work.

- We increase in the knowledge of God.

- We are strengthened with all might according to His glorious power for all patience and long suffering with joy

Let me work backwards on this point. Here is the premise: The fullness of the knowledge of God's will has concrete purpose. Full knowledge has indicators:

1. We walk worthy, fully pleasing Him.

2. We are fruitful in every good work.

3. We increase in the knowledge of God.

4. We are strengthened with all might according to His glorious power.

5. We have patience and longsuffering with joy.

Therefore, if these things are lacking, we are not in God's will. Let's take them one by one:

1. Are you walking worthy? Do you sense that God is pleased with you?

We must answer this both simplistically and deeply. Is what you do, and how you do it worthy of God's goodness? Does it take advantage of anyone? Does it make others poor? Is it ethical, holy, pure, and kind? These are simple questions.

But there is also a subjective question that must be asked and answered: Is God pleased with you? There are many good things to do. There are many options in relationships and ministry. So beyond the integrity of the work or relationship itself, in your spirit do you sense the pleasure of God?

Eric Liddle's sister was concerned that running distracted Eric from mission: "I will be a missionary to China. God made me for a purpose. But He also made me fast, and when I run, I feel His pleasure!"

In what you do, do you sense the pleasure of God? If what you do or in the choice you are making, if the person you connect with helps you walk worthy, be better, kinder, wiser, and more loving than by yourself, if you sense an inexplicable pleasure of God, then you are in His will.

2. Are you fruitful?

Like the above, there is a simple and complex application. Simply, are there results? Are people helped, changes made, a difference accomplished, or significance? Is something good happening? Are you bringing positive change?

On the complex side, fruitfulness is not always nickels and noses. Sometimes fruitfulness is faithfulness and obedience. Sometimes fruitfulness is joyful service for years without noticeable results. Sometimes fruitfulness is not something to be counted, but life to be shared. It is love, joy, peace, patience, kindness, goodness, faithfulness, gentleness, and self-control.

Sometimes it is the lack of anything measurable on the outside that leads to the greatest fruitfulness on the inside.

If what you are doing is making a positive impact on others, and/or leading to the fruit of the Spirit being grown and harvested in you, then you are in His will.

3. Are you increasing in the knowledge of God?

This is a good one. Does your current role, ministry, context, or situation foster growth in knowing the character of God?

I am not talking about Bible study, church, or home group. Those are the will of God, of course. But your daily life, your constant choices, the work, and the task, do they increase your knowledge of God?

Are you faced with things you cannot handle yourself so you learn about God's power? Are you confronted with needs beyond your resources so you learn about God's endless supply? Do giants shout at you so that you learn faith? Does injury lead you to forgiveness? Does hatred cause you to feel mercy and disappointment make you spring forth in joy?

The will of God is not indicated by health, wealth, and happiness. God's will is indicated when circumstances make you increase in your understanding of who He is. When your character is stamped with His image, if you are increasing in the knowledge of God, you are in His will.

4. Are you strengthened with all might according to His glorious power for all patience and longsuffering with joy?

A marvelous thing about the will of God is that He strengthens us for it. You have heard it said, "God's will in God's time in God's way will never lack God's resources."

You may be physically exhausted, but somehow you divinely have the strength to get up and keep going. You have unusual stamina. You have exceptional patience. You have the ability to put up with difficult people, and through it all, you have bubbling joy.

You will know you're out of the will of God if, despite fame, fortune, and prestige, there is no divine energy, no spiritual power, no patience, and no joy. This fourth one, of course, must be balanced with the other three, for there are times for all of us, even in God's general will, when we are weak, exhausted, worn down, impatient, and joyless.

Just because things are rough does not mean we are out of God's will. There will always be rough patches in friendships, marriages, ministries, jobs, and teams. But even in difficult days, God wants to strengthen us, keep us patient, and bathe us in joy.

You can be out of the will of God while you are in it. I mean, God might want you in that situation, but in the situation God wants you in, you are acting in the flesh, which is out of God's will. His will, His way, and His time all must intersect.

Even in difficult seasons, God's will is for us to be strengthened with power, patience, longsuffering, and joy. If we are experiencing and growing in these, we are in the will of God.

The fullness of God's will has definite purpose and indicators:

- We walk worthy of the Lord, fully pleasing Him
- We are fruitful in every good work
- We increase in the knowledge of God
- We are strengthened with all might according to His glorious power for all patience and longsuffering with joy.

When these indicators are true of us, we are in the will of God.

NOT WHAT, BUT WHO

> *…Giving thanks to the Father who has qualified us to be partakers of the inheritance of the saints in the light. He has delivered us from the power of darkness and conveyed us into the kingdom of the Son of His love, in whom we have redemption through His blood, the forgiveness of sins.*
> (Col. 1:12–14)

The fullness of the knowledge of God's will is marked by thankfulness.

I propose to you today that perhaps we spend too much energy wondering if we are in God's will and that our time would be better spent thanking God for what He has willed for us in Christ.

This whole passage in Colossians, speaking as it does of being filled with the knowledge of God's will, speaks so in the context of the preeminence of Christ.

Paul, after praying for the full knowledge of God's will, mentions the benefits (which are also indicators). Then in verses 12 to 14, the text pivots.

He gives thanks to God for His great will and the central place of Jesus in the will of God:

> *Giving thanks to the Father who has qualified us to be partakers of the inheritance of the saints in the light. He has delivered us from the power of darkness and conveyed us into the kingdom of the Son of His love, in whom we have redemption through His blood, the forgiveness of sins.*

God's will, then, is not so much what, but who! We are consumed with the what and where of God's will: What should I do, and where shall I go? The who questions we ask tend to revolve around friendship with man or woman, not the Lordship and intimacy of Christ. But the center of God's will for us is a preeminent Christ—it's not a role or a place or even another person.

> *[JESUS] is the image of the invisible God, the firstborn over all creation. For by [JESUS] all things were created that are in heaven and that are on earth, visible and invisible, whether thrones or dominions or principalities or powers. All things were created through [JESUS] and for [JESUS]. And [JESUS] is before all things, and in [JESUS] all things consist. And [JESUS] is the head of the body, the church, who is the beginning, the firstborn from the dead, that in all things [JESUS] may have the preeminence.* (Col. 1:15–18)

I want to underline this: JESUS is the center of the will of God. Cosmically, consciously, consistently, Jesus is the center of God's will. *God's will for you is Jesus!* Paul's prayer for the church in Colosse in Colossians 1:9 says: "I pray that you may be *filled* with the knowledge of His will" (italics mine). Then he wraps up this teaching on why we should know His will by stating: "For it pleased the Father, that in [JESUS] all the fullness should dwell, and by [JESUS] to reconcile all things to Himself, by [JESUS], whether things on earth or things in heaven, having made peace through the blood of His cross" (Col. 1:19–20, emphasis added).

Jesus reconciles the will of God to us. Jesus is the full revelation of God. Jesus is the fullness of God's will. *Jesus is the fullness of God's will!* Our time and energy should not be spent in fretting over the will of God. Our passion and emotion, our heart and soul must center on the simplicity of having just Jesus. If we have just Jesus, we will have the will of God. Having Jesus will reconcile the difficulties and mysteries of God's will to us. Let us therefore be a people who spend our energies not in worriedly seeking God's will in the abstract, but in passionately seeking God's will in the person of Jesus Christ. Let us live thanking God for every provision, every direction that He makes clear to us in Christ.

Times and roles change. We rotate through places. People come and go. But one central will of God remains for us—the fullness of being in Jesus! United with Him in baptism, raised with Him in resurrection, *Jesus is the sweet will of God.* Let our energies be spent in seeking Jesus and we will find ourselves in the middle of the fullness of God's will.

Leila Morris put it this way:

> *My stubborn will at last hath yielded;*
> *I would be Thine, and Thine alone;*
> *and this the prayer my lips are bringing,*
> *Lord, let in me Thy will be done.*
> *Sweet will of God, still fold me closer,*
> *till I am wholly lost in Thee.*
> *Sweet will of God, still fold me closer,*
> *till I am wholly lost in Thee.*[109]

Yesterday, today, forever, Jesus is the same. All may change but Jesus never. Glory to His name!

Three Journeys

Adoniram Judson sat in jail. A pioneer missionary to Burma (modern day Myanmar), he labored for years with no converts and his translation work met obstacles. Now he was in prison. He was marched overland barefoot, and now at night his feet were shackled and attached to a bamboo pole, hoisted in the air. For several years he slept at night with only his shoulders touching the dirty floor.

Imprisoned with an unbelieving European, Judson was mocked: "What think ye now of the prospects that any Burmese will be converted?"

Picture this with me. Judson in ragged and dirty clothes, scarred feet and chain-chaffed ankles, feet in the air, sweat on his brow, replied, "The prospects are as bright as the promises of God!"

I am here to advocate for the glory of God among all peoples. I am here to declare that God is being glorified in the Arab world. I am here to testify that the prospects for Muslims to be saved are as bright as the promises of God. I am also here to be faithful to the facts and to issue an appeal for laborers.

We are losing ground. Yes, Arab Muslims are coming to Jesus in unprecedented numbers. Yes, there has never been a more exciting day to live and serve in the Middle East. But at the same time, Arab Christians flee the Arab world in record numbers and natural birthrates still far outpace spiritual rebirths. There is a lower percentage of faithful, believing Christians in the Arab world than at any point in history. And it is my belief that there are men and women hearing this today who will live and die to change this unfortunate reality of current history. In this room are men and women that God is calling. Will you say "yes" to Jesus and to His glory in the Arab world?

Before you answer that question, let me be fair with you. Let us be brutally honest about what we are facing. Today, I want us to reflect together on the spirits that empower Islam and three possible responses of the people of the one true God.

THE SPIRIT OF THE ANTICHRIST

Christianity existed in the Arabian Peninsula before the birth of Mohammed. The Bishop of Oman was reported to have attended the council of Nicea

(325 AD).

The *Shahada*, which is the heart of the Muslim confession of faith, states: "I confess there is no God but God, and Mohammed is the prophet of God."

Orthodox Christianity disagrees with both lines of the creed despite a seeming agreement with the first. We are Trinitarian monotheists. The Shahada, when understood contextually, is a direct rejection of the deity of Christ. The Tawhiid (absolute unity of God) is the cardinal doctrine of Islam. Many Muslims say that the summary of Islam is found in these Qur'anic verses:

> *In the name of God most gracious, most merciful*
> *Say, He is God, the one and only*
> *God the eternal absolute*
> *He begetteth not, nor is He begotten*
> *And there is none like Him.* (Ikhlas 112:1-4)

Contrast these verses to what the Scriptures say:

> *Who is a liar but he who denies that Jesus is the Christ? He is the antichrist who denies the Father and the Son.* (1 John 2:22)

> *Every spirit that does not confess that Jesus Christ has come in the flesh is not of God. And this is the spirit of the Antichrist.* (1 John 4:3)

> *He who has the Son has life; he who does not have the Son of God does not have life.* (1 John 5:12)

The spirit of Islam is an anti-Christ spirit. Islam denies that God is our Heavenly Father. Islam denies that Jesus is the divine Son. The spirit of Islam screams: Jesus is not God! Every creed, every prayer call, every doctrine is against the deity of Jesus. The spirit of Islam is the spirit of anti-Christ.

What is our response to the antichrist spirit of Islam? We must boldly respond to this unimaginable insult by elevating, praising and proclaiming in no uncertain terms that Jesus is God.

For the moment, secular humanism and Islam are friends. It's puzzling, as their views on abortion, alcohol and homosexuality are so opposed. But this friendship will not last long for neither ideology can live with the other over time. Still, the one great commonality that all false ideologies share is this—they deny the deity of Jesus Christ.

I want to unequivocally declare that any ideology or person that denies the deity of Jesus is rebellious and insulting. Any ideology or person that does not glorify Jesus as God will be judged and destroyed. The Bible says in 1 John 2:22, "Who is a liar but he who denies that Jesus is the Christ? He is antichrist who denies the Father and the Son." Any ideology that denies God is our Father and Jesus is the divine Son of God—that is, God made flesh to dwell among us—is a lying, antichrist spirit.

Jesus, very God of very God, is daily insulted. His deity and absolute authority is refused. Perhaps no insult is as great as that of the people of God who, cowed and intimidated by the spirits of the age, no longer declare with POWER that Jesus is God and must be glorified as such.

I live in Cairo, and Egyptians are the friendliest people in the world. Whenever I get in a taxi, the conversation goes something like this:

Me: Peace!
Taxi Driver: Peace.
Me: How are you?
Taxi Driver: Praise God, wonderful. You?
Me: Good. Praise God.
Taxi Driver: You speak Arabic well. Are you a Muslim?
Me: No, thanks be to God. I am a follower of Jesus.

Now at this point, my kind Egyptian host will invariably say: "No problem. There is only one God, and we all must serve Him." *Kullu Wahid* in Arabic—it's all one. And I have a choice. I can smile and nod and go along with this general agreement, for the God of the Bible and the God of the Qur'an are indeed similar in their non-transferable attributes: omniscient, omnipresent, and omnipotent.

Or I can go to the heart of the issue. And in these moments I like to slap my taxi driver on the knee with a big smile and say: "I am so glad you believe Jesus is God." I then watch him choke and stutter, "No, no, no, no," for he believes nothing of the kind. But now we can have a real, eternal conversation.

Whether here in America, across the Arab world or globally, this is the heart of the issue: God is the God of Glory, Jesus is God, and Jesus is to be glorified above all other names.

Speak all you want in general terms and you can be loved and accepted, whether in Congress or in Karachi. But extol, magnify, and lift up Jesus as the glorious God of all, and immediately face censorship and rebuke as a bigot. This, friends, is the unavoidable reality of our day.

I want to exhort you today that we must glorify Jesus as God. I want to declare that Jesus himself did not veil His deity. Revisionists with their Western or Islamic bias look back at Scripture and at best propose Jesus veiled His deity. More often they simply refuse to acknowledge Jesus clearly claimed to be God. But the Scripture thunders back the opposite. Jesus led with His divinity—and so must we.

Andrew Thompson tells a story from Oman in his book *Jesus of Arabia*.[110] A missionary reads the story of Zacchaeus to a group of Omani Muslims. This was their response:

"This is absolutely outrageous behavior," said one Omani to the agreement of the others. "How could Jesus be so impudent to invite himself to another man's house! In our culture we would not dream of inviting ourselves into a neighbor's house unless we were explicitly invited by the host. Not even the Sultan of Oman has the right to walk into the most humble citizen's home—he must wait to be invited. The only person who would have that privilege would be God himself." His comments trailed off as he realized the import of what he had just said.

Even the Muslim mind must acknowledge that Jesus' claims and speech demand recognition as deity. Jesus is the Son of Abraham, blesser of all nations. Jesus is the Son of David, sovereign of all peoples. Jesus is the Son of God; He has authority over all kingdoms. Jesus is the Son of Man, divine deliverer among humanity. The title "Son of Man" does not refer to humanity. It is a reference to the book of Daniel and the divine coming down to walk with men in the furnace of earth. Jesus' favorite title for himself pointed to deity. In Mark 2, Jesus forgives sins and then heals. And who can forgive sin but God alone? Jesus calls himself the Good Shepherd. What did this mean to the first century Jew? It is a double claim to divinity. Jehovah is my Shepherd (Psalm 23). Only God is good. I am God the Shepherd. I am God the Good. I AM the I AM. "For this reason we kill you, not for your signs but because you make yourself equal with God." Even the religious leaders understood the divine claims of Christ. The Bible tells us Jesus was proved to be the divine Son of God by His resurrection from the dead. And when the Apostles preached resurrection, they were preaching deity: Peter at Pentecost, Paul in Athens, and the magnificent passages in Colossians.

Jesus is God. He demands allegiance. He deserves worship. He is worthy of glory. He is coming soon as King of Kings with fire in His eyes and a sword in His mouth to judge and to reign. And those who pierced Him shall mourn; those who insulted Him shall be punished; and those who obeyed Him shall be rewarded.

Jesus is the God of glory and He demands and deserves the glorious worship of the nations. Jesus is insulted when Islam denies His deity. Jesus is offended when secularism reduces Him to a caricature. Jesus is mocked when reduced to one of many lesser gods by Hinduism. Jesus is angered when animism tries to manipulate lesser powers. As God, Jesus demands and deserves to be glorified by all.

It is time the Church rises up vocally, gets off the back foot of shame and uncertainty, lifts up our anthems of praise as heralds of the divine Jesus, and proclaims His absolute authority over all powers and ideologies. Now on to the front foot of proclaiming Jesus as God! So, lean into the wind of doubt and mockery. Pay the inevitable price this declaration evokes. Overcome the insults of a world that dishonors His majesty to shout from the rooftops: "Jesus is very God of very God. He is the King of Glory!"

No one knows the critical need to glorify Jesus as God better than those who have been saved out of a religion that is based on the denial of the deity of Jesus. A group of brave believers (Muslim background believers or MBBs) in the Arab world were recently giving out Bibles in the street. An irate

Muslim man approached them and began to rip one up, tossing the pages into the air as he ripped them out. As he did so, his arm froze—while up in the air. He could not draw it back to himself. He walked home—arm in the air—and the believers followed him. "You know what would happen to someone who ripped up a Qur'an," they said to a group of Muslim youth in the street. "Watch how followers of Jesus handle this insult!"

"We will pray for you," they said to the man, "but on this condition. We will pray in the name of Jesus, and when Jesus heals you, you must declare that He is God, leave Islam, and follow Him." The man agreed, and the believers got down on their knees and prayed in tongues for an hour, whereupon the man's arm was healed. The believers led him to the Lord, explained baptism, and offered to baptize him in his tub.

"No," he said. "I insulted Jesus and His Word publicly. I want to be baptized publicly." They went into the street of the village and found a tire repair shop. They emptied the bin used for finding air leaks in tubes, and a bucket brigade filled it with clean water before baptizing the new brother.

If a band of brave believers in the heart of the Arab world does not even consider a brother saved unless he confesses Jesus is God and makes public allegiance through baptism, then surely we who live in the West can lift our voices in the public sphere and proclaim that Jesus is God.

Among these same people, a mother and her grown son accepted Jesus as their divine master. The mother was playing a contextualized chant of the life of Jesus, words straight from the gospels, words glorifying Jesus, truths that Jesus alone is worthy of glory, worthy of worship. Her husband arrived home and when he heard the chanting of Jesus' fame, was incensed. He began to beat his wife. His grown son tried to intervene, but the father threw his son against the wall, cracking his head and knocking him unconscious. The mom rushed to her son's aid, bending over him in concern, as the husband ran to the kitchen, grabbed a large knife and rushed back to slit his wife's throat. But because she was bent over her son and struggling, her husband missed her throat and slit her across her clavicles. She screamed and the neighbors came running.

The husband was taken to jail and promptly released when he said his wife had become a Christian. The wife was taken to the hospital where her life was saved. The believers from before gathered and the Spirit gave them an idea. They gathered more tapes about the life of Jesus and the same verses in printed form, and they descended on the hospital where the woman was. They walked through the halls distributing the life of Jesus in oral and written forms and demanded, "You read or listen to these words of Jesus. You tell us whether or not someone should have her throat slit on account of these words!" These formidable believers used persecution to elevate the worth of Jesus. This indeed is glory.

Upon being released from the hospital, the woman did not feel safe returning to her husband, but she felt God wanted her to forgive him. So she visited him saying, "I forgive you. I love you. Your son loves you. Jesus loves you." Without collusion her son visited his father the next day and said, "Dad, I love you and forgive you. Mom loves you. Jesus loves you." That night the man had a dream and Jesus appeared to him saying, "Your wife loves you. Your son loves you, and I love you."

This precious man gave his heart to Jesus, and remarried his wife in a public Jesus-glorifying ceremony. He honoring the wife he tried to kill, the wife Jesus used to bring him life. He gladly, publicly stood up for Jesus, fighting through that spirit of the antichrist, the spirit that would seek to muzzle us all.

THE SPIRIT OF THE ORPHAN

Even a Muslim offended by my words cannot deny that central to Islam is a denial of the deity of Jesus and the Fatherhood of God. The Bible simply says this is the spirit of the antichrist and the people of God should indeed be offended when the King of Kings is insulted. But there is a second, surprising spirit behind Islam, and this one should make us sympathetic.

Genesis 21:8-21 tells the story of the rejection of Ishmael. Can you imagine how Ishmael felt? Abraham, the only father he had known. He had been cherished, loved, groomed, played with, honored for 13 years. The pride and joy of Abraham, the center of his affections, abandoned to the desert by his own only father!

Mohammed was an orphan. His pain affected his view of God the Father.

The origin of the Taliban began with orphans from the civil war in India. Muslim India (Pakistan and East Pakistan) separated, leaving many orphans of Muslim fighters to be raised by women in orphanages. These orphans formed the militias to fight the Soviets in the 1970s in Afghanistan.

Matthew 18:10 says, "Take heed that you do not despise one of these little ones, for I say to you that in heaven their angels always see the face of my Father who is in heaven." Who are the little ones? Children? Matthew 18:1–2 could lead us to believe that. Actually "little ones" is explained in the verses that follow: "For the Son of Man has come to save that which was lost… Even so it is not the will of your Father who is in heaven that one of these little ones should perish" (Matt. 18:11, 14).

How do you view Muslims? As the sons of Ishmael? Giants? Terrorists? Scary? Intimidating? Powerful? Bullies? Or scared little boys, lost little ones, crying in the desert because they have been orphaned! God sees Islam/ Muslims as scared little orphan boys, as a lost little ones, as boys whose angels see His face always! We don't believe in praying to the saints, but the saints pray. Hebrews tells us that Jesus "always lives to make intercession for them" (7:25). The saints (under the altar in Revelation 6:10) pray and plead with Jesus, "How long, O Lord?"

In 2014, Libyan Muslims beheaded 21 martyrs in orange jumpsuits. The atrocity was videoed professionally. The martyrs' last words were "Lord, Jesus Christ." Twenty of 21 names were released; they were Christian names. The last name was reportedly a Muslim, a man who watched the Christians suffer and was won to Jesus through their example, choosing to die with them. What does he now say in heaven? Is he an "angel" who pleads for his mother, father and Libyan relatives? Could he not even now be pleading for lost little ones?

When you look down at Muslims from the throne, you look down and share the compassion of the Father. Muslims are not scary or intimidating. They are precious little children whom the Father wants to bring home.

In the Arab world recently, a young man began to question Islam. He shared his concerns with his family. The family brought in a group of elders, including sheikhs, to help this young man stay safely in the Islamic flock. The meeting turned volatile. One of the sheikhs, a bully, began to slap the young man around. He didn't mean to kill him, but tragically one of his punches to the head ended the young man's life.

In this particular part of the Arab world, God is doing amazing things. More than 1,000 have been baptized in the last two years. These believers heard about the tragedy and decided to pay the killer a visit. The Spirit led them to an unusual response. They visited the murderous man and tied him to a cement pillar inside his house. Then one by one, they sat down, directly in front of him, and compelled him to listen to their testimonies. They shared how Jesus had saved them and how they came to worship Jesus as Lord. The old man was furious, but he had to listen to testimony after testimony. After they untied him, he was still spitting nails.

The next day they returned to see him again. He was so angry, and they recognized he was tormented by demons. A great, heavenly compassion welled up in them. They no longer saw him as an intimidating murderer; they saw him as a lost little one, bound by the devil and his lies. They saw him as an orphan who desperately needed a Father. They began to pray in the Spirit and laid hands on him. Demons were cast out, and this man, who had unfortunately killed a young seeker, was himself found by the great Shepherd of his soul and joined to the family of faith.

Another believer happened to be a black belt in karate. The local imam sent three thugs to beat him up. He could have taken them all at once, but he allowed them to attack him and knock his teeth out. He then marched to the house of the imam and said, "You and I both know that I could have destroyed those three guys, but I wanted them and you to see how a follower of Jesus treats those who hate him."

Another believer had his shop burned down with Molotov cocktails. It was a small village so everyone knew the men who had done it. The believer went to their homes, put Molotov cocktails in front of their doors, put matches next to them, and left this note:

You know how revenge works in the Arab world, but I am a follower of Jesus. We love those who persecute us.

A family, mostly women, in the Arab world became disillusioned with Islam.

They saw the hypocrisy in their local imams. They traveled to America and became just as offended by the excesses and greed of American pastors. They returned to the Arab world where they came in contact with believers. This family of mostly women indicated they wanted to be baptized. The believer went to their house, but upon entering the women turned on him, shouting, yelling, hitting him with their shoes, and spitting on him. He was thrown from the house. It is shameful in the Arab world to be hit with a shoe and even more so to be spit on.

Furious, he sought his mentor and asked what he should do. "What would Jesus do?" his mentor asked him. The believer bought a cake and took it to the women's house. He knocked on the door and no one answered. He went back the second day with a cake, and no one answered. He went back a third day with the cake and knocked again. The ladies opened the door beaming. "Come in," they said, "the bathtub is filled and we are ready to be baptized. We wanted to see if you were a real follower of Jesus or not. And the only way we could see what was inside you was to treat you shamefully. We wanted to see if the love of the heavenly Father is your real motivation."

These brave Arab men and women! Look with the Father's eyes at those who have caused so much harm. These eyes see little orphan children—who more than anything—need the love of the Father.

THREE JOURNEYS

There are three ways we can respond to Islam. There are three journeys in history to compare.

1. Mohammed to Medina:

Hijrah is considered the most important date in the Islamic calendar. Mohammed leaves Mecca and goes to Medina where religious, political and military powers are combined in one man. Mohammed now has the power to force his view of God. To the Muslim, this idea is vindication and proof of God's blessing. Really, this is very Old Testament in ideology. Islam is a giant leap backwards to the Old Testament; a rejection of the revelation of the character of God as revealed in Jesus.

Do we respond to Muslim coercion with political means? Do we respond to the Islamic insult to King Jesus by amassing political, economic and military power to coerce Muslims into the kingdom? Do you think fear mongering, hate speech, sanctions and Gulf wars help the gospel?

2. Constantine to Rome:

Constantine was vying with Maxentius for control of the Roman Empire. On the eve of battle, he sees a cross in the sky and hears, "Under this sign, conquer." He has a cross painted on his shield and wins the battle. He then issues an edict of toleration for Christianity (which ends persecution). His successor, Theodosius, will make Christianity the official religion of the empire, which is the beginning of its decline. Christian soldiers become the norm, and the Crusades become the fruit or result of Constantine's thinking.

Bosnian Muslims can tell you of the war in the mid-1990s where Serbian nominal Christians crossed themselves before executing men, women and children. A Muslim said of the cross, "I always thought the cross was a symbol for killing your enemy!" A Christian in Lebanon in June 2015 captured an ISIS soldier and proceeded to decapitate him. Do we respond to Muslim violence with our own violence in the name of the cross? We tried the Crusades once. God have mercy on us if we ever try that again.

3. Jesus to Jerusalem:

Jesus fed 5,000 people, and the Zealots, in rebellion to Rome, said, "Wow, he can feed an army! What a weapon!" Jesus rejected them making him King and rebuked Peter. He lived the reality Paul would express: The foolishness of cross is the power of God (1 Cor. 1:18). Jesus centered His response on suffering.

Let's look at one more quick illustration for this. In Syria in 2014, ISIS abducted a Christian man. They tortured him, cut a cross tattoo off his shoulder, and threw it to the dogs to eat. They then cut off his head. They filmed all of this torture on his smart phone and sent the video to everyone on his contact list. His wife, Rose, saw the video and fled to Bulgaria via Turkey.

She began to heal in the camps and joined a ministry that served refugees. One day they pick up a new family from Syria, and Rose recognized that family as being from the area that killed her husband. They were members of ISIS. Rose gathered herself, ministered to the family, and even took one of the pregnant women into her home and saw her through to a safe delivery.

Yes, Islam is the spirit of the antichrist and we must respond with bold elevation and proclamation of Jesus as God. But don't forget the orphan spirit. Muslims are scared little ones, lost and longing for a Father.

Followers of Jesus cannot respond to the insults and coercive ideology of Islam with our own violent and coercive ideology. Not like Mohammed with political power and not like Constantine with military force, but rather like Jesus. We must love Muslims. We must love Muslims enough to die for them. We must love Muslims enough to live with them. We must love Muslims enough to get out of our homes to do life with them; leave our homelands to live and die in theirs; love the smoke-filled cafes where they hang out; give up our 9 p.m. bedtime so we can meet them when they really discuss issues (gospel conversations in the Arab world happen in the smoking section after 11 p.m.); start businesses that allow us to thrive in and serve their communities; learn their language and love their food; go to their soccer games, weddings and circumcision parties and not just endure them, but enjoy them; spend time with them; and love them by opening our mouths and declaring to them the unsearchable riches of Christ.

The only one who will justly balance a rejection of Islam and a love for Muslims is the one who is willing to lay down his life that Muslims might be found and reunited with their Heavenly Father. Jesus came to seek and save the lost—the little ones.

As I speak, we need missionaries—and not just single women, vital as they are. We need strong young men. We need young couples with kids. We need mid-life families. We need empty nesters. We need the retired and available. In Yemen, Syria, Algeria, Saudi Arabia, Iraq, Lebanon, Gaza, Bahrain, and dozens of other places in the Arab world and beyond. Is there anyone here who will be an angel, who will live and die in the Arab world, so some little orphans can come home?

Jesus is calling. Is there anyone here willing to say "yes"?

Standing

as if

Slain

REVELATION 5:1-14

What are the first five words of the book of Revelation?

"The Revelation of Jesus Christ" (1:1).

What is the Greek word for "revelation?"

Apokalupsis.

What does it mean?

It means "to unveil."

A text without a context is what? Pretext.

The unveiling of Jesus by Jesus — this is our hermeneutic as we work our way through this Scripture.

The fact that Jesus needs to be unveiled implies that He has in some form been veiled to us. There is an element of mystery and transcendence. Our past and our contextual environments, our experiences and our pain, our perspective have somehow become clouded, opaque, perhaps even distorted.

Thus, a study of Revelation is a wonderful salve to our spirits. It clarifies and reminds: Just exactly who is this Jesus? What is He like? Is the Jesus I carry in my heart and head the Jesus of Scripture? It is a wonderful opportunity for all of us. Jesus is more radical, more disturbing, more merciful, and more gracious than we really understand.

Let's peer into His Word again and trust for a further unveiling. Let's look at Revelation 5:1–14:

> *And I saw in the right hand of Him who sat on the throne a scroll written inside and on the back, sealed with seven seals. Then I saw a strong angel proclaiming with a loud voice, "Who is worthy to open the scroll and to loose its seals?" And no one in heaven or on the earth or under the earth was able to open the scroll, or to look at it.*
>
> *So I wept much, because no one was found worthy to open and read the scroll, or to look at it. But one of the elders said to me, "Do not weep. Behold, the Lion of the tribe of Judah, the Root of David, has prevailed to open the scroll and to loose its seven seals."*
>
> *And I looked, and behold, in the midst of the throne and of the four living creatures, and in the midst of the elders, stood a Lamb as though it had been slain, having seven horns and seven eyes, which are the seven*

Spirits of God sent out into all the earth. Then He came and took the scroll out of the right hand of Him who sat on the throne.

Now when He had taken the scroll, the four living creatures and the twenty-four elders fell down before the Lamb, each having a harp, and golden bowls full of incense, which are the prayers of the saints. And they sang a new song, saying:

> *"You are worthy to take the scroll, and to open its seals;*
> *For you were slain, and have redeemed us to God by your blood*
> *Out of every tribe and tongue and people and nation,*
> *And have made us kings and priests to our God;*
> *And we shall reign on the earth."*

Then I looked, and I heard the voice of many angels around the throne, the living creatures, and the elders, and the number of them was ten thousand times ten thousand, and thousands of thousands, saying with a loud voice:

> *"Worthy is the Lamb who was slain*
> *To receive power and riches and wisdom,*
> *And strength and honor and glory and blessing!"*

And every creature which is in heaven and on the earth and under the earth and such as are in the sea, and all that are in them, I heard saying:

> *"Blessing and honor and glory and power*
> *Be to Him who sits on the throne,*
> *And to the Lamb, forever and ever!"*

Then the four living creatures said, "Amen!" And the twenty-four elders fell down and worshiped Him who lives forever and forever.

A cry, a comfort, and a conundrum.

A CRY

God in majesty sits on the throne. In His hand rests a scroll. God's plan, His solution for a fallen world is bound up and sealed with seven seals. As the seals on the scroll are broken, God's plan will be progressively revealed and implemented.

To a world of sin will come cleansing. To a world of pain will come peace. To a world of evil holiness will be brought. All that we long for, all that we seek is contained for us in that plan of God. As that scroll is unrolled, God's will is revealed, enacted, and our redemption brought near. The opening of the scroll is our hope.

But Houston, Heaven, we have a problem. An angel questions with a loud voice, "Who is worthy to open the scroll and to loose its seals" (v. 2)? No one is found worthy. Not on earth, nor in heaven, nor under the earth is anyone there found worthy to open the scroll. No one is worthy to read it. No one is even worthy to look at it, and John the Apostle who records this scene for us begins to weep.

I suppose every one of us would also weep if we were present and understood what was happening. The plan that will end all sorrow, the plan that will right all wrong, the plan that will forever banish evil and establish truth remains sealed up and unused.

What use is a master plan if it cannot be implemented? What good are clouds to a man dying of thirst if they withhold rain? John weeps for he realizes what could be and yet he is powerless to affect it.

We live in a world of pain. Tears are the ambassadors of broken human hearts. We know how things could be, even how they should be, and that compounds the agony. We know that there are answers so when we fail to receive them the grief seeps in a little deeper. We know God can heal. We have perhaps experienced healing ourselves, and so when the mother of three infants dies from cancer despite our prayers, it hurts and we cry.

We know God protects. We realize He is a "shield about us," so when our precious child is molested by an uncle, it hurts and we cry. We understand God provides, we read about "the cattle on a thousand hills," and so when we go to bed hungry, when visas do not work out, when handsome husbands do not fall from the sky, it hurts and we cry.

If God was not real, unanswered prayer would be no great surprise. If God was without a master plan, pain and chaos would be understandable. But there is a loving God. He does answer. He does act. He does have a master plan. In fact, He holds that plan right in His hand. We therefore find it hard to understand when no answers come, no act delivers us, and no plan is affected, and out of our hurt, we cry.

My wife Jennifer and I lived in Samburu, Kenya in 1994. It was among the best times of our lives. Our friends Kevin and Miriam came and helped us build our house. No water. No electricity. We dug a pit toilet ten meters from the back door. I made the rafters too short; they barely reached the walls. When it rained, the sound of rain on tin was deafening and the rain coming through the gap sprinkled on us. We had snakes and rats in the house. We sat on our simple wicker chairs and heard "scratch, scratch," followed by a dirt clod falling from the wall. A mouse stuck his head out as if to join our conversation, looked around, and then withdrew into the wall. One day we found a snake coiled up under our wicker chair and after killing it found a rat inside. We were so excited—we killed two with one blow. At night by lantern we listened to lions roar and hyenas howl as they dug up the dead in the shallow graves of the village.

The Samburu are related to the better known Maasai. They still live very traditionally and inhabit the semi-desert of north central Kenya. On one occasion, we took a team of young people to a remote area to evangelize some villages. We camped by a river and every morning set out on long hikes to visit these distant settlements. We preached, sang, testified, and prayed for the sick. Many responded to the gospel message, others were prayed for, and several healed.

During one of those days we visited a settlement in which there was a child who was deathly ill. The crisis brought tribal elders from miles around in order to decide what to do. It was a divine opportunity. Up to this point we found it very difficult to reach the men of the tribe, and here were several of them assembled for us.

We asked permission to pray for the baby and to hold a short service.

The men agreed and led us into the thorn-enclosed ring of huts where all the women sat on cow skins around the crying child. As we approached, the baby threw up and a scruffy dog whistled in to hungrily lap up the vomit.

We gathered around that baby, full of faith and expectancy. The elders squatted down on their heels in the shade of an acacia tree, eyeing us curiously. We believed with all our hearts that this power encounter could be the event that sparked revival in the whole area. We had prayed for an opportunity for the Holy Spirit to move in a miraculous way. We laid our hands on the baby and prayed for healing. The baby quickly fell asleep as we began our service.

One of our team members (who had been healed from a terminal disease) stood and testified of God's healing power. He told the people he believed God could heal the baby just as God had healed him. Another team member stood and began to testify of his own healing experience.

We were all in one accord. We were confident that God was going to heal that baby and show Himself omnipotent. As a result, revival would sweep across the land and transform the people. We just knew the baby we prayed for would wake up whole.

What actually happened was quite the opposite. In the middle of a testimony the baby awoke and went into convulsions. The people ignored us and rushed to administer traditional medicine. Our service came to an abrupt end. There was no closure, just a shunning of us, and we left that settlement confused, ashamed, humiliated, and angry at God.

Have you ever felt the same way? Have you ever gone out on a limb and sincerely trusted God only to receive what felt like a stiff arm? Have you ever cried? Not a little self-pity whimper, but a deep, agonized, tearing of your innards because a God who is love and good feels cruel and withholding?

Our world has. In fact, our world constantly weeps. Slaughter in Rwanda, Bosnia, Cambodia, Sudan, and East St. Louis. Abortion, murder, abuse, and random violence abound. Rejection, despair, loneliness, emptiness, bereavement, and disappointment. Many layered and faceted injustice. Some of it makes us sad; some of it makes us mad. On every side, we stare into the ugly eyes of some form of perversity, sickness, sorrow, suffering, or death.

I have friends, as probably do you too, who have been molested, raped, and murdered. Perhaps you yourself have been on the wrong end of some crime or abuse, or even a slight or oversight. Regardless of the reasons, we all cry. Our world weeps also—sometimes silently and without visible tears.

"God, we know you are real. We know you have a plan. We know you are able to intervene on the behalf of the innocent, and thus when you do not, we do not understand."

Instead we hurt, we grieve, and we cry.

There are answers. Sometimes given by well-intentioned friends who have never walked through the depth of your particular struggle. There are truths and comforts to be found. God is not dead, deaf, nor degrading.

But for a moment, in raw honesty, let us not deny our pain. Let us admit that living in a fallen world hurts. Let us join our tears with those of John the Revelator and weep for our sinful world and the lack of answers.

Weep for ourselves and the difficulty of life. Weep for our loved ones and friends for the burden they must bear. Weep for Muslims who are so bound and deceived. Weep for the lost that wander so unwittingly. Weep for the erring one; lift up the fallen.

Working among Muslims, a constant danger is that we forget how to cry. Overwhelmed by the masses, unable to care for them all, we cease caring for any.

Let us mourn with those that mourn. Let our pain, personal and collective, be an alarm that helps us long for our eternal deliverance. Let us yearn for the return of Christ when all that is wrong is banished and all that is right prevails. Let our tears be the rain that softens barren ground. Let the tears of the sower and the songs of the reaper mingle together in joy by and by.

A COMFORT

As John cries, one of the elders walks over to him, puts an arm around his shoulders and says: "Do not weep. Behold, the Lion of the tribe of Judah, the Root of David, has prevailed to open the scroll and to loose its seven seals" (v. 5).

In a world of pain and tears, we have three simple reasons not to cry:

1.   Jesus is the Lion of Judah.

2.   Jesus is the root of David.

3.   Jesus always prevails.

Jesus as Lion

Lions are built for strength. At 350 to 600 pounds, they can drag something as heavy as a ton. "Saul and Jonathan were beloved and pleasant in their lives, and in their death they were not divided: they were swifter than eagles, they were stronger than lions" (2 Sam. 1:23).

Jesus revealed is a Jesus who beat people (in the Temple), knocked soldiers on their rears with His words in the garden, passed effortlessly through an angry mob (Luke 4), carried a cross after being beaten and scourged, will return to judge the living and the dead with fire in His eyes, sword in His hand, consigning billions to physical and spiritual suffering in eternal hell. Yes, indeed, a lion and a lamb.

According to *Encyclopedia Americana*, "lions after the kill usually rip the carcass open and commence eating the entrails, heart and liver."[111]

Regal, violent, final, strong, dangerous, but not tame or safe, at least not according to C. S. Lewis:

> "If there's anyone who can appear before Aslan without their knees knocking, they're either braver than me or else just silly."

> "Then he isn't safe?" asked Lucy.

> "Safe?" said Mr. Beaver. "Don't you hear what Mrs. Beaver tells you? Who said anything about safe? Course he isn't safe. But he's good. He's the King, I tell you."[112]

Jesus as Root

The biblical context, of course, means that Jesus comes before David while paradoxically being born after him. Jesus is the foundation of the Kingdom.

Jesus is the foundation of God's rule.

But I want to draw attention to another aspect of roots. They are hidden. It is the unusual tree that displays its roots. Most roots are hidden, silent, life-giving structures behind the scenes.

Yes, Jesus rips apart with His lion teeth. Yes, Jesus establishes eternal kingdoms. Yes, Jesus sometimes works silently, invisibly. And Yes, sometimes He roots when we most badly want Him to lion. For Jesus is not our puppet. He does not dance at our request. Nor does he mourn when we are melancholic.

Jesus is not above being hidden. Thus, too, must we embrace the hidden nature of "roothood." You will remember what author Alicia Chole said: "In anonymous seasons we must hold tightly to the truth that no doubt strengthened Jesus throughout His hidden years. Father God is neither care-less nor cause-less with how He spends our lives. When He calls a soul simultaneously to greatness and obscurity, the fruit — if we wait for it — can change the world."[113]

Which leads directly to the third revelation of Jesus in this fifth verse of chapter 5.

Jesus as Prevail-er

The word prevail comes from two Latin words: Pre (before) and valere, from which we get our word "valor" meaning "have power." Literally it means "above all powers." Again, I know this is academic, but Christianity so often is not about new truths discovered but old truths amplified.

Above all powers, above all kings, above all nature, and all created things, above all wisdom, and treasures of the earth.[114]

Above all Muslims, above all threats, above all dangers, and all assorted debt, above all demons, and all the wiles of man.

Above all longings, above all sins, above temptation, and all the filth therein, above all sickness, and all the chains of hell.

Above all ideologies, above all hurts, above all bureaucracy, above all deception, above all abuse, above all personalities, above all governments, above all armies, above all worlds, above…

"All hail the power of Jesus' name! Let angels prostrate fall. Let every kindred every tongue on this terrestrial ball to Him all majesty ascribe and crown Him Lord of all!"[115]

Don't cry, John, for Jesus is a destroying, fearsome, unsafe lion. Jesus is annoyingly hidden, yet at life-giving work. Jesus is above all. And what Jesus is to John, He eternally is to us.

Again, we do not deny facts (faith always confronts them). We have legitimate pain. The earth as we know it is full of tears. But from our pain and with the wailing of earth in our ears, we look to Jesus, the unsafe lion, hidden sovereign, omnipotent friend.

A CONUNDRUM (OR A SLAIN LAMB STANDING)

When the baby in that Samburu village began to convulse, all the people acted as if we were not there. I don't know if you have ever been in a setting where church or mission was interrupted so suddenly that it did not end, it just stopped.

We were so full of faith and then boom! It felt like a collective punch in the gut. Stunned into silence, we began a silent, brooding, single-file walk out of the bush, four hours to our cars. Nobody talked. We were dazed. We walked to the top of Mt. Carmel and publicly proclaimed the praises of our Mighty God. We stepped off the cliff in faith, and God embarrassed us. We walked into the den of lions in faith, and they gnawed on us.

To add insult to injury, the village asked us to take the sick child with us. We carried her out and the unspoken reality was, "Please, no more of your empty words and absent potentate. Take this child to the hospital where some real help can be found."

Glum and numb, we walked the many hours to our cars and drove the child several hours to our little village of Wamba. We checked the child into the hospital late that night and dropped into fitful sleep. The baby was in critical condition, but the doctors saved her little life.

After two weeks, the baby was released from hospital into our care. Jennifer watched over her for a while before we climbed into our four-wheel drive truck, drove to the base of the hills, and made the trek into the village. As we walked up to the village with the little smiling baby in our arms, the village went wild. They sang and celebrated. They insisted we stay for a feast. They slaughtered one of their sheep. Everyone had a merry time. I watched them cut the throat of the unresisting sheep. They pulled the neck tight and swiftly ran the knife over the jugular and windpipe. The sheep kicked and convulsed a little. Blood poured out on the ground and then all was still.

I looked at the slain sheep. I looked at the blood. I realized there was absolutely no way the slain sheep could now, or ever again, stand.

And I looked (see verse 6) and there in the middle of the throne, elders, and creatures was a lamb "standing as if had been slain." How does a slain lamb stand? How does an animal that has its throat cut, its blood spilt, its heart stopped, and its brain oxygen-starved get up and stand? Much less as a lion, a root, or a prevailer?

The cross is acceptable to us now, but intrinsically it is a conundrum, a confusing and difficult problem. A dead God, a resurrected human, a virgin birth, a God made flesh. These are impossible concepts.

Jesus slaughtered and standing. Though we think we understand the cross, we still make the principle mistake of John. We miss Jesus, even when He is the center. We miss Jesus, even when He is in the middle of everything. We miss Jesus, even when we are looking right at Him. Because He does not look, act, speak, or decide as we have predetermined He should. Jesus does not show up in the costume we personally designed for Him. So, we go into a funk, get our feelings hurt, and start doubting who He is. Or rather, we are unsettled because the realization smacks us — Jesus is so much bigger than who I want Him to be. The revealed Jesus is beyond my lines of comfort. The real Jesus does not really care that I disapprove.

After we ate the slaughtered sheep in that Samburu village, we sat around in contented silence. The village elders gathered and their spokesman quietly said, "We have now seen with our own eyes that you love our daughter. We would now like to hear more about this Jesus you talk about."

Somewhat stunned, we stumbled over ourselves to inadequately present Him and that whole village bowed their heads in prayer. They welcomed the King of Glory to the thorny gates of their enclosure. And the King of Glory came in.

HE STANDS IN THE MIDDLE

Jesus comes and takes the scroll and everybody falls on their faces. "Jesus, You are worthy!" they say. "You have redeemed us. From every nation, You have saved us. You have made us kings and priests. We shall reign on the earth."

Then the choir starts in. Angels and creatures and 100,000,000 million voices plus: "Worthy is the Lamb. Worthy to receive power and riches and wisdom and strength and honor and glory and blessing."

And then the crescendo. Every creature on heaven and earth and under the earth and such as are in the sea, and all that are in them, all creation can no longer hold back and they burst forth: "Blessing and honor and glory and power be to Him who sits on the throne and to the Lamb — Jesus — forever and ever and ever."

And the weak-kneed elders and creatures again flop on their face and say, "Amen, amen, truly, truly, truly." Let it be.

What do you think of Jesus? Unsafe lion? Hidden root? Above all powers? A slain Lamb standing? We often miss Jesus, even when He is in the middle of our circumstance because He does not look or act as we expect or sometimes demand of Him.

We cry because we feel hopelessness.

We cry because it all seems so unjust.

We cry often because we have missed the slain Lamb who stands.

And He stands right in the middle of everything.

Overcome

REVELATION 12

It is a privilege to worship in a sanctuary again without fear. No secret police, no spies, no informers. I hope you don't take that liberty for granted. It is humbling to stand before you, for you have stood with us through the generosity of your giving and the lifeline of your prayers. You held up our arms, and it is because of you that the battle goes on, for make no mistake about it, we are at war.

As we enjoy the luxury of worshipping together in this place, I want to call your attention to the regions beyond. Even while we recognize that every place and every ministry faces hardship, while we admit that every church and every Christian have their particular giants to face, we also must declare that the easy places are gone. The servants of the King have advanced His gospel upon this earth and by the grace of God, we together have taken the plains.

But the mountains remain.

If you plot on a map the hottest countries of the world...

If you plot on a map the highest percentages of Islam...

If you plot on a map the most desolate and barren of lands...

If you plot on a map the location of most of the unreached tribes and kindreds, you will have pinpointed exactly where the bulk of our missionaries, pastors, and Christians...are not.

There are practical reasons, of course, like restricted access. But I agree with an old Swedish missionary who says that there are no closed countries or areas. There is always a way in; it just may not be traditional or easy.

If we are to be faithful to our missions mandate, we must now assail the high places. We must now go and live in the very bastions of evil. We must now set up camp where the climates are the fiercest. We must pitch our tent where the resistance is the strongest. We must survive there, and beyond that, we must thrive.

I want to speak to you today about overcoming. I want to challenge the young people here to listen for the call of the Harvest Master. I want to relate what the Lord has done and is doing in the Sudan. My text comes from Revelation 12: "And war broke out in heaven...and they overcame him by the blood of the Lamb and by the word of their testimony, and they did not their lives to the death" (v. 7, 11).

THEY OVERCAME HIM BY THE BLOOD OF THE LAMB

Revelation can be an intimidating book, but I find refuge in its first five words: "The Revelation of Jesus Christ." The Greek word for Revelation is *apocaalipsos*, and from it we derive the word "apocalypse," which to us gives connotations of doom and gloom. The literal translation is "unveiling." This is the unveiling of Jesus Christ — the curtain pulled away and our wonderful Jesus made known.

Let me set the context of our text. John the Apostle is in prison. In a vision, he is taken to heaven, and he is told to record what he sees and hears. In Revelation 1-3, he records a message for seven different churches, messages relevant to the church of that day and to ours. In Revelation 4-5, he gives us a peek into heaven. He shows us the glory given to God by every ethnic group on this earth. In Revelation 6-7, he records the seven seals that will be opened, and each opened seal moves us closer to the end of man-centered history. The last seal has seven trumpets mentioned in Revelation 8 and 9. You can feel the tension mounting. The violent war of good versus evil, truth versus falsehood, love versus hate, God versus Satan is coming to a climax, and in Revelation 11, the loud voices in heaven proclaim: "The kingdoms of this world have become the kingdoms of our Lord and of His Christ, and He shall reign for ever and ever" (v. 15). In the beginning of chapter 12, the woman gives birth to a male child who will rule all nations, and he is caught up to God and His throne. Then war breaks out in heaven.

Sudan, the country in which we served, is a land at war. Since 1956, with little respite, this land has been tearing itself apart. In the last few years alone, more than two million souls have perished as a direct consequence of war. More people have died recently in Sudan than in Rwanda, Somalia, Bosnia, and Kosova combined. The Muslim majority of the north is aligned against the Christian minority of the south, as racism plays a role, too, in this Arab versus African clash.

More people die for their Christian faith in the Sudan than in any other country of the world, and more people are stolen and sold as slaves in Sudan than anywhere on the globe. Children are snatched away as infants, educated in Islam and the Qur'an, and then sent back to turn their own towards the God of Islam. I heard the story of one pastor whose church was set on fire. He was thrown in, the doors were sealed, and he burned to death. I heard about another pastor, buried alive face down, only his feet above ground, and then his feet were set on fire. A young child loitering outside a church was handed a live grenade and prodded to enter. She waddled down the aisle only to disintegrate with others as it exploded in her hands. An evangelist was bound hand and foot to the outside of a tank. The tank was driven out into the desert and parked; the evangelist was left to roast on the hot metal in 140-degree heat. A prominent Islamic lecturer offered blood money to anyone who will kill a Christian. Yes, Sudan knows all about being at war.

And yet we recognize that despite all the atrocities committed against the outward man, there is a war raging that is much more serious and much more deadly. It is a war over the souls of men, and in this most vicious war of the ages, we overcome the devil by the blood of the Lamb. Spirit is aligned against flesh, good versus evil, God versus Satan. Every one of you is a fellow soldier with our beloved Sudanese in this struggle. Each one of us, whether we face the Goliath of Islam or the giants of secularism and seduction so rampant in America or even the wretchedness of our own natures, we will overcome by the blood of the Lamb.

What exactly does that mean? It means that we must live, breathe, and operate under the precious blood of Jesus. It means that the answers are not found in our wisdom, effort, intelligence, or theology, but only in the person of Christ. It means that the hard places will fall not because of you or me, but because of Jesus and our submission to His Lordship. Jesus will win the battle.

I want to remind you today that as we face the challenge of assaulting the hard places that remain, we will only do so by the blood of Jesus. It is only as we are at rest in Him. It is only when we are secure under His precious blood that we overcome the hard places and see the giants fall.

THEY OVERCAME HIM BY THE WORD OF THEIR TESTIMONY

There is a direct correlation between witnessing and persecution. Some of the best evangelistic sermons in Acts were not given in church. They were not given in the Temple and they were not given in the market. Some of the boldest and most direct testimonies of Jesus were given at trials, in courtrooms, and before hostile crowds.

"There is no other name under heaven given among men by which we must be saved," Peter declared to the Sanhedrin in direct opposition to their attempt to silence him (Acts 4:12). Stephen's whole sermon in Acts 7, Paul and Silas in the Philippian jail, Paul in Ephesus and Jerusalem — all these great proclamations were made in situations of conflict and danger.

We must have a proclaimer's mentality in order to survive and thrive in the hardest of places. We cannot sacrifice the very core of who we are — proclaimers. We understand that our very proclamation will arouse opposition, but this cannot deter us. If everyone welcomed our message, it would not be a hard place, would it?

A pastor recently felt led to hold an open-air meeting, preach, and distribute Bibles. This tactic, you can understand, has not been often tried in this Islamic nation. He asked his church to fast and pray for him and they did so for three days. On the third day, our friend approached the market and began to preach. A fanatical Muslim tried to shut him down by out shouting him, but he mysteriously developed a racking cough that removed his ability to speak. So, our friend preached on, giving the gospel message and offering a free Bible to any who would like one. As he finished preaching, he offered everyone who would like a Bible to step forward and receive it.

Not a soul moved.

Suddenly out of nowhere a violent dust storm blew in. Thick red sand swirled around and the visibility dropped to zero. The sudden flurry passed swiftly, and when the dust had settled...literally, every single one of the Bibles had been snatched away.

We overcome by the word of our testimony as we assail the hard places and as we witness to friends and co-workers. Our message is not always going to be received with ticker tape parades and brass bands, but we cannot compromise our message nor cease to proclaim it. Jesus himself was turned away from places. Paul was thrown out and refused. Our expulsion or rejection should not be treated as heroic or shameful if we are doing our job.

It should be normal. We overcome by the word of our testimony, a testimony in direct opposition to the powers of this age.

It will be resisted, and we will continue to proclaim. They will attack the messenger, and we will continue to proclaim. They will beat us, and we will continue to proclaim. They will kill us, and we will continue to proclaim.

We do not overcome by silence.

We do not overcome by misunderstood social ministry.

We do not overcome by education.

We do not overcome by compromise.

We overcome by the word of our testimony.

We must be proclaimers through the dark night unto the beautiful dawn.

There is power in proclamation. I always thought I was tough. I always thought that at moments of extreme duress I would stand out as a beacon, a shining example of grace under pressure. My first trip to jail shattered my delusion.

Just over two years ago I was arrested with three others by security for carrying Bibles. We were four hours north of the capital in the middle of the desert. We were on route to another village, a day's drive through the sand. No one knew that we were being held because they expected us to be hundreds of miles away.

As the interrogation continued hour after hour, my little faith packed its bags and fled. I could not pray. I could not rejoice. I could not hope. I was in despair. Wanting to be strong, I found myself cowering. After 24 hours of repeated interrogation, I was allowed two hours of sleep on a barren floor. The dawn brought the sound of soft singing from the cell next to me. A Sudanese brother lifted his voice in song and started to worship the Lord. As he proclaimed his allegiance, the chains shackling hearts fell away. The presence of the Lord filled our jail. We will overcome by the word of our testimony.

AND THEY LOVED NOT THEIR LIVES UNTO DEATH

If we are, in our age, going to see the hard places fall, it is going to require great sacrifice. I want to assure you that our Sudanese brothers and sisters know very well what it means to lay down their lives, whether that means their wills, their wallets, or their very bodies. Sudanese are giving all to overcome.

Recently I was at a youth conference. It was the closing ceremony, and the leader was about to wind up the proceedings. A young man approached the microphone and timidly said, "I feel the Lord wants us to take an offering." In true African style, the offering baskets were placed on the front row. The people marched joyfully to the front and placed their offerings in the baskets. The man I was next to danced back to his seat and then spun on his heel and returned to the front. When he next reappeared from the throng, he was without shoes but had a beautiful smile. He danced back to me and picked up his water jug. His wife joyfully laid her purse on the altar. The Holy Spirit fell and the youth began to give everything they had pens, books, Bibles, shirts, shoes, belts, head scarves, watches, and sweaters. Sudanese have modeled sacrifice for us.

A few days later in a pastor's prayer meeting, one of the leaders of our church felt impressed that the pastors should give also. He gave his fridge, his electric fan, and his radio. This might not seem like much to you, but this was his savings. He has no bank account and no other resources. These were the things he was saving in case his wife or child got sick. This was his savings, his stocks, and his retirement — this was his everything. Another pastor gave every single item from his simple house — every bed, every chair, every book, every utensil. He sleeps now on the mud floor. Our Sudanese brothers are an example to us. Many of them have given every available resource they have.

I mentioned earlier that more people die in Sudan for their Christian faith every year than in any country in the world. Through fair means and foul, Islam pushes its agenda. Through rape, slavery, and starvation the radical regime endeavors to Islamicize the land. When Christians become Muslims, they are shown on TV and celebrated. When Muslims become Christians, they disappear.

There stands a prison in Khartoum called Kober. It houses common criminals, murderers, and politicians on the wrong side of the regime. It also holds those who have rejected Islam and turned to the truth. A man had been sentenced to death, and on the day of his execution he was called before the chief warden. "If you renounce your faith and become a Muslim, we will let you live." The warden gave him the chance to be pardoned if he renounced his faith. He refused, and the warden said, "OK, you will be hung and buried in the Muslim cemetery."

The man protested saying, "You cannot bury me there. I am now a Christian."

"Too late," the warden said, "the grave has already been dug."

"Bury me where you will then," responded the condemned, "but let me tell you something. One of these days the trumpet is going to sound. One of these days the eastern sky is going to split. One of these days the clouds will recede. One of these days my Jesus will come back, and when He does, I am going to leave you Muslims behind. You bury me where you want but I am telling you this: I am going to rise!"

The warden again in fury decreed his death.

It is not an unusual thing in the Sudan to die for Jesus. I personally know people who have been stabbed. I personally know people who have been tortured. I personally know people who have been imprisoned.

The week before we left, a Muslim converted to Christianity and determined to share his faith with his family. His corpse was found with the head severed from the body. The police arrested the murderer, but the family of the deceased approached the authorities. "This man did what was right to kill our son and cut off his head. Please release him and let him go," and the man was immediately released.

Most likely, many of you know someone who has suffered for the gospel. Perhaps you know martyrs yourself, but let me end with this. The time is coming to an end in which the convert loses his life and the missionary writes the newsletter. The time will soon end in which the African Christian dies and the American Christian reads about it as he sits in his Lazy Boy. We are at war, friends. Please do not be lulled to sleep by the false security of our homeland. The time is soon coming where it will be very unpopular to be like Jesus right here in the U.S. If we really are going to reach the hard places, it is going to take some of our lives. If in the world, we are to see in our generation the giants come down, it is going to happen at the cost of our lives.

The immediate reaction to such drastic proclamation is "Well, it is much harder to live for Jesus, than to die for Him." If I may respond to that by quoting my wife, "If we really live for Jesus, people will want to kill us." Jesus gave His life for the hardness of our hearts. The Apostles all died because of their faith. It was the rule, not the exception.

We stand at the threshold of the last days. We are in the final thrust of the eternal war. The Lord at Calvary won the war, but there are still the high places that hold out. We will take them — we have been promised that much — but not without cost and not without loving our lives to the death.

Please do not think that America will shield you. Our country, as much as we love her, has sold her soul to the god of this age. The time is coming when it will be as unpopular to be born again in the Midwest as it is in Mecca. We are all in this together, and we are foot soldiers together under the Lord of Hosts. Please do not forget that.

And war rages on in heaven, and we will overcome by the blood of the lamb.

And war rages on in heaven, and we will overcome by the word of our testimonies.

And war rages on in heaven, and we will overcome by not loving our lives unto death.

ENDNOTES

[1] Oswald Chambers. "April 10." *My Utmost for His Highest, Classic Edition* (UK: Oswald Chambers Publications, 1927).

[2] Elisha A Hoffman. "Is Your All on the Altar." 1905.

[3] Chambers. "April 22."

[4] Francis Brook. "My Goal Is God Himself." 1890.

[5] Oscar C. A. Bernadotte. "I'd Rather Have Jesus." 1888.[3] C

[6] *The Lord of the Rings*, Director Peter Jackson, New Line Cinema, 2001. Film.

[7] Story told to me by Darryl Welling, a 40-year veteran SIM missionary to Sudan.

[8] Nik Ripken shared this in a seminar he gave to the Cairo Live Dead team in 2013.

[9] Ibid.

[10] *London Calling*. Issues 1-64. British Broadcasting Corporation, 1940.

[11] *The Lord of the Rings*, Director Peter Jackson, New Line Cinema, 2001, Film.

[12] The Antioch Initiative is a partnership between Assemblies of God World Missions and North Central University (Minneapolis, MN), focused on the unreached of the world. Learn more at www.theantiochinitiative.com.

[13] "The Princess Bride." Dir. Rob Reiner.Perf. Cary Elwes, Robin Wright, Mandy Patinkin. Twentieth Century Fox, 1987. Film.

[14] David Platt. *Radical: Taking Back Your Faith From the American Dream* (Colorado Springs: Multnomah, 2010), 31.

[15] G. K. Chesterton. *Manalive* (Adelaide, Australia: The University of Adelaide, 2014), https://ebooks.adelaide.edu.au/c/chesterton/gk/manalive/part2.2.html.

[16] Russell K. Carter. "Standing on the Promises." 1886.

[17] Edward Perronet. "All Hail the Power of Jesus' Name!" 1780.

[18] The Ice Bucket Challenge, or ALS Ice Bucket Challenge, involved dumping a bucket of ice and water over a person's head to promote awareness of the disease amyotrophic lateral sclerosis (ALS, or Lou Gehrig's disease). It went viral on social media in summer 2014.

[19] Speed the Light is a ministry of the Assemblies of God National Youth Department through which students raise money for essential transportation and equipment for Assemblies of God World missionaries.

[20] John Piper and David Mathis, eds. *Finish the Mission: Bringing the Gospel to the Unreached and Unengaged* (Wheaton, IL: Crossway, 2012), 14.

[21] William Shakespeare. *Julius Caesar.* Tom Smith, ed. (Oxford: Globe Theater Press, 2005). Act 4, Scene 3. Print.

[22] Rudyard Kipling. "Fuzzy-Wuzzy" (Bartleby.com). http://www.bartleby.com/246/1128.html.

[23] I preached this message in Khartoum, Sudan in 2002. At the time, the leaders listed were involved in the peace talks between northern Sudan and southern Sudan. Abel Alier is a South Sudanese politician; Hassan Al Turabi was a religious and Islamist political leader in Sudan; John Garang was a Sudanese politician and leader; Omar Al-Bashiir is the president of Sudan; Mohammar Qadaffi was the leader of Libya; Hosni Mubarak was the

president of Egypt; Yoweri Museveni is the president of Uganda; and Daniel Moi was the president of Kenya.

[24] Mary Ann Thompson. "Christians, Make Haste." *Celebrating Grace Hymnal* (Macon, Georgia: Celebrating Grace, Inc., 2010).

[25] E. M. Bounds. *Power Through Prayer* (New Kensington, PA: Whitaker House Publishers, 2005).

[26] Janet Benge and Geoff Benge. *Gladys Aylward: The Adventure of a Lifetime (Christian Heroes: Then and Now)* (Seattle: YWAM Publishing, 1998).

[27] A practice in which the feet were literally bent in half while supple.

[28] Benge.

[29] Ibid.

[30] Ibid.

[31] Ibid.

[32] Ibid.

[33] Ibid.

[34] Ibid.

[35] Darrin Rodgers. "Paul Bettex: Early Pentecostal Linguist, Missionary, Martyr." Flower Pentecostal Heritage Center. https://Ifphc.wordpress.com/. Accessed 26 February 2015.

[36] Elisabeth Elliot. *These Strange Ashes: Is God Still in Charge?* (Grand Rapids, MI: Revell, 2004).

[37] Ibid.

[38] Elisabeth Elliot. *Through the Gates of Splendor* (Carol Stream, IL: Tyndale Momentum, 1981).

[39] John Harrigan. *The Gospel of Christ Crucified* (Paroikos Publishers, 2015).

[40] George Duffield. "Stand Up! Stand Up for Jesus!"

[41] A. B. Simpson. *Days of Heaven Upon Earth*. Public Domain.

[42] Harvey.

[43] Ibid.

[44] Lily Douglas. *Labourers in the East: Or Memoirs of Eminent Men Who Were Devoted to the Service of Christ in India* (Philadelphia: Presbyterian Board of Publication, 1840).

[45] Edward Payson, Asa Cummings and Ann Louisa Payson. *A Memoir of the Rev. E. Payson* (Thomas Ward & Company, 1835).

[46] Alfred Ackely. "Take Up Thy Cross and Follow Me." 1922.

[47] *My Fair Lady*. Director George Cukor, Warner Bros., 1964. Film.

[48] Helen Keller. *Let Us Have Faith* (New York: Doubleday & Company, 1940).

[49] World Missions Summit 3 was held in Ft. Worth, Texas in January 2013. National Chi Alpha, in partnership with Assemblies of God World Missions, hosts a strategic gathering of university students, called World Missions Summit, that focuses strictly on God's mission to reach the lost around the globe.

50 Rodgers and Hammerstein. "My Favorite Things." *The Sound of Music.* 1959.

51 Oswald Chambers. "The Baffling Call of God." *Called of God: Extracts from My Utmost for His Highest on the Missionary Call* (Grand Rapids. MI: Discovery House, 1936).

52 Dietrich Bonhoeffer. *The Cost of Discipleship* (New York: Touchstone, 1959).

53 C. S. Lewis. *God in the Dock: Essays on Theology and Ethics* (New York: Harper, 1944).

54 Charles H. Spurgeon. *My Sermon Notes: A Selection from Outlines of Discourses Delivered at the Metropolitan Tabernacle,* Part IV (New York: Funk and Wagnalls, 1888).

55 Anita P. Forbes. *Modern Verse, British American.* (New York: Henry Holt and Company, 1923).

56 Elisabeth Elliot. *Shadow of the Almighty: The Life and Testament of Jim Elliot* (Peabody, Mass.: Hendrickson Publishing, 2008), 4.

57 Platt, 35.

58 Ibid.

59 C. S. Lewis. *Screwtape Letters* (London: Geoffrey Bles, 1942).

60 John Piper. *A Holy Ambition: To Preach Where Christ Has Not Been Named* (Desiring God, 2011).

61 John Piper. *Let the Nations Be Glad: The Supremacy of God in Missions* (Grand Rapids, MI: Baker Academic, 1993).

[62] Thomas Cahill. *How the Irish Saved Civilization* (New York: Knopf Doubleday, Nan A. Talese, 1995).

[63] John Piper. "How Few There Are Who Die So Hard" (Desiring God, 2003). http://www.desiringgod.org/messages/how-few-there-are-who-die-so-hard.

[64] William P. Merrill. *Excursions in Literature*. Donna Lynn Hess, ed. (Greenville, SC: BJU Press,1997).

[65] David Larsen. *The Company of Preachers* (Grand Rapids, MI: Kregel Publishers, 1998).

[66] "The Fear of Death." The Imaginative Conservative. http://www.theimaginativeconservative.org/2012/07/tecumseh-quotes-fear-of-death.html.

[67] A. W. Tozer. "The World: Battleground or Playground." (Christian Publications, 1989).

[68] Harvey. *They Knew Their God*, vol. 6.

[69] I heard Eli Gautreaux share this in a message to missionaries in 2013.

[70] Samuel Zwemer. "The Glory of the Impossible." *Perspectives on the World Christian Movement*. Winter and Hawthorne, eds. (Pasadena, CA: William Carey Library, 1981).

[71] Nik Ripken. *The Insanity of God: A True Story of Faith Resurrected* (Nashville: B&H Publishing Group, 2013).

[72] Harvey. *They Knew Their God*, Vol 1.

[73] Zwemer.

[74] J. M. Sherwood and Arthur T. Pierson. *The Missionary Review of the World*,

vol. 11 (New York: Funk and Wagnalls, 1888), 188-190.

[75] Lillian Harvey. *They Knew Their God*, vol. 6. (Old Paths Track Society, 2011).

[76] George Matheson, *Searchings in the Silence: A Series of Devotional Meditations.* (London: Cassell and Company, 1895), 93-94.

[77] Williams, 22.

[78] Richard Baxter and Theodisia Alleine. *Life and Death of the Rev. Joseph Alleine* (New York: Robert Carter, 1840), 191.

[79] Williams, 25.

[80] John Piper. "A Call for Christian Risk." *Desiring God.* May 29, 2002. http://www.desiringgod.org/articles/a-call-for-christian-risk

[81] Bob Blincoe. "Don't Weep for Jesus," *Think It Not Strange: Navigating Trials in the New America.* John Piper and David Mathis, eds. (Minneapolis, MN: Desiring God, 2016).

[82] John T. Benson. "I Live." 1976.

[83] Samuel Pollard was a missionary to China. After several years of learning the language and culture, he had seen no fruit. He became desperate and began to seek Jesus. After a week of prayer and fasting, he writes, "I had the promise at that meeting that we are going to have thousands of souls." [William A. Grist, *Samuel Pollard: Pioneer Missionary in China.* (New York: Gassell and Company, 1971), 44.]

[84] Piper, http://www.desiringgod.org/articles/a-call-for-christian-risk.

[85] Anna Hampton and Stuart Briscoe. *Facing Danger: A Guide Through Risk* (New Prague, MN: Zendagi Press, 2016).

[86] Thomas Chalmers. "The Expulsive Power of New Affection," Sermon, http://www.christianity.com/christian-life/spiritual-growth/the-expulsive-power-of-a-new-affection-11627257.html

[87] Sherwood, 188-190.

[88] For a more thorough exegesis on this passage, see my dissertation: *Abiding Mission: Missionary Spirituality and Disciple-Making Among Muslim Peoples of Egypt and Northern Sudan* (Eugene, OR: Wipf and Stock, 2016).

[89] F. J. Huegel. *Bone of His Bone: Going Beyond the Imitation of Christ* (Fort Washington, PA: CLC Publications, 2012), 105.

[90] Church Missionary Society.

[91] Constance Padwick. *Temple Gairdner of Cairo* (London: S.P.C.K., 1929), 325.

[92] Excerpt from "Auguries of Innocence" by William Blake: http://www.online-literature.com/blake/612/

[93] Richard Foster. Prayer: *Finding the Heart's True Home* (London: Hodder & Stoughton, 1992), 74.

[94] James Stewart. *She Was Only 22: The Story of Helen Ewan of Scotland, a Fragrant Dynamic Life* (Asheville, NC: Revival Literature, 1966).

[95] Ibid.

[96] Ibid.

[97] Ibid.

[98] Ibid.